SELF-REGULATION
IN CYBERSPACE

For other titles in the Series see p. 239

INFORMATION TECHNOLOGY & LAW SERIES (16)

SELF-REGULATION
IN CYBERSPACE

Jeanne Pia Mifsud Bonnici

T·M·C· ASSER PRESS

The Hague

The *Information Technology & Law Series* is published
by T·M·C·Asser press
P.O. Box 16163, 2500 BD The Hague, The Netherlands
<www.asserpress.nl>

T·M·C·Asser press English language books are distributed exclusively by:

Cambridge University Press, The Edinburgh Building, Shaftesbury Road,
Cambridge CB2 2RU, UK,
or
for customers in the USA, Canada and Mexico:
Cambridge University Press, 100 Brook Hill Drive, West Nyack, NY 10994-2133, USA

<www.cambridge.org>

The *Information Technology & Law Series* is an initiative of IT*e*R, the National Programme for Information Technology and Law, which is a research programme set up by the Dutch government and the Netherlands Organisation for Scientific Research (NWO) in The Hague. Since 1995 IT*e*R has published all of its research results in its own book series. In 2002 IT*e*R launched the present internationally orientated and English language *Information Technology & Law Series*. This series deals with the implications of information technology for legal systems and institutions. It is not restricted to publishing IT*e*R's research results. Hence, authors are invited and encouraged to submit their manuscripts for inclusion. Manuscripts and related correspondence can be sent to the Series' Editorial Office, which will also gladly provide more information concerning editorial standards and procedures.

Editorial Office
eLaw@Leiden, Centre for Law in the Information Society
Leiden University
P.O. Box 9520
2300 RA Leiden, The Netherlands
Tel. +31(0)715277846
E-mail: <ital@law.leidenuniv.nl>
Web site: <www.nwo.nl/iter>

Single copies or Standing Order
The books in the *Information Technology & Law Series* can either be purchased as single copies or through a standing order. For ordering information see the information on top of this page or visit the publisher's web site at <www.asserpress.nl/cata/itlaw11/fra.htm>.

ISBN 13: 978-90-6704-267-3
ISSN 1570-2782

Cover and lay-out: Oasis Productions, Nieuwerkerk a/d IJssel, The Netherlands
Printing and binding: Koninklijke Wöhrmann BV, Zutphen, The Netherlands

SUMMARY OF CONTENTS

TABLE OF CONTENTS

LIST OF ABBREVIATIONS

ADNDRC	Asian Domain Name Dispute Resolution Centre
ADR	Alternative Dispute Resolution
AFA	Association des Fournisseurs d'Accès et de Services Internet
AIIA	Australian Internet Industry Association
B2C	Business to Consumer
BCP	Best Current Practices
CcNSO	Country-Code Names Supporting Organization
CcTLD	Country Code Top-level Domain Name
CDT	Centre for Democracy and Technology
CEN	European Committee for Standardisation
CIETAC	China International Economic and Trade Arbitration Commission
CIPA	Children's Internet Protection Act
CPR	Centre for Public Resources Institute for Dispute Resolution
CPTWG	Copy Protection Technical Working Group
CSS	Content Scramble System
DMCA	Digital Millennium Copyright Act
DNS	Domain Name System
DOC	United States Department of Commerce
DRM	Digital Rights Management
DVD	Digital Versatile Disc
ECODIR	Electronic Consumer Dispute Resolution
EESSI	European Electronic Signature Standardization Initiative
ESP	E-mail Service Provider
ETSI ESI	European Telecommunications Standards Institute
EU	European Union
FEDMA	Federation of European Direct and Interactive Marketing
GAC	Governmental Advisory Committee
GTLD	Generic Top-level Domain Name
HKIAC	Hong Kong International Arbitration Centre
HTTP	HyperText Transfer Protocol
IANA	Internet Assigned Numbers Authority
ICANN	Internet Corporation for Assigned Names and Numbers
ICP	ICANN Corporate Policy
ICRA	Internet Content Rating Association
IE 6	Internet Explorer 6
IESG	Internet Engineering Steering Group
IETF	Internet Engineering Task Force
IP	Internet Protocol

IPv6	Internet Protocol version 6
IRIS	Imaginons un Réseau Internet Solidaire
ISO	International Standards Organisation
ISP	Internet Service Provider
ISPA	ISP associations
ITLD	Infrastructure Top-level Domain Name
ITU	International Telecommunications Union
IWF	Internet Watch Foundation
JHA	Justice and Home Affairs
LINX	London Internet Exchange
MAC	Medium Access Control
MoU	Memorandum of Understanding
NGO	Non-Governmental Organisation
ODR	On-line Dispute Resolution
ODRS	On-line Dispute Resolution System
OECD	Organisation for Economic Co-operation and Development
OJ	Official Journal (of the European Union)
P3P	Platform for Privacy Preferences
PICS	Platform for Internet Content Selection
PKE	Public Key Encryption
RFC	Requests for Comment
RIAA	Recording Industry Association of America
ROKSO	Register of Known Spam Operations
SASF	Semi Autonomous Social Field
SDMI	Secure Digital Music Initiative
SMEs	Small and Medium Enterprises
TLD	Top-level Domain Name
TPM	Technical Protection Measure
UDRP	Uniform Domain Name Dispute Resolution Policy
UK	United Kingdom
UN/CEFACT	United Nations Centre for Trade Facilitation and Electronic Business
UNECE	United Nations Economic Commission for Europe
US	United States of America
USD	United States Dollar
W3C	World Wide Web Consortium
WAIA	Western Australian Internet Association
WGIG	Working Group on Internet Governance
WIPO	World Intellectual Property Organisation
WSIS	World Summit on Information Society
XML	Extensible Markup Language

Chapter 1
INTRODUCTION

1.1 INTRODUCTION

In the beginning … there were States.[1] The Internet came later. Much later.

States are places with legal systems. Places with (more or less) clearly defined territorial boundaries outside of which their legal systems have no jurisdiction. Men have worked out a system of rules to regulate behaviour within states and between states or individuals whose behaviour has an impact across state boundaries.

The Internet is not a place. It is a collection of places, a multiplicity of spaces. The people that use the Internet inhabit a physical space, as do the machines, the computers and cables that provide the technical infrastructure that underlies the Internet. Before they log on and while they are logged on, the same people are subject to the 'laws of the land', the State, where they happen to be located (as are the machines and the cables). Once they are logged on, they are also in 'Cyberspace', which is not a tangible territory but which is a vast space nevertheless, a space (or possibly a collection of spaces) that was promoted as having no national boundaries.

The realisation that there exists a virtual space or cyberspace and the discussion of what goes on inside that space excited a number of people from the very beginning. We find people indulging in or at least exploring the notion of a space where traditional legal systems have no jurisdiction, where a new order can be built by the inhabitants of that space and not imposed from above by states.[2] The extent to which this notion of a stateless Internet is a reality or a fantasy has been the subject of much discussion and many books over the past ten years since the Internet exploded on the international scene. Various authors have, often in a rather partisan manner, come out for or against the notion that the Internet is or should be governed by rules imposed by states or by rules made by users of the Internet. The latter approach, that is, regulation by 'rules created by the administrators and/or users of the Internet' is, for the purposes of this introductory stage of this book, what is meant by 'self-regulation'.[3]

This is the point at which this book commences. It sets out to map where self-regulation really stands on the Internet, how it got there and where it is possibly

---

[1] Of course in the very very beginning there were no states. But states in some form or other have been around for a long time and more distinctively since the Treaty of Westphalia (1648).

[2] Barlow (1996) with his 'A Declaration of the Independence of Cyberspace' was amongst the most notorious and vociferous proponents of this position.

[3] The working definition of self-regulation is discussed in Chapter 3.

going. I do not have a political cause and thus no partisan thesis to promote. I will not try to convince the reader that state regulation rules supreme even with regards to the Internet and that self-regulation is dead. Nor will I try to seduce the reader with the notion that self-regulation has all the makings of a panacea, which is capable of providing all the forms of regulation that the Internet will ever need.

As a practicing lawyer, I am accustomed to consider that clients' behaviour is not regulated only by state law but also by a variety of rules of the social groups they belong to. We live our daily lives in spaces regulated by a plurality of rules. Could this be also the case on the Internet? I suspected that the Internet is no different to other places where legal pluralism is the norm. My hypothesis, therefore, is that self-regulation has been and is likely to remain an important but never the sole form of regulation of the Internet.

This idea for this book was stimulated by the fact that states had been busy at trying to regulate the Internet, almost from the very moment in time that the Internet started connecting people. The exponential growth of the Internet in Western society may be traced back to the mid-nineties. At the same time, in 1996, the major countries where the Internet was most widely used began meeting in Strasbourg in order to try and tackle older and new forms of crime that can be committed using the Internet. By 2001, this effort had led to the European Convention on Cybercrime,[4] the first (and until now the only) international treaty that attempts to regulate some forms of behaviour on the Internet and that was drafted specifically for the Internet.

Although restricted to criminal behaviour, the Cybercrime Convention showed that if States were determined enough to get together and come up with a minimum set of rules for the Internet they could do so. If States acting in unison can regulate the Internet insofar as crime is concerned they could conceivably also agree on sets of rules that govern commerce and various other forms of behaviour that do not attract criminal sanction.

Set against a background where states were clearly muscling in on the regulation of the Internet, it appeared perfectly legitimate to ask,

> 'So is all the fuss about self-regulation finally over? Is self-regulation dead, dying or otherwise on the way out? Is the Internet really not so special after all but just simply something else which is and should be subject to a system where rules are increasingly made by the State or by several States acting in unison?'

These questions might not have appeared important had the Internet remained a toy for academics. By 2001, it was obvious that the vast commercial potential of the Internet leads to situations that require some form of regulation. While it was not perfectly clear as to which businesses could thrive and which could not survive in

---

[4] Council of Europe Convention on Cybercrime (ETS No. 185) opened for signature in Budapest, Hungary on 23 November 2001 and came into force on 1st July 2004 (found at <http://conventions.coe.int/Treaty/en/treaties/html/185.htm>).

an Internet environment (hence the '.com' collapse) it was increasingly apparent that ordinary people could buy and sell things over the Internet with an ease that made this new marketplace very attractive indeed. It was the new transactions made possible by all this buying and selling that was getting some lawyers excited. For who is going to decide matters if a dispute arises once, inevitably, some deals start to go wrong? Even before one gets to that stage one has to know which rules are going to be applied. Moreover, if rules there must be, who is going to make them or do they already exist somewhere out there so that all that needs to be done is to adapt them or simply apply them with no change at all?

These uncertainties are compounded by the lack of homogeneity of the participants on the Internet. Participants coming from different national and territorial origins having different (and often opposing) cultural traditions, moral or religious beliefs, legal and regulatory traditions, participate in different transactional spaces. Achieving global consensus between the different participants to regulate activities on the Internet is difficult if not impossible.

Lawyers and states awoke to the fact that the Internet had grown piecemeal and was not necessarily subject to existing laws, especially those on jurisdiction. As lawyers developed an interest on the Internet, they found that transactions were governed, when they were, by a mixture of self-regulation and state regulation. The exact mix, however, remained unclear.

In this book, I explore some of the different modes of self-regulation that one can find in operation. In each case, I examine the historical development and limitations of such self-regulation. The outcome shows that there are many instances where self-regulation was and remains the best tool for the job. But there are many other instances which are simply beyond what self-regulation can achieve. The most glaring example of the latter is the issue of jurisdiction, a perennial problem, intrinsic to the very transborder nature of the Internet and basic to identifying the most appropriate forum and governing law. I will conclude that self-regulation intertwines and complements other forms of regulation, particularly state legislation, in a complex and essential manner which may not have been the result of a preordained design but which remains healthy and essential nonetheless.

1.2   WHAT THIS BOOK AIMS TO DO

As indicated above, this book was born out of the hunch that the task of governing the Internet is, in practice, not performed by one source alone, even if states endeavour (from time to time) to assume the power of governing the Internet. Possibly to the chagrin of a number of authors, there is no one comprehensive treaty – a 'Cyberspace Treaty' – that provides for the regulation of all the activities taking place on the Internet and that identifies the responsibilities of the different (public and private) actors in the regulation. The picture, from the very outset, appeared to be more complex: the governance of the Internet guided by the rules that shape its utilisation, developed and adopted by governments, private industry groups and civil society. The aim of this book is to identify the actual function of self-regulation in the regulation of the Internet and its relationship with the other sources of regulation, specifically state regulation.

The main question addressed in this book is therefore 'What is the actual function of self-regulation in the regulation of Internet activities?' Apart from its scientific (theoretical) interest, the answer to this question can be used to explain possible normative successes and failures of self-regulation, to estimate possible developments in the regulation of the Internet and to propose improved relations between state regulation and self-regulation for a better regulation of activities in Internet.

The approach taken to answer the main question is to address two sub-questions. One of these concentrates on the need to clarify the phrase 'self-regulation on the Internet' – who are the groups involved, what form or type of regulation are they involved in and what Internet activities are being regulated? The second question aims at describing and explaining the links, where they exist, between the self-regulation arrangements and states and state regulation.

I have accepted from the outset that self-regulation can be an important form of regulation on the Internet and that it can co-exist with other forms of regulation. This assumption finds support in theories of legal pluralism that show how in any given space more than one legal order can exist.[5] The difficulties that the Internet poses for state regulation and the existence of self-regulation as a response to the need of private groups for some form of regulation are by no means unique to the Internet.

I examine self-regulation in four main areas of Internet activity:

(i)   the regulation of Internet content (in Chapter 4);
(ii) the administration of the domain name system (in Chapter 5);
(iii) the setting of technical standards in cyberspace (in Chapter 6);
(iv) the provision of dispute resolution for on-line disputes (in Chapter 7).

The choice of the four areas was arrived at after a systematic review of academic writing on Internet regulation. There are a number of reasons why these four particular areas of activities and regulation were chosen:

(a)   on the basis of the quantity and quality of the existing literature;[6]

---

[5] Cf., Griffiths 1986, 2001, de Sousa Santos 1995 and Twining 2000.

[6] Reference to cases of self-regulation in three other areas of activities is also found in the literature. These are (a) the regulation of e-commerce; (b) the regulation of on-line privacy; and (c) the regulation of behaviour in on-line communities, such as in chat lists. While this study does not include these three areas of activities, the most important subjects of self-regulation in connection with e-commerce (such as the regulation of digital signatures and dispute resolution arrangements) and of on-line privacy are included in the discussion of the four areas mentioned above, in particular in the description of the setting of technical standards and in the provision of on-line dispute resolution. A

(b) because they cover a wide variety of self-regulatory instruments, for example, codes of conduct, contracts, technical standards, industry standards;

(c) because they cover a wide variety of private groups active in the regulation of the activities so that the study is not limited to self-regulation of one sector of the Internet industry; and

(d) because they cover activities taking place at different levels of the Internet network.

The facts reported in the study were collected between September 2001 and November 2005 primarily from publicly available documentation such as research reports, Internet sources, academic writings, legislation, policy documents, parliamentary discussions and reports, memoranda of various groups, information provided by private groups, etc. Some interviews with key actors involved in the self-regulation process or in state policy setting were done to clarify the written information. The multiple sources for facts on each case-area of self-regulation permit some fact triangulation.

Previous studies of self-regulation and cyberspace are limited to an examination of self-regulation of one area of activities and one category of private groups. The work of Price and Verhulst,[7] for example, focuses only on industry self-regulation in the regulation of Internet content. They argue that all forms of self-regulation are present in the debate over content control on the Internet[8] and hence that the area is representative enough to enable generalisations about 'self-regulation and the Internet'. The problem with this approach is that industry self-regulation is not the only sort of self-regulation going on in the Internet or in the regulation of content. Looking at more than one area of activities permits a more comprehensive description of different arrangements of self-regulation going on in the Internet.

I do not attempt to describe or map every different self-regulation arrangement found in each area of activity. My purpose is not to establish the frequency of self-regulation on the Internet but rather to describe and explain the presence of self-regulation in the regulation of Internet activities. The book, hence, deals with a sample of self-regulation initiatives.

Taking the cases of self-regulation individually, a wide variety of different arrangements emerge. However some important general characteristics of self-regulation could be identified: that self-regulation provides customised solutions tailored to the needs of the group, that self-regulation is active in the regulation of transnational activities, that self-regulation creates rules that are later adopted or acknowledged by states, and that self-regulation fills in for missing procedural steps and substan-

---

description of self-regulation of behaviour in on-line communities falls outside the scope of this research since this study describes 'formal' arrangements of self-regulation rather than the 'informal' norms of behaviour, also referred to (confusingly) in the literature as self-regulation, used between members in on-line communities.

[7] Price and Verhulst 2005.

[8] Id. 2005: 4.

tive measures in state law. This examination shows that self-regulation and state regulation on the Internet intertwine and complement each other. The literature usually describes and explains one direction of interaction between state and private regulation, such as, that state regulation substitutes for private regulation,[9] or that state regulation complements private regulation,[10] or that private regulation substitutes for state regulation. This study shows that the relationship between self-regulation and state regulation of the Internet is reciprocal, that is, self-regulation both complements state regulation and is complemented by state regulation.

The intertwining and complementary relations between self-regulation and state regulation can be explained by the presence of an underlying interdependence between state regulation and self-regulation. This interdependence is dictated by the nature of the Internet, the kind of activities that take place and the creation of multiple communities based on shared interest(s). The relations are also encouraged by current trends in regulation due to globalisation.

1.3   THE STRUCTURE OF THIS BOOK

Following this introduction, in Chapter 2 I briefly trace the history of self-regulation on the Internet. I then introduce the three main theoretical approaches to the function of self-regulation on the Internet found in the literature.

In Chapter 3, I discuss three aspects of the term 'self-regulation' as used in this book. Mainly the term 'self-regulation' refers to (a) a type of regulation; (b) a set of rules voluntarily developed and accepted by those who are taking part in an activity;[11] and (c) a rule-making process followed to develop and apply the set of norms. Chapter 3 explains each of these aspects. I have used these aspects when examining self-regulation in the regulation of the different Internet activities.

In Chapters 4 to 7, I discuss the function of self-regulation in four areas of Internet activities: Internet content (in Chapter 4); the domain name system (in Chapter 5); the setting of technical standards (in Chapter 6) and the provision of dispute resolution for on-line disputes (in Chapter 7). In each chapter, I describe who carries out the regulation, what rules are created and enacted and I discuss the reasons for the process of self-regulation. At the end of each chapter, I conclude by discussing the relationship between state regulation and self-regulation in the regulation of the particular activity.

Based on the findings in these four chapters, in Chapter 8 I draw a number of general conclusions on the nature of self-regulation on the Internet and I give some answers to the main research question of this study: what is the function of self-regulation on the Internet. Predominantly, I explain how an intertwining and comple-

---

[9] For example, Macaulay 1963: 55-70 (in particular pg 64).

[10] For example Lazzarini, Miller and Zenger 2001.

[11] Trudel 2000: 204.

mentary relationship between self-regulation and state regulation has emerged. Together they cast a mesh of rules that currently regulate many aspects of the four Internet activities discussed in the preceding chapters. I argue that this relationship has evolved because of an underlying interdependence between states and private groups, the nature of the Internet and the activities taking place there, the reality of multiple communities of interest and recent trends in regulation due to globalisation.

Chapter 2
THEORETICAL APPROACHES TO SELF-REGULATION ON THE INTERNET

In this chapter, I describe the historical and theoretical background to this book on self-regulation on the Internet. Since today's self-regulation arrangements find their roots in earlier developments, I first give a brief account of the historical development of self-regulation on the Internet. Then I discuss the three main theoretical approaches found in the literature on the function of self-regulation on the Internet: the co-regulation approach, the hybrid arrangements approach and the substitution approach. These three approaches form the main theoretical frames of reference in the subsequent analysis of the current arrangements of self-regulation.

In the last part of the chapter, I introduce two ideas from legal theory – legal pluralism and network/mesh regulation – that have influenced my assessment of the three theoretical approaches.

2.1 A BRIEF HISTORY

The shift on the Internet from a predominantly academic and research network – as it was originally planned and used – to a network accommodating many participants including their commercial interests, marked the beginning of the Internet regulatory challenge (predominantly for states).

As long as the Internet was a closed space, open only to a limited number of researchers and institutions, internal regulatory systems and community rules were the main source of regulation of Internet activities. These private, somewhat basic, rules were not sufficient when the shift in access to the Internet by the wider public took place. In other areas, the shift from private to public would have lead to state regulation filling the regulatory gap. In the case of the Internet, however, this was not so simple. Two dimensions made it particularly challenging for state regulation. Internet activities take place in a *decentralised technical space* that states were (at least initially) unaccustomed to, about which they had no expertise, and for which traditional legal concepts seemed inappropriate. Secondly, the activities had *a global aspect* that made legislation by one state alone incapable of regulating the activity successfully. Gradually, with the increase in the number of users, a third dimension challenged state regulation: the Internet accommodates growing *digital communities* upon which national and international legal systems seem to have little grip. Some events,

J.P. Mifsud Bonnici, Self-Regulation in Cyberspace
© *2008, T·M·C·ASSER PRESS, The Hague, and the author*

such as the alleged infringement of copyright by Napster users,[1] found states un-prepared and mostly unable to intervene effectively.

The use of the idea of 'self-regulation' in the early debates on the regulation of the Internet thus comes as no surprise. Self-regulation – rules (voluntarily) developed and accepted by those who take part in an activity[2] – is not a new concept. Self-regulation is a well-known phenomenon in the regulation of professions, sports and voluntary or not-for-profit associations, and in sectors such as financial services, advertising, insurance, corporate responsibility, medical care and the press.[3] There is also a growing body of examples of self-regulation in transnational contexts such as in environmental protection,[4] human rights[5] and multinational business practices and transnational commercial transactions.[6]

Furthermore, there are historical examples where self-regulation has emerged and developed in situations where public authority had difficulty regulating the particular area of activities. For example, Greif and Milgrom[7] argue that medieval guilds arose because state sovereignty and state power had not yet become stable enough to afford a solid basis for commercial transactions. Traders who wanted to trade in different cities needed mutually guaranteed security (similar problems beset e-commerce today). Since state institutions could not provide the required structures of mutual security, private arrangements of traders developed the missing regulatory structures. The Hanseatic League between the guilds in some of the northern European trading towns is a particularly striking example.[8]

In the early debates on the regulation of the Internet, the idea of self-regulation was advanced by some as a freer method of regulation when compared with state regulation. Johnson[9] and others[10] argued that if the Internet had to be regulated at all, self-regulation seemed able to meet the demand for regulation without being too invasive. Regulation of the Internet should be left in the hands of the people who participate in the activities: they have an interest in determining what behaviour is permissible, in following the resulting norms, in devising ways of maintaining these norms and of sanctioning deviant behaviour. The term 'self-regulation' was

---

[1] Napster was one of the first on-line music sharing software. Its technology allowed music fans to easily share and download music. The music industry alleged that this software allowed for massive infringement of copyright and sued Napster for damages. The originality of this case found courts and states legally unprepared, even if ultimately the courts managed to adapt existing legislation to the case. (More information at <http://en.wikipedia.org/wiki/Napster>).

[2] Trudel 1988-89.

[3] See Baldwin and Martin 1999: 125-137; Weyers and Stamhuis 2003.

[4] See for example van Gestel 2005.

[5] See for example, Frost 2002 and Van Tuijl and many others.

[6] See for example Cutler 2003.

[7] Greif and Milgrom 1994.

[8] Id. 1994: 761.

[9] Johnson 1997.

[10] See for example, Barlow 1996.

hence associated with an independent form of regulation created and developed by a group of people to regulate their interactions.

Proposals for self-regulation rather than regulation by states triggered a debate on which form of governance would best meet the requirements of the Internet. One side of the debate, first promoted by Johnson and Post[11] and then followed by others, argued that 'bottom-up' non-legislative norms based on contracts and private agreements suit the Internet better than a 'top-down' state-led approach. Proponents of state regulation[12] argued that while it was evident that for cyberspace existing forms of state regulation were faced with a number of difficulties, this did not mean that the state was incapable of adapting to the needs of the new medium.

By 1997, the 'pro-self-regulation' side was further strengthened by the proposal of the United States government to promote self-regulation. In July 1997, the United States issued a document called 'Framework for Global Electronic Commerce'[13] proposing industry self-regulation as a way to help cyberspace grow and prosper. The European Union similarly came out in favour of self-regulation. Since the early stages of EU policy on 'information highways', in 1993 and 1994, industry self-regulation has been seen as an important strategy to be followed. In the Bangemann Group Report,[14] the authors argued in favour of a market-driven approach to the regulation of the information society. The group argued that the EU should introduce direct regulation only where necessary to ensure that the markets within the Union had a common competitive and regulatory position. Furthermore, after the Maastricht Treaty, the EU was committed to the principle of subsidiarity and the Bangemann Report approach helped reinforce the commitment to subsidiarity.[15] In 1996, when the EU launched three initiatives dealing with the regulation of Internet content, the preference for industry self-regulation was unequivocal.[16] Other international organisations, such as the OECD, also came out in support of self-regulation in the regulation of cyberspace.[17]

---

[11] Johnson and Post 1996. They argued that the flexibility of private regulation suited the Internet better than the rigidity of state regulation.

[12] See for example Perritt 1997.

[13] <http://www.technology.gov/digeconomy/framewrk.htm> (accessed 3 March 2004).

[14] In 1993, the EU issued a 'White paper on Growth, Competitiveness and Employment – the Challenges and Way forward into the 21st Century' (COM(1993)700 5 December, 1993). This was followed by the Bangemann Group report on 'Global Information Society'. The Bangemann Group Report was prepared for the Corfu Council meeting (24-25th June 1994). The conclusions of the report were endorsed at the Corfu Council meeting. <http://www.eff/org/global/multinational/g11/bangemann_report> accessed 3 March 2004.

[15] Cf., Poullet 2004.

[16] a. Council Resolution on illegal and harmful content on the Internet (*OJ* C70 6 March 1997); b. Commission Communication on illegal and harmful content on the Internet (COM(1996)487 16 October 1996); c. Commission Green Paper on the protection of minors and human dignity in audiovisual and information services (COM(1996)483 16 October 1996).

[17] OECD (1998) Proceedings of the OECD/BIAC Forum on Internet Content Self-Regulation held in Paris, 25 March 1998. Doc. dated 14 December 1998 Doc. Ref. DSTI/ICCP(98)18/FINAL.

A number of proponents were quick to point out that in fact the regulation of the Internet was not a dichotomous situation: state only or private only regulation. There were a number of different types of rules regulating activities in cyberspace. Some authors, like Reidenberg[18] and Trudel[19] pointed out that the technical architecture of the Internet can impose limits on how users can behave in certain activities, for example, it can be designed to limit or allow access only to specific users. Others, like Radin and Wagner,[20] argued that private ordering (such as contracts and private agreements) cannot stably exist without an established background of state law to enforce these agreements.

Gradually over the ensuing years, it became clear that multiple sources are involved in regulating activities in cyberspace. In *Code and Other Laws of Cyberspace*, Lessig identified four constraining forces present: (i) state law; (ii) social norms; (iii) architecture and (iv) the market.[21] He argued that each of these constraints has important implications for the behaviour and fundamental rights and freedoms of individuals on the Internet.

2.1.1 Increase in state regulation of cyberspace activities

From the late nineties to the present day states have been increasingly involved, at a national, regional and inter-state level, in enacting legislation to regulate activities in cyberspace.

At an inter-state level, in 2001 – after a drafting and negotiation process of more than five years – the first international convention dealing specifically with the regulation of some cyberspace activities opened for signature. The Council of Europe Convention on Cybercrime[22] attempts to regulate crimes committed via the Internet and other computer networks, dealing particularly with computer-related fraud, child pornography and violations of network security. It also, more importantly perhaps, provides for collaboration in the enforcement of these crimes between enforcement agencies in different states. States involved in the drafting of the Convention included, apart from the (forty-six) Member States of the Council of Europe, five non-Member States – the Holy See, the United States, Canada, Japan and Mexico. The convention is also open for signature and ratification by other non-Council of Europe Member States. This is still the only international treaty specifically drafted to regulate activities in cyberspace. Since the Convention has come into force only in 2004 and the 'big' players such as the United States

---

[18] Reidenberg 1998.
[19] Trudel 2001.
[20] Radin and Wagner 1998.
[21] Lessig 1999: 87.
[22] ETS No. 185 opened for signature in Budapest 23 November 2001 (found at <http://conventions.coe.int/Treaty/en/treaties/html/185.htm>).

have only ratified the Convention in 2006,[23] it is still too early to evaluate the effect of the Convention.

Some international conventions, such as the WIPO Copyright Treaty,[24] though not specifically drafted to regulate copyright issues on the Internet, have been applied by some states to activities on the Internet.[25] At a regional level, the European Union has enacted a number of Directives and other legal frameworks aimed at regulating different aspects of activities on-line. One example is the e-Commerce Directive (2000/31/EC) that regulates the provision of e-commerce services in the European Union.

At a state level, states have enacted legislation to regulate various Internet activities, such as legislation protecting intellectual property rights in a digital context, anti-cybersquatting legislation, the recognition of electronic signatures and so forth. The application and administration of this national legislation is limited to the jurisdiction of the enacting state and in many instances, a single state is unable to sanction non-compliance. The difficulties states (at a national and international level) face in the application and enforcement of state law on the Internet prompt them to promote self-regulation.

The difficulties facing state legislation have shifted the focus on self-regulation toward more attention on the alleged objections to self-regulation. On the one hand, states acknowledge that many Internet activities are regulated by self-regulation rather than by national or international law. Indeed, states often expect self-regulation to regulate certain Internet activities. Self-regulation is perceived to be better suited to regulate certain activities.[26] It is generally claimed[27] that, due to the collective expertise of the group making the regulation, self-regulation offers a better (or more appropriate) regulatory solution that fits the needs identified by and known to the group. Self-regulation is flexible enough to satisfy different regulatory needs. In addition, some authors claim that self-regulatory arrangements are less costly than the drafting and application of state legislation. It is capable of regulating activities independent of territorial considerations, offering a global solution enforced through technical means.

---

[23] The US ratification has come into force on 1 January 2007.

[24] The Copyright Treaty was adopted by the World Intellectual Property Organisation Member States in December 1996 (found at <http://www.wipo.int/treaties/en/ip/wct/trtdocs_wo033.html>).

[25] See for example the US Digital Millennium Copyright Act 1998 (found at <http://www.copyright.gov/legislation/dmca.pdf>) and the EU Copyright Directive (2001/29/EC).

[26] Cf., European Parliament Report on the Commission proposal for a Council Decision adopting a Multiannual Community Action Plan on Promoting Safe Use of the Internet (Rapporteur Mr Gerhard Schmid – 9 June 1998) (doc. Ref. A4-0234/98) at p. 32 – '[choosing self-regulation] does have the advantage of being realistic and practicable. European legislation to control the content of the Internet is obviously difficult to bring about, in view of technical difficulties and the Internet's worldwide nature.' ... 'Our preference is for flexible solutions, not least because the Internet is still in full development and this could be hampered by tough legislation.'

[27] See for example Lerouge 2002.

On the other hand, a number of objections to self-regulation have been voiced. The principle objection, found in the literature, is that self-regulatory arrangements do not sufficiently protect the fundamental rights of users usually protected by state legislation in democratic states.[28] A related objection is that self-regulation does not adequately protect the 'public interest' involved in the activities being regulated. Self-regulation favours the interest or goals of the group creating and developing the regulation and does not necessarily protect the general interests of the community of Internet users as a whole. This leads to a third objection: the legitimacy and accountability of self-regulation arrangements is questioned. The remedy for these objections, various authors suggest, is stronger state involvement in the self-regulation process.

2.2   SELF-REGULATION AS CO-REGULATION, AS A HYBRID ARRANGEMENT AND AS SUBSTITUTION

Although state documents and commentators have long acknowledged that many Internet activities are regulated by self-regulation rather than by national or international law, there is hardly any agreement on what the term 'self-regulation' actually means. It is used interchangeably to describe a wide variety of issues: a rule-making process by a non-state group; a set of rules developed by a non-state group – such as a code of conduct; a process of enforcement of the rules; and a comprehensive regulatory system.

Nor is there agreement on what function self-regulation actually fulfils in the regulation of Internet activities. There are at least three main approaches to the function of self-regulation on the Internet. One position, the 'co-regulation' approach, followed by the European Union and European authors, argues that the role of self-regulation should be dictated by states and state regulation. Another position, the 'hybrid approach', argues that the role of self-regulation is to create, together with state regulation, hybrid regulatory arrangements that are based on both private and state regulation. A third position, the 'substitution approach', argues that self-regulation should develop independently of state regulation at least until state regulation substitutes for self-regulation. The substitution approach finds more following in the United States. Both the United States and the European Union promote the use of self-regulation in the regulation of the Internet. For example, at least four European Union Directives[29] make a direct reference to and encourage industry self-regulation for matters relating to the Internet. However, an examina-

---

[28] See for example Kaspersen, et al. (1999) for a criticism of self-regulation in the regulation of Internet content.

[29] E-Commerce Directive (2000/31/EC), Electronic Signatures Directive (1999/93/EC); Copyright Directive (2001/29/EC); Data Protection Directive (1995/46/EC).

tion of the academic and political debates reveals differences between the ways that the United States and the European Union look at self-regulation.

2.2.1 The co-regulation approach

The concept of co-regulation implies that state regulation and self-regulation co-operate in the regulation of particular activities. (Indeed, some authors, like Grewlich, use the term 'co-operative self-regulation'[30] rather than co-regulation.) In the literature, 'co-regulation' generally refers to a situation where state legislation provides a specific framework within which self-governing institutions create rules and administer them.

The literature reveals two approaches to the relationship between self-regulation and the state in a situation of co-regulation. The first, predominantly followed (albeit implicitly) in EU policy documents, is that the authority to regulate of self-regulation comes from the state and hence, following traditional concepts of delegation of power self-regulation on the Internet should develop within a framework provided by state legislation.

The second approach denies that the link between state regulation and self-regulation is one of allocation of authority. The link is rather one of 'control'. As Poullet argues, 'there could be no question of rejecting self-regulation as a normative source in the fullest sense of the term'.[31] However, it is the state's responsibility to control self-regulation. Poullet argues further that a state

'cannot simply resign, but rather, without pretending to police the network in a thorough manner, it should duly call attention to the social values that enshrine the norms, even if this is only in order to provoke appropriate self-regulatory reflexes and to serve as their basis.'[32]

The main argument in favour of a dominant role for state regulation is that only the state can ensure that the public interest and respect for fundamental rights are respected in the regulatory process. Authors like Poullet[33] argue that this is particularly important on the Internet where individual rights are easily overridden by technological measures. In arguing for the co-regulation approach, Poullet[34] invokes the intervention of the European Union to protect the rights to a private life and personal data: the EU Data Protection Directive (95/46/EC) provides a legislative legal framework for self-regulation. Indeed, the Directive dedicates an entire chapter[35] to the drawing up by trade associations

---

[30] Grewlich 1999: 110, 291.
[31] Poullet 2000.
[32] Poullet 2001a: 105-106.
[33] Poullet 2001a.
[34] In particular in Poullet 2001a.
[35] Chapter V, Art. 27 of Directive 95/46/EC.

and other bodies of codes of conduct intended to implement the provisions of data protection.[36]

Perhaps unsurprisingly, especially in view of the argument that the state has a responsibility to protect citizens' rights, the concept of co-regulation is primarily promoted, in the literature, in connection with the regulation of Internet content-related activities. Studies of the potential role of self-regulation in the regulation of Internet content commissioned by both states[37] and the private sector[38] argue in favour of co-regulation. Indeed, Price and Verhulst[39] argue that co-regulation not only 'should' be the norm but 'is' the norm (in the regulation of Internet content) even if the best models of regulation are still being developed.[40]

While European authors generally agree that self-regulation (on the Internet) should be controlled,[41] not all agree that having a strict legislative framework is the best way to do so. Some authors, like Fenoulhet,[42] argue that the state's authority and laws of general application are enough to control self-regulation. Others, like Brousseau,[43] argue in favour of an institutional framework to control self-regulation.

Some problematic elements of the co-regulation approach need particular attention. The first is the implication that there is a hierarchy between state regulation and self-regulation: state regulation is assumed to be more authoritative or effective than self-regulation. This seems to foreclose the possibility that there might not in fact be such a hierarchy at all, that self-regulation might be the only or predominant form of regulation with state regulation playing a minor role, if any, in the regulation of a given activity.

The second problematic element in the co-regulation approach is, as Poullet[44] argues, that it seems to set fixed partitions between competencies of state regulation and self-regulation where in fact these divisions might not exist. The relationships between state regulation and self-regulation are still in the process of development.

[36] Poullet (2001a) argues that the European Union's co-regulatory approach to data protection is a better approach to protecting citizens' privacy than the US approach of self-regulation without a legislative framework, even if as Bomse (2001) argues, the US government agencies do play a role in putting pressure on industry to formulate and publish privacy positions. Simitis (1998) and Rodotà (2001) follow the same line of argument.

[37] OECD, EU, the UK; also Marsden (2004) on a more recent study commissioned by the EU DG Information Society.

[38] One of the first studies was commissioned by the Bertelsmann Foundation. The results and the position papers produced in the study were eventually published in 2000 in a book edited by Waltermann and Machill 2000.

[39] Price and Verhulst 2005:136.

[40] However, the book where they conclude that co-regulation is the norm, includes the same contribution they made when arguing that co-regulation should be the norm.

[41] Indeed some authors promote 'regulated self-regulation' – that is, self-regulation regulated by direct or indirect state regulation based on constitutional principles. See for example Schultz and Held 2001.

[42] Fenoulhet 2002.

[43] Brousseau 2001.

[44] Poullet 2001a.

With the frequent changes in the economic, social and technical activities taking place on the Internet, the interactions between state and non-state groups fluctuate to accommodate new needs.[45]

A third objection is that the co-regulation approach seems to ignore that Internet activities can take place across different states and that these states may have conflicting approaches to the way the activities are to be regulated. The proponents of the co-regulation approach seem to look at the co-existence of self-regulation and state regulation only from the perspective of an individual state or at most that of the regional arrangement of the European Union. They fail to acknowledge that the position of states in the actual regulation of Internet activities (and other emerging transnational activities) may no longer fit the classic Westphalia legal positivist model. The co-regulation approach fails to take account of changes in the role and effectiveness of state regulation involved in the governance of the Internet.

2.2.2   The hybrid arrangement approach

A second approach sometimes written about is what can be called the 'hybrid arrangement' approach. The expression 'hybrid arrangement' is not found in the literature but it is used here to describe an approach that refers to 'hybrid' institutions and 'hybrid' agreements.

In this approach, the function of self-regulation is that of building together with state regulation combined arrangements that can regulate particular activities that would be problematic for either state regulation alone or self-regulation alone. The only way to regulate such activities is to create 'hybrid arrangements' that while containing elements of both state and self- regulation, can in effect be called neither.

Farrell,[46] an important exponent of this position, argues that what is actually happening, contrary to the co-regulation proponents, is not a situation where state regulation gives authority to or exercises control over self-regulation but rather the development of new hybrid arrangements formed by the action of both self-regulation and state regulation. The example he uses is the creation of safe harbour arrangements in the United States to address the requirements set by data protection law in Europe for the transfer of personal data to third countries that do not have adequate data protection safeguards.

There are two ways to interpret the need for such institutions, according to Farrell. One is to say that the involvement of the private sector shows that the power of the state is diminishing. The interpretation he favours, however, is that hybrid arrange-

---

[45] Indeed, Marsden (2004: 190), when arguing in favour of co-regulation of the media and Internet sectors, confirms that 'regimes must be adjusted to the needs of each sector and other circumstances (technological change, changes in policy to respond to changes in technology, a country's legal system, case law of European courts and so on).'

[46] Farrell 2002.

ments do not show a decrease in state power and corresponding increase in private sector power but rather that new global situations (namely globalisation and the spread of new communications technology) require novel ways of interfacing between different legal systems.[47] State and private regulation work together to create new hybrid arrangements that bridge legal systems while relying extensively on these legal systems for meaning and backup.

Nevertheless, as in the case of the co-regulation approach, the approach seems inadequate to account for what is actually happening. At least two important problems can be identified. The first is the implication that self-regulation, like state regulation, has no effective power over Internet activities. While this may be true for some, the implication ignores all those situations where self-regulation effectively regulates Internet activities. The second difficulty lies with the implication that all problems of regulation in cyberspace involve a 'conflict of laws' and hence require a hybrid arrangement as an interface between conflicting legal systems. This fails to account for all those situations where what is involved is not conflict of laws, but rather problems of co-ordination, of technical access, of conflicting cultural traditions or just a need for an autonomous law.

2.2.3   The substitution approach

The substitution approach is characteristic of much of the literature coming from the United States. The difference between the US approach and the European approach lies primarily in the way the function of the state – of public power – is seen in the interaction with self-regulation. From a European perspective, as described above, self-regulation functions within the parameters set by a legislative framework that both gives self-regulation its authority and delimits the direction self-regulation should follow. The regulation of the Internet is seen as a process of co-regulation involving state regulation and state-led self-regulation.

In the US approach, self-regulation is expected to develop independently of the state or state regulation. Self-regulation is often promoted as a pre-emptive effort to avoid government involvement.[48] There is an implicit faith that private regulation based on contractual arrangements and on conflict resolution through negotiations and alternative dispute resolution[49] can work better than direct government regulation.

From a US perspective, self-regulation (or, as referred to in the US literature 'private ordering')[50] and state regulation co-exist in the same space but have separate and different aims. When interaction between self-regulation and state regulation occurs, this is because state regulation steps in to substitute for self-regulation.

---

[47] Id. 2002: 26.
[48] Newman and Bach 2004.
[49] Grewlich 1999:110.
[50] Macey 1997; Radin and Wagner 1998.

Self-regulation is seen as 'first choice' regulation for the Internet: only when self-regulation is incapable of regulating the activity satisfactorily shall government step in with legal regulation. Where, in the co-regulation approach, the function of state regulation is that of giving authority to self-regulation or guiding the process of self-regulation, in the substitution approach it is rather that of 'quality control'. The self-regulation process is autonomous as long as private regulation meets (declared or undeclared) regulatory goals.[51]

Poullet[52] comments that in recent years the US government has not retained its commitment to self-regulation policy in all sectors of Internet activities. It has legislated intensively in the areas of intellectual property and has only retained its preference for self-regulation in cases such as the protection of privacy or the setting of limits to freedom of expression. One might argue that in fact, this is not a change in policy at all but rather an example of the substitution approach. State regulation steps in to substitute for self-regulation in areas where self-regulation does not satisfy the goals of the US government. This explains the emphasis on the 'failures' of private regulatory arrangements in the US academic literature. In contrast, where the US government is reluctant to intervene, such as in the protection of personal information or to set limits to freedom of expression, self-regulation is still expected to play the role of primary provider of regulation.

As with co-regulation and hybrid arrangements, the substitution approach can be somewhat problematic as a description of the current co-existence of self-regulation and state regulation. The major criticism of the substitution approach is that it views regulation of cyberspace activities dichotomously, that is, either government (state) regulation or self-regulation. It fails to account for the possibility that there might be situations where state regulation and self-regulation interact in the regulation of activities.

The idea of state regulation substituting for private regulation has been suggested in other areas of regulation. In the classic work of Macaulay[53] on contractual relations in business, state rules only substitute for informal non-contractual relations between business parties when what is achieved through non-contractual relations is not considered acceptable. Similarly, Ellickson,[54] in his description of the settlement of cattle-related disputes between neighbouring ranchers, argues that private rules co-exist with state rules and that state rules are invoked by private parties and hence substitute for private rules only when some of those involved do not accept the private rules.

---

[51] One can argue that the substitution approach is also a form of co-regulation. The main difference however, is that the authoritative legal context is private law (and not public law as understood in the co-regulation approach).

[52] Poullet 2001b.

[53] Macaulay 1963.

[54] Ellickson 1991.

2.3   LEGAL PLURALISM AND MESH REGULATION

Differences of opinion reflected in the three approaches described above seem to derive largely from limited and non-representative knowledge of how self-regulation actually works on the Internet. Indeed, the three approaches found in the literature are mainly hypothetical prescriptive positions – that is, self-regulation 'should' perform a particular function – and not descriptions of what self-regulation actually 'is'.

I argue, based on the findings set forth in the coming chapters, that the three approaches are, at best, partial and incomplete positions of what is actually happening in the regulation of the Internet. Two legal theory positions have influenced my assessment of whether self-regulation developed in the way argued for in the literature: legal pluralism and network/mesh regulation. The former refers to the idea that more than one source of rules often coexist in any regulatory space. The latter refers to the idea that sources of rules today have shifted from a hierarchical pyramidal structure with state legislation at the top of the hierarchy to networked or meshed regulation where different sources of rules co-exist and interact to form a complex whole.

2.3.1   Legal pluralism in Internet regulation

As Griffiths states,

> 'the concept of legal pluralism refers in the most general sense to situations in which the "law" that obtains in a social field consists of more than one set of binding rules, whose behavioural requirements are different and sometimes conflicting.'[55]

Central to the concept of legal pluralism is that in any social space, state law is not the only 'law'. 'Law' is not a single monolithic, unified set of rules flowing from the State's hierarchy. 'Law' refers to all the (binding) rules created by the state or private groups within a social field. A corollary of the idea that state law is not the only law is that there are many groups making rules in the same space, not only the state.[56] For some authors, the central idea in legal pluralism can be extended further to include not only the existence of a plurality of rules and a variety of groups making the rules in any given space but also that the various rules interact and are interrelated. As de Sousa Santos argues 'Rather than being ordered by a single legal order, modern societies are ordered by a plurality of legal orders, interrelated and socially distributed in different ways.'[57]

---

[55] Griffiths 2001: 8650; also Griffiths 1986.

[56] See for example the classic work of Moore 1973.

[57] de Sousa Santos 1995: 114; also Griffiths (2003) for detailed analysis of various sorts of interrelationships.

The concept of legal pluralism affords us the 'freedom' to move away from a positivistic approach to 'law'. Through the concept of legal pluralism, 'self-regulation' can be considered as a form of 'law' (largely) independent of the state. This shift in looking at self-regulation as (possibly) primarily autonomous is an important element in the way cases of self-regulation on the Internet are described. The contrast with the co-regulation approach (described earlier) is particularly sharp.

While initially 'legal pluralism' was a term used to characterise the presence of multiple legal orders and groups within states or territorial arrangements, the concept(s)[58] of legal pluralism have also been applied to explain transnational and supra-state orders in international contexts.[59] These studies show that there is an emerging transnational 'law' formulated primarily by non-state groups, for example, a *lex mercatoria* for the regulation of transnational arbitration processes.

Authors such as Jones[60] and Berman[61] have argued for the use of the concept of legal pluralism in understanding Internet regulation. By using the concept of legal pluralism, authors can formally accept that there are in fact multiple sources of regulation on the Internet and can focus on determining what the contribution of each source actually is and on the emergence of a transnational law for the Internet.

In using the concept of legal pluralism as a theoretical basis for this book, I make two assumptions. One is that self-regulation on the Internet is a form of legal ordering (created and administered by private groups for their own behaviour) and not simply a set of social norms. The second is that self-regulation co-exists in the same regulatory space as other sources of regulation including state regulation.

2.3.2 Mesh regulation – networked regulation

The work of Ost and Van de Kerchove[62] and others[63] support the suspicion that there may be no hierarchical relationship between state regulation and self-regulation on the Internet. Ost and Van de Kerchove argue that there is a paradigm shift moving in many fields of law away from a pyramidal process of rule creation to a network or mesh process. In a pyramidal model, the relationship between state regulation and other sources is hierarchical. State legislation and structures determine the scope and limits of self-regulation. In a network or mesh model, the relationship is primarily one of interconnectedness.

---

[58] I use here 'concepts' in the plural primarily because in the literature there is no one concept of legal pluralism. There is a central understanding of the concept surrounded by different nuances that have been added to the initial descriptions of legal pluralism. For a presentation of the different nuances see Melissaris 2004.

[59] For example the work of Teubner 1997, Snyder 1999, Twining 2000.

[60] Jones 1998.

[61] Berman (2002) uses legal pluralism to explain the need to acknowledge the presence of private rules in choice of law decisions and the reshaping of existing legal regimes in cyberspace.

[62] Ost and Van de Kerchove 2002.

[63] Schultz 2005; Cannataci and Mifsud Bonnici 2006; and Poullet 2006.

In the concept of 'mesh regulation', the analogy utilised is that of the steel mesh in reinforced concrete structures or the mesh in fishing nets, where, when put together, different strands provide a structure much stronger than that of the individual components.[64] The origin of the strands, whether from self-regulation or state regulation is immaterial: what is important is the flexibility and strength of the structure provided. In mesh regulation various forms of regulation, that is, state regulation, self-regulation, and so-called 'hybrid' regulation have evolved and continue to evolve, sometimes independently and sometimes in interaction with each other to produce a mesh of rule-systems where the sources, creation and implementation of rules depends on interconnected operation of states and private groups.

The concept of 'mesh regulation' is used in the literature to identify new solutions to problems caused by transactions in cyberspace. It is argued that the need for real-time remedies for users/citizens pushes both self-regulation and states to collaborate in the development and administration of rules. While each creates rules and fora to meet the needs of its respective constituency, disputes are increasingly settled through mechanisms established by a combination of self-regulation and state regulation. Lawyers pursuing solutions for the problems encountered by their clients in cyberspace, weave together solutions from market norms, private regulation and state regulation. The observation of Knill and Lehmkuhl to the effect that there are increasingly 'more synergetic relationships [between private and public regulation], with private and public activities partially reinforcing each other'[65] reinforces the need to look at regulation on the Internet from a network/mesh perspective rather than the traditional hierarchical perspective.

---

[64] Cannataci and Mifsud Bonnici 2006.
[65] Knill and Lehmkuhl 2002: 42; also Reidenberg 2004b and Ferdinand 2005.

Chapter 3
IDENTIFYING SELF-REGULATION

As Price and Verhulst point out, 'The initial problem of every approach to self-regulation pertains to definition and semantics.'[1] The meaning given to the term 'self-regulation' varies from sector to sector, from time to time and depends on whether the reference comes from the perspective of the state or of the private sector. Black lists the different variables that lead to different self-regulation arrangements. She points out that

> 'self-regulation may vary not only in its relationship with the state but in the nature of its participants (which may be solely members of the collective or may be outsiders), its structures (there may be separate agency or it may be a cartel), its enforcement (it may enforce its own norms or it may rely on individuals to enforce), and its rule type (its rules may be of legislative, contractual or no legal status, be general or specific, vague or precise, simple or complex).'[2]

Various references in the literature seem to allude to an undeclared common understanding of self-regulation.[3] However, while both the United States and Europe promote self-regulation, the meaning attached to the term is often different.[4] The term 'self-regulation' in Europe often refers to 'codes of conduct' or to a type of regulation by private parties in conformity with and backed up by a state legal framework and legislation. The meaning in the United States, on the other hand, usually implies a minimalist legal environment model,[5] or what Post and Johnson[6] call 'decentralized, emergent law-making' – implying a system independent from a state public law framework.

In this book I use the term 'self-regulation' when referring to three distinctive features of 'self-regulation': (a) a flexible type of regulation model; (b) a set of rules developed and accepted by those who are taking part in an activity;[7] and (c) a

---

[1] Price and Verhulst 2000b: 58.

[2] Black 1996: 27-28.

[3] See, among others, Lerouge 2001, Berleur and de Wespin 2001.

[4] Grewlich 1999: 110. See also Chapter 2.

[5] Grewlich 1999: 110.

[6] Post and Johnson 1997.

[7] Trudel 2000: 204 'L'autoréglementation fait référence aux normes volontairement développées et acceptées par ceux qui prennent part à une activité.'

J.P. Mifsud Bonnici, Self-Regulation in Cyberspace
© 2008, T·M·C· ASSER PRESS, *The Hague, and the author*

regulatory process.[8] Each reference to the term self-regulation in the coming chapters assumes this understanding of the term.

3.1   SELF-REGULATION AS A TYPE OF REGULATION MODEL

In general, self-regulation is a type of regulation – a middle way between command and control systems of regulation identified with state regulation and 'laissez-faire'.[9] State regulation is considered the most rigid: exclusively competent legislator, fixed process of rule formation, certainty of rule content and formalism in the enforcement and application of the rules. Market-driven regulation ('laissez-faire capitalism') is viewed as the most lax: in that the organisation/firm tracks the requirements of the market and adapts accordingly.

Self-regulation is considered[10] as somewhere in between the two: 'a private norm'[11] created by private groups who have 'rule-making capacities and the means to induce or coerce compliance'.[12] As Newman and Bach comment,

> 'In an environment still characterized by rapidly changing business models, market structures and technological advances, private sector self-regulation carves out a regulatory middle ground between government intervention and pure market mechanisms. Self-regulatory systems are often more flexible and less intrusive than formal regulation by governments; at the same time, they reduce uncertainty and enhance consumer confidence beyond levels attainable by the market alone.'[13]

3.2   SELF-REGULATION AS A SET OF RULES

As a point of departure, I use Trudel's definition of self-regulation as 'a set of rules voluntarily developed and accepted by those who are taking part in an activity'.[14] Furthermore as Black argues, the term self-regulation

> 'describes the situation of a group of persons or bodies, acting together, performing a regulatory function in respect of themselves and others who accept their authority.'[15]

---

[8] Black (1996:26) argues that any description of self-regulation should also include a description of its relationship with the state. For her there are three constituent elements to self-regulation: the self, the regulation and the state.

[9] Gunningham and Rees 1997: 365.

[10] Id. 1997: 364-365.

[11] D'Udekem-Gevers and Poullet 2002.

[12] Moore 1973: 720.

[13] Newman and Bach 2004: 387.

[14] Trudel's 2000: 204

[15] Black 1996: 27.

Both definitions, however, need some further explanation of the 'self' who creates the rules and of the 'rules' developed by this 'self'.

3.2.1   The self

I find it useful in identifying the 'self' in self-regulation to use Moore's[16] concept of a 'semi-autonomous social field' (SASF).[17] What distinguishes the 'self' in self-regulation from any private arrangement of people is that the SASF, hereinafter called 'the group' consists of members who regulate their own behaviour (to some extent).[18]

The members of the group can be natural and/or artificial persons who share a number of similar or common interests and goals and accept regulation by the group they participate in.[19] The interests shared may be based on a common profession or occupation, industry, business community, not-for-profit action or a combination of interests.[20] The reason to be part of the group and accept its rules is, as Moore puts it 'induced by the desire to stay in the game and prosper'.[21] The group is 'capable of managing collective resources, undertaking group action, and carrying on external affairs'.[22]

The group for my purposes does not include the state, nor is the state a member of a self-regulating group. This does not mean that the group is wholly independent of the state or state regulation. For example, in discussions of self-regulation of the domain name system, while the Internet Corporation for Assigned Names and Numbers (ICANN) can be identified as a possible 'self', intervention of the state has given rise to a debate on whether ICANN can be considered a self-regulatory body or not. Some authors[23] claim that ICANN is not really a self-regulatory body since it is dependent to some extent on the US government and Department of Commerce and since states have some influence on the decisions of ICANN through the Governmental Advisory Committee. Influence of the state or a public authority on the group and its regulatory process is an important factor, but not inconsistent with the concept of self-regulation.

Moore[24] uses the concept of 'semi-autonomy' precisely to make this point clear. In regulating its own behaviour, a group is partially (semi-) autonomous. It can

---

[16] Moore 1973.

[17] The SASF concept developed by Moore can be used to explain the relationship between private groups involved in rule setting and states. In her article she examined the membership and behaviour of two groups involved in setting rules: one involved in the garment industry and the other, the Chagga tribe of Mount Kilimanjaro. (See Moore 1973).

[18] Griffiths 2003.

[19] Boulding 2000: 134.

[20] Gunningham, and Rees 1997: 370-380.

[21] Moore 1973: 729.

[22] Griffiths 2003: 23.

[23] For example Froomkin 2000b.

[24] Moore 1973.

regulate its affairs only to a certain extent – to the extent 'allowed' by regulation coming form other sources of regulation predominantly state regulation. As Griffiths points out

> '(T)hus, under normal conditions, the state – one of the most prominent and for many purposes the most inclusive of the SASFs in modern society – substantially constrains the autonomy of other SASFs.'[25]

Identifying the groups involved in the self-regulation of Internet activities can be difficult. Self-regulatory efforts are often neither public nor reported, and they take different forms in different parts of the world.[26] Furthermore, the membership of the relevant groups depends on the activity to be regulated. It can be expected that members with different expertise and interests will be involved in the regulation of different Internet activities. Hence, for example, members with technical expertise, such as engineers, are more likely to regulate technical activities while industry groups are more likely to be involved in the regulation of activities linked with their line of business.[27]

Given the layered structure of the Internet, the choice of groups involved in regulation also depends on the level at which the activity needing regulation takes place. For example, groups involved in the technical level have a greater incentive and arguably a better possibility to regulate activities at that technical level.

Some authors have chosen to look at one category of groups, for example, industry groups, in the regulation of particular activities. The work of Price and Verhulst[28] on self-regulation of illegal and harmful Internet content identifies the 'self' primarily as industry groups or a collective made up of representatives of the different sectors of industry. This approach is somewhat limited if one considers that the private sector on the Internet is not a uniform block and there is no single 'industry' that speaks for the whole of the Internet.[29] In this study, different groups involved in self-regulation are examined.

Two aspects of the group need to be examined: legitimacy and accountability of the group as rule-makers. In a state, the authority to create rules comes from the community of persons who accept the legality of the rules enacted. Similarly, in this study, I look at whether the persons allegedly bound by the group rules (that is,

---

[25] Griffiths 2003: 24.

[26] Price and Verhulst 2005: 72.

[27] Frieden (2001) argues that given the hierarchical structure of the Internet, the particular groups involved in regulation also depends on the level at which the activity needing regulation takes place. For example, persons involved at the technical level have a greater incentive and arguably a better possibility to regulate activities at that technical level.

[28] Price and Verhulst 2000b.

[29] Price and Verhulst (2005: 68) refer to the work of Albert Gidari, 'Observations on the state of self-regulation of the Internet' prepared for the Ministerial Conference of the OECD (7-9 October 1998).

primarily the members and at times third parties such as customers of a member) accept the validity of the self-regulation rules and of the governing regime.[30] I expected[31] that four elements could influence the acceptance of the legitimacy of the rules and the group.

The formation of the group is one element. Unlike a state, the link between the group and its members is not based on birth and territory but on *shared interest*. The shared interest can be a reason for the members to accept the validity of the rules and the creators of the rules. A second element is *expertise*. Through its technical expertise and familiarity with the activity concerned, the group can determine the actual need for regulation, analyse the implications[32] and design appropriate rules and procedures. Trusting the expertise and familiarity of the group, members and third parties are more ready to accept the validity of the group rules. A third element is *technical access* to the relevant Internet activities. Only some groups have such access and, through (technical) intervention, can effectively regulate (and enforce the regulation of) the activity. The practical power to regulate an activity (in contrast to the, for example, theoretical power of state legislation) strengthens the inclination of the members to accept the validity of the rules of the group. Finally, as some authors[33] point out, groups can also obtain legitimacy through the *acknowledgement/approval of states* or public authorities.[34]

Through a complicated system of checks and balances, states and state agencies can, at least in theory, be held to account for the laws they enact. Are groups held to account? In this study, I use the theoretical model developed by Wapner to identify sources of NGO accountability.[35] He identifies two forms of accountability: internal and external accountability.

Internal accountability refers to systems built into the organisation of the group. These systems can be used to hold the group in check. These systems include: (a) a hierarchical decision-making structure that can provide some internal accountability; (b) internal democracy; (c) payment of membership fees – as Wapner points out 'members also vote with their pocket-books';[36] (d) active engagement of members in the governance of the group; (e) ease of 'exit' from the group.

---

[30] These two issues are taken from a definition of 'legitimacy' in the political science literature. 'Legitimacy is whether or not people accept the validity of a law or ruling or the validity of a governing regime.' (see <http://en.wikipedia.org/wiki/Legitimacy> accessed 19 May 2006).

[31] Based on debates found in legal and political science literature, such as Cutler, Haufler and Porter 1999; Haufler 2001; Hall and Biersteker 2002; and Cutler 2003.

[32] Mifsud Bonnici and De Vey Mestdagh 2004b.

[33] For example , Poullet 2001b.

[34] Poullet (2001b: 100) gives the Dutch Code of Conduct on electronic commerce concluded under the auspices of the Dutch Government as an example.

[35] Wapner develops this theoretical model to question the claim of other authors that private actors cannot be held accountable like states. For Wapner (2002: 198) 'States and NGOs possess various mechanisms of accountability, each of which works imperfectly.'

[36] Wapner 2002: 201.

External accountability refers to external sources of regulation that hold the group to account. States and public organisations are the primary source of external accountability.

3.2.2 The rules

Groups can be involved in any or all of the following aspects of regulation of Internet activities:[37] (a) policy-making, that is, identifying principles and policies that could be used to regulate the actions of a group; (b) rule creation, that is, formulating rules to control specific behaviour; (c) application and enforcement and sanctioning of rules, irrespective of whether the rules were created by the private group or by the state;[38] and (d) dispute-settlement, that is, offering a forum for resolving disputes arising from activities in a particular area.

The rules involved in self-regulation are expressed in a variety of instruments. The instruments used and the rules they contain or implement show what activities self-regulation regulates in fact. The most popular instruments of self-regulation are codes of conduct.[39] At times, a reference to a 'code of conduct' is (almost) synonymous with the term 'self-regulation'. Some authors[40] list other instruments of self-regulation. These include the use of 'rule-based' instruments such as model contracts, memoranda of understanding,[41] guidelines, consumer charters,[42] voluntary and co-operative agreements,[43] covenants, negotiated compliance systems, partnerships, management systems, corporate reporting, accounting and self-auditing systems and licensing systems. Reports of international organisations[44] on self-regulation on the Internet also include 'technology-based' self-regulatory instruments.

There often are particular reasons why certain instruments are used instead of others. For example, one can argue that the predominant use of codes of conduct as self-regulatory instruments is linked to the funding and support for self-regulation from states and international organisations that require codes of conduct as instruments of self-regulation.[45]

---

[37] See Price and Verhulst 2000b: 62.

[38] See Moore 1973 and Griffiths 2003.

[39] At times these are also called 'codes of practice' or 'codes of ethics'.

[40] For example, Lerouge 2002.

[41] Micossi 1999.

[42] UK National Consumer Council 2000: 8.

[43] Sinclair 1997: 532.

[44] OECD (1998) Proceedings of the OECD/BIAC Forum on Internet Content Self-Regulation held in Paris, 25 March 1998. Doc. dated 14 December 1998 Doc. Ref. DSTI/ICCP(98)18/FINAL pp 4-11 and see also Johnson and Post 1998.

[45] The EU for example has funded research on the use and content of codes of conduct in the regulation of Internet content (see Programme in Comparative Media Law and Policy at Oxford University 2003) in order to issue guidelines on good practices to be followed in the compilation and use of codes of conduct by private actors.

Legal effect of the rules

What is the legal effect of the self-regulation rules? Do the rules of self-regulation have a similar legal effect to laws created by states? In this book, I formulate three criteria usually associated with state rules to examine the legal effect of self-regulation rules. The first considers the binding effect of the rules. State rules have a binding effect irrespective of whether a particular law is enforced by public authority or not (although it can and has been doubted whether a legal rule with no effect whatever is really a rule at all). The binding quality of non-state rules is an empirical matter to be established by looking at the mechanisms foreseen by the creators of the rule to ensure that the rule is followed and to sanction non-conformity.[46] The means to induce or coerce compliance can include technical means.

The second criterion considers the transparency of the rules and the rule-making process. State rules are published and hence knowable. Are self-regulation rules on the Internet similarly transparent? The third criterion is legal certainty. Legal certainty can be examined by looking at the stability (that is, whether the rules are subject to frequent change or improvisation), the clarity and the public nature of the rules.

3.3   SELF-REGULATION AS A RULE-MAKING PROCESS

In a national law-making context, identifying the procedure followed for the enactment of law is usually not too difficult a task. The national law-making process, whether by Parliament, delegated to specific authorities or by judges, follows well-established steps. In comparison, the rule-making process of groups may sometimes seem hard to pin down.

Using the steps followed in the formation of state legislation (by the legislature), I understand the idea of a 'rule-making process' to involve the following five stages:[47]

(i)   identification of need: the process is set into action by the recognition that a particular activity needs to be regulated;

(ii)   valuation: action is only taken on those activities deemed of substantial importance, as measured in terms of the moral, financial and political values of the group;

(iii) implementation: the valued need is translated into a norm, that is, the group decides what it considers to be desirable behaviour and formulates this as a legal rule;

---

[46] Poullet 2001b: 82.

[47] This theoretical framework for 'law' formation is discussed in Mifsud Bonnici and De Vey Mestdagh (2004b).

(iv) application: the text or instrument containing the rule acquires binding force;
(v)   enforcement and sanction: the rule is enforced and non-compliance sanctioned.

In *pure self-regulation*[48] the private group, independent of any direct government involvement, carries out both the rule-making and enforcement.[49] Price and Verhulst[50] argue that pure self-regulation does not exist in connection with the Internet, especially in the case of Internet content.[51] One may argue, however, that that part of the self-regulation exercise that regulates the internal working of the private groups themselves is an example of pure self-regulation. The rules include rules on membership of the group, the basis for the group getting together, rules of behaviour in the group, rules on participation in the rule-making process and rules on enforcement and sanction of group rules.

In the majority of cases, the rule-making process involves some state involvement. In the self-regulation literature, several authors[52] have formulated categorisation schemes to classify the different self-regulation arrangements that groups are involved in. I use the following typology, an amalgamation of different lists found in the literature, to identify the various rule-making processes on the Internet and consequently identify the function of self-regulation. The list consists of four categories:

(a) *Statutory self-regulation*:[53] private groups are required or 'encouraged' by state regulation to engage in self-regulation. State regulation acts as a framework within which the private groups can engage in the regulation of activities. Poullet[54] contends that examples of self-regulation concerning the use of personal data in Europe are an example of statutory self-regulation.[55]

(b) *Mandated or delegated self-regulation*:[56] although private groups formulate the rules and carry out the rule-making and enforcement, the private rules are either officially sanctioned by the state or are monitored by an official body (for example, the Director-General of Fair Trading in the United Kingdom) to keep check on the success and efficiency of the self-regulation. This form of self-regulation is mostly found in areas where self-regulation arrangements are funded (or partly funded) by the state. At times, the self-regulation is not only mandated but it is delegated, that

---

[48] Geelhoed's 1993; 'voluntary self-regulation' in Gunningham and Rees 1997.
[49] Gunningham and Rees 1997: 366; Black 1996: 27 and Geelhoed 1993.
[50] Price and Verhulst 2005.
[51] See also Programme in Comparative Media Law and Policy at Oxford University 2003.
[52] Gunningham and Rees 1997: 366; Black 1996: 27 and Geelhoed 1993: 49.
[53] Gunningham and Rees 1997: 366; Price and Verhulst 2005: 65; and Black 1996: 27.
[54] Poullet 2001b.
[55] See EU Data Protection Directive (95/46/EC).
[56] Gunningham and Rees 1997: 366; Price and Verhulst 2005: 65; and Black 1996: 27.

is, the state formally delegates the authority to regulate a particular activity to the private sector.

(c) *Coerced self-regulation*:[57] while the self-regulation is carried out by private groups, the initiative to do so is in response to perceived government threats of statutorily imposed regulation, or intended to pre-empt possible state involvement in the regulation[58] or in response to government political pressure (especially in areas where the state cannot readily impose statutory self-regulation). Coerced self-regulation can be found in situations where important industry resources are at stake, where government or private sector inertia could lead to a (financial or economic) loss for the industry.

(d) *Agreed self-regulation*:[59] a form of self-regulation negotiated between private groups. Such an arrangement generally takes place when regulation is needed to solve a co-ordination problem so that the different private groups benefit from the self-regulation arrangement. Often this sort of self-regulation involves the creation of a 'code of conduct' – rules negotiated or at least discussed (either formally or informally) between an industry body, on the one hand, and for example consumer organisations on the other.[60]

3.4 CONCLUSION

In this and the preceding chapters, I have sketched a broad background for this book. In Chapter 1, I introduced the central research question of this study – 'what is the function of self-regulation on the Internet?' In Chapter 2, I gave a short account of the historical development of self-regulation in the regulation of activities on the Internet. Essentially, the development of regulation has followed the development of the Internet: in the early years when the Internet was closed to the public, the main form of regulation was self-regulation. Once the Internet was open to the public and people realised that money can be made and lost on the Internet, other forms of regulation, particularly state regulation, increased.

In Chapter 2, I also described the three main theoretical approaches found in the literature on the function of self-regulation in relation to the Internet: the co-regulation approach, the hybrid arrangements approach and the substitution approach. These three approaches form the main theoretical frames of reference for the analysis of the current arrangements of self-regulation examined in this study.

---

[57] Price and Verhulst 2005: 65; and Black 1996: 27.
[58] Maxwell, Lyon and Hackett 2000: 584.
[59] Geelhoed 1993:49.
[60] See UK National Consumer Council 2000: 13.

The findings set forth in the coming chapters, show that the three approaches are, at best, partial and incomplete reflections of what is actually happening in the regulation of the Internet. At the end of Chapter 2, I introduced two ideas from legal theory that have influenced my assessment of whether self-regulation developed in the way argued for in the literature: legal pluralism and network/mesh regulation.

In this chapter, I have discussed three aspects of the term 'self-regulation' as used in this study. The term refers to (a) a type of regulation; (b) a set of rules developed and accepted by those who are taking part in an activity;[61] and (c) a rule-making process.

Armed with the necessary background, I proceed in the coming chapters to examine the function of self-regulation in Internet content regulation, in the administration of the Domain Name System, in the setting of technical standards and in the provision of dispute resolution for on-line disputes.

---

[61] Trudel 2000: 204.

Chapter 4
SELF-REGULATION OF INTERNET CONTENT

4.1 INTRODUCTION

Undoubtedly the most important contribution of the Internet is that it offers a straight-forward means for publication, distribution, storage and access to a wide range of content. Searching, accessing, downloading and putting information on the Internet are certainly the most common uses participants make of the Internet.

The Internet has changed the flow of content in society. It allows individuals, groups, businesses, governments, etc. to disseminate information to a potentially global audience at relatively low transaction costs. Equally simple, users located in any place can access information in real time, often virtually free of charge, irrespective of the territorial origin of the content.[1]

Though states are familiar with regulating flows of content in society, the changes in the flow of content brought about by the Internet challenges traditional regulation of content by individual states. The difference is primarily that the content to be regulated exists in a global space where different traditions of regulating content conflict, where different cultural values of countries and users clash, and where communities with different histories of content regulation meet and interact. Put simply, the problem in the regulation of content on the Internet is that the same content on the Internet can be considered illegal in one state, (merely) harmful in another state and even legal or desirable in a third country.

Groups have long been involved in the regulation of Internet content. A number of authors have argued both in favour and against the involvement of self-regulation in the regulation of Internet content, at times by comparing the situation to self-regulation of content in other media, for example print media or broadcasting.[2] In a study on the potential role of self-regulation of content commissioned by the Bertelsmann Foundation, Price and Verhulst[3] argued in favour of self-regulation acting together with state regulation. D'Udekem-Gevers and Poullet[4] take a similar position. The 'Memorandum on Self-Regulation' published by the Bertelsmann Foundation in 1999, based, *inter alia*, on the contribution of Price and Verhulst,[5]

---

[1] Cf., Newman and Bach 2004: 399.

[2] For example in the UK self-regulation of journalists has a long standing tradition. The Code of Conduct of the National Union of Journalists in Britain and Ireland has been in effect since 1936. (Code of Conduct accessed at <http://www.nuj.org.uk/inner.php?docid=59> 15 December 2005).

[3] Price and Verhulst 2000a and also 2000b and 2005.

[4] D'Udekem-Gevers and Poullet 2001-2.

[5] Price and Verhulst 2000a.

J.P. Mifsud Bonnici, Self-Regulation in Cyberspace
© 2008, T·M·C· ASSER PRESS, The Hague, and the author

argues for greater state involvement in the formulation of codes of conduct for Internet Service Providers (ISP) involved in regulating content. In later research, Price and Verhulst[6] and the authors of the Programme in Comparative Media Law and Policy at Oxford University study,[7] commissioned by the European Commission, give specific recommendations on how the State can be involved in the formulation of ISP codes of conduct.[8]

In contrast, Kaspersen, et al., argue that self-regulation 'should not be considered as an ideal solution to any problem'[9] more so in the case of the regulation of Internet content where fundamental rights may be involved. Self-regulation in this scenario could only work with adequate safeguards provided by the State, which safeguards, they argue, are missing.[10]

Kaspersen, et al.,[11] argue that self-regulation in the regulation of content is unilateral. The groups decide on rules to enforce on themselves and the users of their systems. Users have no say in the enactment of the rules and hence some of their rights, for example, their right to freedom of speech and its corollary freedom of information, can be curtailed. Self-regulation is, effectively for some authors,[12] the equivalent of censorship and not legal regulation.

To limit unilateralism, some authors, such as the Centre for Democracy and Technology (CDT),[13] argue in favour of user empowerment to move the decisions on content from ISPs to users. In its report, CDT argues that since central to the concept of user empowerment is 'the recognition that, on the Internet, individuals and *parents* are best suited to make decisions about what information flows into their home',[14] it follows that neither group self-regulation nor State regulation should be regulating what an individual receives. Self-regulation should instead provide tools (such as filtering or rating tools) for individuals to decide what content to receive.

D'Udekem-Gevers and Poullet counter, however, that user empowerment can only function when it is protected by the State.[15] The State can safeguard the right of users to be given appropriate tools to 'empower' themselves and set a legal framework outlining the criteria within which user empowerment tools should be developed by self-regulation.

For Grewlich too, state regulation is the only means to protect users from arbitrary removal of content from the Internet and private censorship. He argues that 'a

---

[6] Price and Verhulst 2005.

[7] Programme in Comparative Media Law and Policy at Oxford University 2003.

[8] See Marsden 2004.

[9] Kaspersen, et al. 1999: 78.

[10] Kaspersen, et al. (1999) focus their criticism on intermediaries, such as ISPs. They argue that there are no proper safeguards to protect the fundamental rights of users from the unilateral action of ISPs in regulating content.

[11] Kaspersen, et al. 1999.

[12] See Starr 2003.

[13] Centre for Democracy and Technology 1999.

[14] Id. 1999: 1.

[15] D'Udekem-Gevers and Poullet 2001: 21.

strict "double-track approach" is needed'.[16] One track is the development of self-regulatory instruments. The second track involves State legislation regulating Internet content, especially by imposing mechanisms to protect users from arbitrary removal of content and censorship.

In this chapter, I identify a number of self-regulation arrangements that are involved in the regulation of Internet content. Based on the characteristics of these arrangements, I explain what is actually happening in practice, that is, that self-regulation of content is widespread and that its coexistence with state regulation is now established. This coexistence, I argue, involves strong intertwining and complementary relations between self-regulation and state regulation.

In this chapter, the term 'content' is at times qualified by the terms 'illegal', 'harmful' or 'unwanted'. This classification of Internet content into 'illegal', 'harmful' and 'unwanted' follows the classification followed in EU policy documents on the regulation of Internet content.[17] The distinction between each category of content is a formal one. In practice, there is an overlap and a gradual transition between the three categories of content and the distinctions are rather subjective.

Content is 'illegal' if prohibited by a state. As argued in the EU Commission Communication on illegal and harmful content, there exists a whole range of legislation, which for various reasons limits the publication, use and distribution of certain content, for example, child pornography. Infringement of such legislation leads to the 'illegality' of the content.[18]

In the phrase 'harmful content', it is not the content *per se* that is harmful but the perceived effect of the particular content on certain individuals or groups. The perceived effect depends on the individual or groups' beliefs, values, interests or cultural traditions. One group can consider harmless what another considers harmful. While there may be general agreement between states that for example children or minorities need specific protection from the effect of the publication of certain content, there is hardly any general agreement between states on the level of protection or on the specific content, which needs regulation.

The EU Commission introduced the distinction between 'illegal' and 'harmful' content as an important criterion in identifying what regulation was required in the regulation of content in the audiovisual and information services sector (including Internet). The two major initiatives launched contemporaneously in 1996 by the European Union to regulate content – that is the Commission Communication on illegal and harmful content on the Internet[19] and the Green Paper on the Protection

---

[16] Grewlich 1999: 298.

[17] Proposal for a Decision of the European Parliament and of the Council on establishing a multi-annual Community programme on promoting safer use of the Internet and new on-line technologies (COM(2004)91 final 12 March 2004) at p. 3-5.

[18] COM(1996)487 final p. 10 and d'Udekem-Gevers and Poullet 2001: 374.

[19] Communication to the European Parliament, The Council, The Economic and Social Committee and the Committee of the Regions (COM(1996)487 16 October 1996).

of Minors and Human Dignity in audiovisual and information services[20] – use the distinction between 'illegal' and 'harmful' content as an important criterion. The Commission Communication points out that

> 'In terms of illegal and harmful content, it is crucial to differentiate between content which is illegal and other harmful content. These different categories of content pose radically different issues of principle and call for very different legal and technological responses. It would be dangerous to amalgamate separate issues such as children accessing pornographic content for adults, and adults accessing pornography about children.'[21]

While the formal definitions and distinctions imply that there is global agreement on what content is illegal and harmful, global agreement in fact only exists with regard to child pornography. Furthermore, in spite of the recognition that 'illegal' and 'harmful' content require different treatment,[22] the terms 'illegal' and 'harmful' are often used interchangeably in policy documents and in the literature.

'Unwanted content' refers to all content that the recipient of the content had not specifically asked for or sought to access. It is also often referred to as 'spam'. The role of regulation here is to protect users from being exposed to unwanted content (including the danger of viruses), having their computer and their Internet access overloaded by it, and more generally to protect the Internet from overloading. In EU documents, this category of content was added later to the discussion of the regulation of content on the Internet. The increase in sending and receipt of unsolicited bulk email has increased the attention to 'unwanted content'.

4.2   THE PREVALENCE OF SELF-REGULATION IN THE REGULATION OF INTERNET CONTENT

Self-regulation is common in the regulation of Internet content. There are several groups involved in the regulation of Internet content. They exhibit an extensive variety of different self-regulation arrangements and rules.

In the literature,[23] ISPs are invariably highlighted in any discussion on self-regulation of content. However, ISPs, while an important industry group, are not the only groups involved in self-regulation. Any group that has an interest in controlling the flow of content accessed or received by them (and by others) is involved in some aspect of regulation of content. These include religious groups, groups who share a common belief, ideology, interest or value and so forth.

---

[20] COM(1996)483 final 16 October 1996.
[21] COM(1996)487 final 16 October 1996 at p. 10.
[22] Ibid.
[23] For example, Price and Verhulst 2005.

4.2.1 **The different self-regulation groups**

The groups involved in the regulation of content can be (loosely) classified in the following manner:

(a) Groups that have technical access to Internet content such as ISPs and Internet exchanges. In the current technical structure of the Internet, ISPs are important players. They provide the technical link and services by which the majority of customers have access to the Internet. As intermediaries, ISPs have technical access to content hosted on their servers and content that goes through their servers. Given this position, ISPs, for a variety of reasons (discussed below) are actively involved in the regulation of content (even if the guiding principle in ISP regulation is that ISPs are not responsible for the content that is hosted on or goes through their servers).

Whilst some individual ISPs have created their own individual rules to regulate Internet content, mostly ISPs act together in associations. ISP associations (ISPAs) (now) exist in many countries.[24] There are also regional ISPAs.[25] The UK ISPA, for example, currently represents around 90% of ISPs that offer Internet access and services in the United Kingdom.[26] The members of the UK ISPA vary in market size, number of employees, customers and services offered.[27] Membership in an ISPA is voluntary but once a member, an ISP is expected to follow the association's rules.

There are other groups, such as Internet exchange points, that may also have technical means to regulate content. The London Internet Exchange (LINX), for example, is the largest Internet exchange point in Europe. The members of the Internet exchange point are ISPs from different countries or that act globally. LINX provides a physical interconnection for its members to exchange Internet traffic. The interconnection is based on co-operative peering agreements.[28]

---

[24] A recent approximate count shows more than twenty national organisations or associations of ISPs (e.g., in Australia, Austria, Belgium, Canada, Denmark, France, Germany, India, Indonesia, Ireland, Italy, Japan, Luxembourg, The Netherlands, Pakistan, Slovenia, South Africa, Spain, UK, US).

[25] Regional ISPAs are usually made up of a number of national ISPAs, for example, the Spanish, French, Italian, Austrian, German, Irish, Dutch and UK ISPA are all members of European Internet Service Providers Association (EuroISPA). EuroISPA represents more than 850 ISPs in the EU Member States. (see <http://www.euroispa.org>/ and Rotert 2005) There are four regional organisations worldwide: The European organisation (EuroISPA); the Asian & Pacific Internet Association (APIA), the South American and Carribean Association (Federacion de Lationamerica y El Caribe (eCOMLAC)) and Association of African Internet Service Provider Associations (AfrISPA).

[26] As reported in the Council of Europe Cyberforum country information accessed at <http://www.coe.int/t/e/cyberforum/country..../United_Kingdom(E)> on 16 April 2002.

[27] Membership fees relate to the annual revenue of the ISP: corporate (multinational companies), large (over £1 million per annum), medium (revenue of £500,000 to £1 million per annum), and small (revenue up to £500,000 per annum).

[28] Accessed at <http://www.linx.net/index.thtml> on 27 April 2005.

(b) Internet industry groups such as The Australian Internet Industry Association (AIIA). The AIIA members include telecommunications carriers, content creators and publishers, web developers, e-commerce traders and solutions providers, hardware vendors, systems integrators, banks, insurance underwriters, technology law firms, ISPs, educational institutions, research analysts, and those providing professional and technical support services.[29] AIIA has a dual role: it acts as a lobby group with government in the passing of new legislation related to the sector and sets minimum rules of practice that the members of the association follow in the regulation of specific issues such as the regulation of unwanted Internet content. The AIIA rules on unwanted content are based on Australian legislation on unwanted content.[30]

(c) Groups protecting particular interests – for example groups involved with child protection. Given the different groups involved in the protection of children the rules created by the groups vary widely. One such group is the Internet Content Rating Association (ICRA). ICRA,[31] established in 1999,[32] is an international non-profit organisation dedicated to developing tools for parents to determine what content their children can access. Its mission is

'to develop, implement and manage an internationally acceptable voluntary self-rating system which provides Internet users world wide with the choice to limit access to content they consider harmful, especially to children.'[33]

(d) Groups protecting shared cultural interests, religious beliefs, ideologies and other interests.[34] The group creates rules to control access and the receipt of content that the group considers 'harmful'. Given the countless numbers of groups based on shared common interests that the Internet accommodates, I will present only some illustrations of the type of rules created by groups sharing common interest(s).

---

[29] Accessed at <http://www.iia.net.au/about.html> on 27 April 2005.

[30] Indeed the AIIA rules were formulated to meet the requirements of the then new Australian legislation on unwanted content.

[31] See <http://www.icra.org/about/> on 22 April 2005.

[32] It evolved from the pre-existing Recreational Software Advisory Council (RSAC) established in 1996. The members of the organisation are major international (from Europe, the North America and Japan) Internet industry players (such as AOL and Microsoft), telecommunications companies (such as Cable and Wireless, Bell Canada, British Telecom), content providers, private organisations (such as the Bertelsmann Foundation) and child protection bodies.

[33] See FAQ 4.1 What is ICRA? Accessed at <http://www.icra.org/faq/abouticra/> on 22 April 2005

[34] At times, the link within the group is solely determined by shared interest in one (or more) particular area. For example, one can belong to a group of rose lovers irrespective of whether the other members share the same nationality, religion, and racial traits. The group can choose to create a space where any content that does not support their love for roses is deemed harmful and thus blocked out. The singular reason for the group is the (perhaps trivial) singular interest of love of roses.

(e) Groups protecting the 'free' use of the Internet, such as anti-spam Organisations and Internet user organisations. Anti-spam organisations, as the name indicates, are organisations set-up specifically to develop means to regulate unwanted Internet content. The set-up and membership of these organisations varies. For example, the anti-spam organisation Spamhaus is a non-profit limited liability company run by volunteers all over the world and sponsored by a number of important Internet industry enterprises.[35] Anti-spam organisations specialise in developing predominantly technical ways to regulate unwanted content. The common interest of the members is to reduce the flow of unwanted content that unnecessarily obstructs valuable space on servers and slows networks.

Internet user organisations, such as the Western Australian Internet Association (WAIA),[36] are usually civil associations[37] made up of Internet users – both individuals and business users – in a particular geographical territory. The objectives and aims of the organisations vary.

(f) Industry groups using the Internet in their main line of business, such as direct marketing business associations. For direct marketing businesses the Internet is an essential tool to approach, inform and retain customers, as well as providing customer relationship services.[38] European direct marketing associations[39] (such as the Federation of European Direct and Interactive marketing (FEDMA)) are actively involved in creating rules on the sending of e-mail in bulk.[40]

(g) Groups offering a service to which users can report the finding of illegal content on the Internet, such as groups offering a 'hotline service'.[41] The focus of most

---

[35] Accessed at <http://www.spamhaus.org/organization/index.html> on 26 April 2005.

[36] WAIA was formed in 1995. Its members come from both the Internet industry and individual users. The WAIA rules on unwanted content pre-date the enactment of specific legislation in Australia on unwanted content. (see <http://www.waia.asn.au/info/constitution.shtml> accessed 27 April 2005).

[37] That is, associations registered under civil law and not commercial law.

[38] See for an explanation of importance of direct e-marketing strategies information on FEDMA site accessed at <http://www.fedma.org/code/page.cfm?id_page=1> on 27 April 2005; see also The Economist Special Report (2005).

[39] Direct marketing associations in other countries, such as in the US and Australia, are also involved in the regulation of unwanted content. For example, the Australian Direct Marketing Association (ADMA) has developed rules in line with Australian legislation on the sending of unwanted content that members should follow when using the Internet for marketing purposes. The eMarketing Code of Practice was registered with the Australian Communications Authority in March 2005. (see <http://www.adma.com.au/data/portal/00000947/content/67206001111096604001.pdf> accessed 27 April 2005).

[40] Especially in the period between the drafting of the EU e-commerce directive and the drafting of the Privacy and Electronic communications Directive. Having established self-regulation rules meant that the groups had an already established position from which to lobby in the drafting of the Privacy and Electronic communications Directive.

[41] The reported alleged illegal content is accessed and assessed by the hotline. If the content is found to be potentially illegal, it is reported to law enforcement agencies and to the ISP hosting the

of the hotlines is on the reporting of child pornography or child abuse images. Some hotlines also 'investigate' claims on Internet content that is racist or obscene. Hotlines are mostly collaborations between ISPs and child welfare organisations.[42] Perhaps unsurprisingly, hotlines are mostly found in European countries although there are also hotlines in the United States and in Australia. One of the more important hotlines is the (UK) Internet Watch Foundation (IWF).[43] In 2004, IWF received 17,255 reports of alleged illegal content.[44] IWF has contributed to significant law enforcement operations related to illegal Internet content. It is representative of how other hotlines work or (aspire to work).

4.2.2   Reasons to self-regulate

To address legal vulnerability

The first court cases instituted in 1996 against ISPs for hosting content, brought to the fore the vulnerability of ISPs for content hosted by third parties on their servers. Creating rules on content was a way for ISPs to co-ordinate the handling of content hosted on their servers, to collaborate *a priori* with law enforcement agencies, and to reduce the possibility of court action against them. The German ISP rules were set in the light of a particularly high profile court case. In the *Felix Somm* case,[45] the managing director of CompuServe GmbH, an ISP, was criminally prosecuted and convicted for facilitating the dissemination of pornography by allowing newsgroups hosted on the ISP servers to provide violent, child or animal pornography. Even though the conviction by the lower court was later overturned on appeal,[46] it was enough to alert ISPs to their vulnerable legal position.[47]

Similarly, the UK ISP Association (ISPA UK)[48] was established in 1995 at the time of the first legal action against an ISP in the United Kingdom for allegedly

---

content to take down the content. The law enforcement agencies may take legal action against the wrongdoer.

[42] The first hotlines to be set-up was in The Netherlands – Meldpunt Kinderporno – in spring 1996. This was followed by initiatives in Norway, Belgium and the UK before the end of 1996. (For a more comprehensive history see Williams 1999).

[43] The IWF is mainly occupied with content involving child pornography. The members of IWF are companies that are involved in the provision of internet services and on-line facilities and tools including; ISPs, Content Service Providers, filtering companies, mobile operators & mobile manufacturers, search engines, software providers and so on. The membership is divided into full and associate members. Associate members are members who do not host Internet content. IWF currently has over 50 members (See Akdeniz 2001 and <http://www.iwf.org.uk/funding/page.59.htm> accessed 16 April 2005).

[44] See IWF 2004 Annual Report accessed at <http://www.iwf.org.uk/documents/20050204_annual_report_2004.pdf> 15 April 2005.

[45] Amtsgericht München, *Bavaria* v. *Felix Bruno Somm* File No.:8340 Ds 465 Js 173158/95.

[46] For a detailed evaluation on the effect of the *Somm* case see Sieber 2001: 235, 237-239.

[47] Cf., Mifsud Bonnici 2003.

[48] <http://www.ispa.org.uk>.

hosting content defamatory of the plaintiff in the action.[49] Establishing rules of conduct for ISPs was a way to establish some legal certainty in an area that was yet developing.

Although specific legislation (such as the EU e-Commerce Directive (2000/31/EC)) has formally limited the responsibility of ISPs for content by specifically excluding the obligation to monitor content hosted or transmitted,[50] ISPs still have an interest in clarifying what role they actually play in the blocking or 'taking down' of content. This is particularly true in the case of 'harmful' content, where the definition of what is 'harmful' (unlike the case of 'illegal' content) is not backed up by state legislation. Creating written rules on the handling of harmful content is one way to clarify the role of ISPs.

In response to 'pressure' from states

Another reason for engaging in the regulation of content comes from 'pressure' from states to regulate harmful content by means of self-regulation. In a number of countries, for example the United Kingdom, law enforcement agencies put pressure on ISPs to collaborate in the enforcement of legislation on illegal content. In August 1996, the UK Metropolitan Police issued a letter to UK ISPs naming 133 Usenet newsgroups believed to contain illegal pornography. The wording of the letter was perceived as an implicit threat of prosecution for ISPs who failed to take action to drop the groups from their servers.[51] ISPs and other content-related industry players, in response to the pressure from law enforcement agencies, set-up the (UK) Internet Watch Foundation (IWF), which now runs the UK hotline.

Besides pressure to assist in the enforcement of state law, groups are also pressured to create rules on content where legislation may not be politically appropriate. For example, while states may be aware that a strict approach to the regulation of harmful content could undermine the positive contributions of Internet, they are still keen to see activities regulated, preferably through self-regulation[52] instead. States have 'persuaded' groups, particularly ISPs, to regulate harmful Internet content through self-regulation.

In some instances, this 'pressure' is accompanied by financial support given by states for groups participating in regulation of content. From as early as 1997, the European Commission funded initiatives to support hotlines for the reporting of illegal content. Under the Daphne programme,[53] the European Union funded a

---

[49] *Godfrey* v. *Demon Internet Ltd.* 26 March 1999, per Morland J [2001] QB 201 QBD.

[50] See Art. 15 of the EU e-Commerce Directive (2000/31/EC).

[51] This is confirmed in Dixon 2001.

[52] See recital P of European Parliament Resolution 24th April 1997 on Commission Communication on Illegal and Harmful Content on the Internet (*OJ* C150 19 May 1997 p. 38).

[53] <http://europa.eu.int/comm/justice_home/project/daphne/ilustratives_cases_en/case_2_en.htm> accessed 15 April 2005. The Daphne programme funds activities aimed to combat violence against children, young people and women. See <http://europa.eu.int/comm/justice_home/funding/daphne/funding_daphne_en.htm>.

pilot project for the creation of a Europe wide network of hotlines. Under the Multi-annual Community Action Plan and successive Action plans[54] on promoting safer use of the Internet by combating illegal and harmful content on global networks (Safer Internet Action Plan)[55] the European Union funded a number of self-regulation initiatives.

The involvement of the European Union is not surprising. Politicians around the world were (are) under pressure to respond to the fears of citizens based on the easy accessibility of illegal, harmful or unwanted content on the Internet. In launching the funding programmes, the European Union was aware of the difficulties the Council of Europe was facing in trying to reach some consensus on the regulation of (criminal) illegal Internet content in the drafting of the Cybercrime Convention. The funding of self-regulation arrangements to assist in the enforcement and regulation of content is seen as a more practical approach.

In response to specific legislation

Some groups are involved in the regulation of content in response to specific state legislation. For example, since the entry into force of the German *Jugendmedien-schutz-Staatsvertrag* in 2003, ISPs are expected to ensure that minors do not have access to harmful content. To meet this obligation ISPs develop rules to apply and enforce this state legislation.[56] Similarly, libraries in the United States (or associations of libraries like the American Library Association) have developed rules to meet the requirements of the US Children's Internet Protection Act (CIPA) enacted in 2000.[57]

To dampen the effect of existing or potential state legislation

Another reason for self-regulation is to limit the impact of state legislation. Groups involved in regulating unwanted content sometimes do so to forestall legislation for as long as possible, or to have a base from which to negotiate once the state decides to regulate. Rule-making by direct marketing associations is an example.[58] Similarly, the Internet Content Rating Association (and its predecessor the Recreational Software Advisory Council) first identified the need for the creation of rules to

---

[54] The Safer Internet Action Plan for the years 2003-2004 and the Safer Internet *Plus* plan for the period 2005-2008.

[55] The funding of the Safer Internet Action Plan was approved the European Parliament and Council by Decision 276/1999EC on 25 January 1999 (*OJ* L33 6 February 1999 p. 1).

[56] Second Evaluation report on the application of Council Recommendation of 24 September 1998 concerning the protection of minors and human dignity (COM(2003)776 final 12 December 2003) at p. 9.

[57] The Act is available at <http://www.ifea.net/cipa.pdf>. For best practices/rules developed by the American Library Association see <http://www.ala.org/ala/washoff/WOissues/civilliberties/cipaweb/adviceresources/adviceresources.htm>.

[58] Asscher and Hoogcarspel 2006

SELF-REGULATION OF INTERNET CONTENT

regulate the receipt of (illegal) and harmful content specifically to limit the threat of government intervention in the regulation of content.[59]

For economic reasons

From the perspective of Internet infrastructure, unwanted content involves extra costs principally brought about by loss in productivity of the network when the systems are clogged up with unwanted content. In addition, unwanted content may constitute, in a variety of ways, a threat to network security. Threats for the security may have financial implications – in financing ways to counter the threat and from a loss of reputation if information on the threat (and breach) of security reaches the public. This is one of the reasons why ISPs and other groups having technical access are involved in regulating the flow of content.

At other times, a need to follow market/customer needs motivates ISPs to regulate content. ISP self-regulation of harmful content developed to satisfy consumers' wishes for the removal of harmful content (and hence to retain their custom). For example, *Yahoo!* removed 'pro-eating disorders' forums as a result of increased customer concern that such forums are 'harmful' to persons suffering from eating disorders.[60]

To address specific needs of the group

The protection of user privacy is a reason groups – especially Internet user groups – formulate rules to control unwanted content, in particular. Spam annoys users who have not asked for and have little or no interest in the information being sent to them. Internet user groups have a 'personal' interest in not being harassed with unwanted content. Internet industry groups and direct marketing groups also have an interest that their clients are not importuned with unwanted content. Users (at least theoretically) can take legal action against the Internet industry groups and direct marketing groups. In addition, users may opt to change email service provider if another provider offers better protection from unwanted content.

Some groups choose to regulate content that the group considers harmful by participating in 'safe areas', that is, areas where the user has the 'safety' of knowing that the content accessed there conforms to the user's set of values and beliefs.

In reacting to these various needs, different groups regulate different aspects of Internet content, forming a heterogeneous patchwork. As an EU Commission evaluation report[61] comments, 'the heterogeneity of the measures is not surprising, tak-

---

[59] See Press Release (9 May 1996) 'CompuServe Europe to rate its content with RSAC*i*' accessed at <http://penta2.ufrgs.br/gereseg/censura/rsac/960509-2.htm> on 22 April 2005.

[60] See Holahan 2001.

[61] Commission evaluation report on the application of Council Recommendation of 24 September 1998 concerning the protection of minors and human dignity (COM(2001)106 final 27 February 2001).

ing into account both cultural heterogeneity and the variation in development of Internet'[62] in different national, regional and global contexts. The fragmentation and decentralisation of the initiatives reflects the nature of the Internet. The structure of Internet allows for existence of different initiatives and in some ways supports their development. At times, there is some repetition in regulation between the rules of the different groups. The overlap coming from the repetition has a positive effect. It acts as a bridge between the different regulatory arrangements.

4.2.3   What is regulated by self-regulation?

The internal organisation of the group

Self-regulation regulates the internal organisation of the group and the way the group handles particular Internet content. The rules regulating the internal organisation of the group are usually written rules found in 'articles of association'. These sets of rules determine how the group is set-up, the aims of the group, membership and voting rights of members. These rules are often available to the public (mostly on the group's web site).

While the rules of association are important to assess the legal standing of each group, the focus of this section is on the rules regulating content. How and what each group regulates depends on the degree of its technical access to the content and the aims and interests of the group involved. The technical position of ISPs and their aims as businesses explain the strong involvement of ISPs in the regulation of illegal, harmful and unwanted content. Groups having technical access to Internet content, such as ISPs, are mainly involved in two types of rules on content. One set of rules establishes criteria for the blocking and taking down of content. The other set of rules establishes ways to apply state laws on content (where these exist) and on the ways to assist in the enforcement of state laws. These two sorts of rules are often related, especially when, as in the case of the e-Commerce Directive, legislation determines the responsibilities of ISPs in taking down content.

Blocking and taking down of content

Blocking and taking down of content is a delicate issue. ISPs are in a technical position to block and take down content. This exposes them to potential claims of either having taken down content unnecessarily or having failed to take down content when asked to do so. ISPs are generally reluctant to take down content. The rules on blocking and taking down of content they have developed reflect their position that they have 'no general obligation to monitor' content that goes through their systems or that is hosted on their systems. This is often the first rule of the code. The rejection of responsibility for content hosted on or passing through their

---

[62] Conclusion COM(2001)106 final 27 February 2001 p. 14.

systems is followed by a commitment of the members to inform their customers (through their contracts of service) that the customer is individually responsible for the legality or otherwise of the content.

Generally, the rules establish that content will be blocked or taken down only in specific circumstances and under certain conditions outlined in the Code of Practice of the group. These conditions generally require that the ISP has a legal obligation to do so, in particular when the content is illegal and when law enforcement agencies ask for the content to be taken down. This is usually followed by a rule that the contracts of service with customers will specifically provide that the ISP may terminate the contract if the customer uses the ISP services to publish content that is illegal (even if law enforcement agencies have not asked for it to be taken down).

The rules include a requirement that members collaborate and follow the rules and procedures developed with law enforcement agencies and private organisations (such as the UK Internet Watch Foundation and groups that run content hotlines) for the removal of illegal content from web sites and newsgroups.[63] These procedures generally include an obligation to provide a link on the ISP's site to a hotline service for the reporting of illegal content that customers may come across.[64] They also generally include a requirement to provide a 24-hour contact line through which law enforcement agencies can contact the ISP for the removal of illegal content.

ISPs can also block or take down content where the content, though not specifically illegal, is considered harmful by the customers of the ISP. Mostly ISPs refrain from taking direct action to block content but bind themselves to offer filtering tools to customers to choose which content to receive and which to block.[65] In addition, member ISPs may be bound to include a rule in their contract of service with their clients that the services are not to be used to host 'harmful' content (even if the definition of 'harmful' content as such is not clear).

These rules are written in codes of conduct that bind the members of an ISPA. Some ISPAs, such as the French ISPA – Association des Fournisseurs d'Accès et de Services Internet (AFA)[66] – have specific written rules on the handling of illegal and harmful content: the *Charte contre les contenus odieux*.[67] AFA members are bound by this charter to offer customers (parents in particular) the means to monitor the content accessed or received. In this way, the responsibility of deciding what content is harmful to the user and his dependents remains with the customers.

---

[63] For example Art. 5.1 ISPA UK Code of Practice at <http://www.ispa.org.uk/html/index3.html?frame=http%3A//www.ispa.org.uk/html/about_ispa/index.html> accessed 19 April 2005.

[64] See for example Art. 7.4 of ISPA UK Code of Practice and Art III AFA Pratiques et Usages accessed at <http://www.afa-france.com/deontologie.html#confiance> 19 April 2005.

[65] See Art. 7.2 and 7.6 ISPA UK and Art. I 4 AFA.

[66] *Charte contre les contenus odieux* accessed at <http://www.afa-france.com/charte_contrenusodieux.html> on 18 April 2005.

[67] AFA members approved the charter on harmful content in July 2004.

ISPs rely on the rules of other groups, such as hotline service providers and law enforcement agencies, in deciding which (illegal) content should be blocked or taken down. Hotline services for illegal content are often set-up specifically as a way for ISPs not to take the actual decisions on content. Decisions on content are then taken by persons who are trained in examining the legality or otherwise of the content. The rules of hotline service providers identify which illegal content it will act upon; the process of assessing the alleged illegal content reported; the action/s that will be taken upon *prima facie* of illegality; and where applicable the duties of the individual members when illegal content is hosted by them. The code of practice of the UK Internet Watch Foundation (IWF),[68] for example, regulates the way content containing child abuse images and potentially illegal racist and obscene content hosted on members' servers are handled. The rules determine how complaints are reviewed and how the content is accessed and assessed. If IWF deems the content potentially illegal then it informs the relevant ISP and law enforcement authority for the necessary action to be taken. The Code determines how members should respond to IWF advice on illegal content hosted by them (basically by taking down the content). There are also procedures outlined for action to be taken when a member fails to comply with the IWF advice.[69]

Other groups (separate from ISPs) develop the technical measures offered by ISPs for customers to filter and block content. A wide variety of technical means have been developed. The most popular are filtering tools, content rating, site blocking, pop-up blocking, content monitoring, quality labelling tools and systems, and the creation of 'safe' portals.

Filtering tools are technical tools that block or allow access to content according to a pre-selected list of content types and criteria determined by an individual or a group. Content filtering usually works by specifying character strings, which, if matched, indicate the undesirable content that is to be screened out.[70] Some filtering tools are dependent on the existence of labels or ratings (either self-rated or rated by third parties). Other filtering tools are not dependent on pre-existing labels.[71]

---

[68] <http://www.iwf.org.uk/funding/page.60.htm> accessed 15 April 2005. The code of practice was drafted by the Board running the organisation and agreed to by members. The code of practice may be amended by the IWF through a Board resolution following appropriate consultation.

[69] The Code of Practice provides for a sanction for non-compliance of a member. When the IWF advises one of its members to take down specific content hosted by the member's servers, the IWF can check whether the specific member has complied with the take down notification. The IWF can also act on members' non-compliance when third party users report such non-compliance. 'If a Full Member fails to take down the relevant content within a reasonable time following an IWF notification and, following an investigation by the IWF executive, fails to provide reasonable grounds for doing so, the Full Member will receive a formal warning and a report may be filed with the relevant law enforcement agency.' The IWF may even suspend a member from membership if it acts in such a way to bring 'the IWF into disrepute'. 'Failure to Comply' in IWF Code of Practice accessed at <http://www.iwf.org.uk/funding/page.60.htm> on 15 April 2005.

[70] 'What is content filtering' accessed at <http://searchsecurity.techtarget.com/sDefinition/0,,sid14_gci863125,00.html> on 22 April 2005.

[71] Center for Democracy & Technology 1999.

Some groups, such as the Internet Content Rating Association (ICRA), have developed of a set of content descriptors (according to the groups' values and beliefs) to label or rate content.[72] These content descriptors are based on rules set by ICRA defining what content is considered harmful (by ICRA members and users of the ICRA descriptors). The ICRA vocabulary list provides a list of descriptors based on five categories of 'harmful' content:[73] nudity and sexual material; violence; language (such as offensive words); a generic category of potentially 'harmful' content such as the promotion of tobacco, alcohol or drug use; gambling; promotion of discrimination or harm against people; and chat. The descriptors are available not only in English but also in German, Spanish, French, Italian, Japanese and Chinese.[74] The problem with developing a rating system is that precisely because of the cultural differences between users and content providers it is difficult (if not impossible) to create globally acceptable descriptors. The ICRA descriptors attempt to be 'neutral' to attract many content providers to rating their content by the descriptors.

The content descriptors on their own are useless unless there is a set of rules that content providers follow in rating their own content. ICRA provides these rules implemented in label-generating software. Content providers are permitted to use the ICRA logo on their site if they label the content according to the ICRA descriptors and follow ICRA's terms and conditions. ICRA may perform automated or manual checks of the labels against the content.[75] Furthermore, ICRA can also act on complaints received by users on mislabelled content and ask the content provider for the rectification of the content labels.[76]

ICRA has also developed filtering software – ICRA*plus*[77] – that blocks or allows access to labelled sites according to the user selected setting. The ICRA filter also works with additional content descriptors and filters to block or allow access to content.

A variety of filtering tools, developed by commercial and non-profit organisations, are available. One major criticism of filtering tools is that 'harmless' content can 'mistakenly' be blocked together with the 'harmful' content. This has led to debates on the merits and demerits of filtering software as means to control harmful content.[78]

Other groups create 'safe portals', spaces that block all content that is considered harmful or unwanted by the group of users of the portal. A content portal provides access only to 'approved' content on the Internet. It can be used to facili-

---

[72] The descriptors were determined by ICRA members and through a process of consultation with interested parties.

[73] See <http://www.icra.org/vocabulary/> accessed on 22 April 2005.

[74] See ICRA International accessed at <http://www.icra.org/international/> on 22 April 2005.

[75] See ICRA Terms and Conditions Art. 6 accessed at <http://www.icra.org/legal/#tandc> on 22 April 2005.

[76] 'Why you can trust an ICRA label' accessed at <http://www.icra.org/trust/> on 22 April 2005.

[77] ICRA*plus* accessed at <http://www.icra.org/icraplus/> on 22 April 2005.

[78] Such as d'Udekem-Gevers and Poullet 2001; Price and Verhulst 2005 at Chapter 3.

tate searching for domain-specific information and also to limit the access to 'unapproved' (harmful) content. The rules on what content is approved or not by the group are inbuilt in the creation of the 'safe' portal. Content filtering and blocking software are programmed to fit the choices of the group. For example, particular religious groups organise portals through which their members can access content on the Internet. The members, while agreeing to use the portal as their gateway to the Internet, are 'assured' that the content accessed will not include anything 'harmful'.[79]

Blocking software, and spam detection tools, are used by ISPs to regulate the sending and receipt of unwanted content. ISPs rely on tools (and rules) developed by other groups used to trace when the sender's address is masked or falsified and means for ISPs to be able to block the receipt of e-mail sent by an unidentifiable sender. (These tools are based on the rule that electronic mail sent from unidentifiable or false senders is considered spam.)

Some groups (such as Spamhaus) compile blacklists of known spammers. These lists are used to block all mail sent from a known spammer. The groups compile these lists by monitoring and investigating the flow of spam. The lists generated by these organisations, such as the Register of Known Spam Operations (ROKSO)[80] generated by Spamhaus, are used by ISPs and e-mail service providers to block incoming spam[81] and to terminate their service agreements with such senders. Groups generating black lists usually have specific rules that are followed in the identification and labelling of activities as spam operations. For example, to be listed in the ROKSO list the services to a spammer must first be terminated by a minimum of 3 ISPs.[82]

Application and enforcement of state law

Self-regulation is not the only source of rules regulating content. There is a wide variety of state legislation regulating content (including Internet content) such as legislation identifying child pornography as illegal content and anti-spam laws. These state laws need to be applied and enforced on the Internet. Group rules are formulated not only in accordance with the specific legislation but also in a way to apply the state rules. State rules provide a framework within which the rules of the group can act. For example, a state law may identify particular vulnerable groups such as minors that require special protection for certain categories of harmful content. ISPAs, for example then set rules to be followed by the members to ensure the

---

[79] See for example <http://www.catholicexchange.com/> – a Catholic groups' portal; <http://www.worldofislam.info/index.php>; <http://www.musalman.com/> – Islamic groups' portal.

[80] Can be accessed at <http://www.spamhaus.org/rokso/index.lasso>.

[81] The list compiled by Spamhaus lists the Internet Protocol (IP) number (that is the unique number assigned to each computer on the Internet) use by the spammer to send spam. The ISPs then block any content going or coming from the particular IP numbers.

[82] Accessed at <http://www.spamhaus.org/rokso/index.lasso> on 27 April 2005.

application of the state legislation. Rules set by hotline service providers identifying procedures to report alleged illegal content is another example.

Groups having technical access to content develop rules identifying ways to assist in the enforcement of state laws. ISPA rules usually include a rule either developed by the ISPA alone or developed together with law enforcement agencies on data retention for law enforcement purposes,[83] for example by retaining trails showing illegal behaviour. Especially after 11 September 2001, ISPs have received more requests from law enforcement agencies to retain connection data[84] for long periods so that law enforcement agencies can access the information to trace criminal activity. The European Union has just passed legislation on data retention[85] which is considered controversial.[86]

Retention of connection data by ISPs is a controversial issue. On the one hand, state law enforcement officials see data retention as the only way in which critical proof of Internet crime can be traced. On the other hand, ISPs see this as a source of potential civil liability especially since the data retained includes personal data and data reflecting personal preferences that could potentially be abused. Retaining data by ISPs also has financial implications: ISPs must store massive amounts of data that could otherwise be deleted. Some ISPAs such as the French AFA have developed rules on data retention even before the passing of EU legislation binding ISPs to retain data about users. The AFA code of practice identifies which data must be retained by the various AFA Members[87] and specifies the length of time these data are to be kept.

---

[83] Access providers retain login details of the user, including IP address and date and time of connection and disconnection from the service. These details are kept usually for three months. Cache servers operators retain IP address of the user, the server details used by the user, what information was demanded by the user and date and time of each transaction. These details are usually kept between three to five days. The hosting provider retains the login details of the user, the IP details and the date and time of connection and disconnection. See Pratiques et Usages Art. I.2.5 Conservation des données de connexion de l'utilisateur accessed at <http://www.usages.afa-france.com/> on 10 December 2002.

[84] Connection data – includes information about the identity of the customer, when the customer connected to the ISP, when he/she logged-off and the trace of the sites visited during that session.

[85] See Draft Framework Decision on the retention of data processed and stored in connection with the provision of publicly available electronic communications services or data on public communications networks for the purpose of prevention, investigation, detection and prosecution of crime and criminal offences including terrorism. Document of the Council of the European Union COPEN 35 dated 25th February 2005 and Directive 2006/24/EC of the European Parliament and of the Council of 15 March 2006 on the retention of data generated or processed in connection with the provision of publicly available electronic communications services or of public communications networks and amending Directive 2002/58/EC (*OJ* L105 13 April 2006 p. 54).

[86] It is argued by experts in the field that this legislation waters down the 'purpose principle' which is fundamental in the regulation of data protection.

[87] Access providers retain login details of the user, including IP address and date and time of connection and disconnection from the service. These details are kept usually for three months. Cache servers operators retain IP address of the user, the server details used by the user, what information was demanded by the user and date and time of each transaction. These details are usually kept between three to five days. The hosting provider retains the login details of the user, the IP details and the date

Some groups, such as the Australian Internet Industry Association (AIIA), are involved in the application and enforcement of state anti-spam legislation. The AIIA Code of Practice on Spam was drafted after the coming into force of the Australian 'Spam Act 2003'.[88] The rules in the Code flesh out the principles established in the Act. They, for example, list what information ISPs are to provide their customers on the sending of spam and the consequences of breaching the Spam Act; on methods of reducing the receipt of spam using content filtering tools; and on the procedure for reporting the receipt of spam.[89] Some rules may be of a technical nature, such as rules on the configuration of ISP networks in ways to make them less susceptible to spam attacks.[90]

Regulate the sending of spam

Self-regulation rules regulate the sending of unwanted content (even where state legislation does not yet exist). These rules give a definition of spam and list circumstances where the sending of bulk Internet communications is considered unsolicited and hence contrary to the rules.[91] The rules also identify the responsibilities of the group members in the regulation of spam.[92] These responsibilities include not sending spam and not permitting computers or networks over which they have control to be used to send spam. In addition, the rules emphasize the obligation of groups to protect the personal information of users. ISPA rules, for example, require that ISPs keep client information secure.

---

and time of connection and disconnection. See Pratiques et Usages Art. I.2.5 Conservation des données de connexion de l'utilisateur accessed at <http://www.afa-france.com/deontologie.html#conservation> on 15 April 2005.

[88] The code was drafted by an AIIA task force. The task force was made up of different Internet and e-mail service providers and other interested parties. In July 2004, the code was launched for public consultation till 30th August 2004. In November 2004, the amended draft code was presented to the Australian Communications Authority. (Under Australian Telecommunications Act 1997, the Australian Communications Authority is responsible to monitor whether the development of voluntary codes of practice and technical standards are in the public interest and do not impose undue financial and administrative burdens on industry participants. In addition, once an industry codes is registered with the Australian Communications Authority, the Authority can require an industry actor to comply with a code). See Code development and Review at p. 4 of Draft AIIA Spam Code of Practice – accessed at <http://www.iia.net.au/nospam/Draft_IIA_Spam_Code.pdf> on 27 April 2005.

[89] See Arts. 4, 6, 8-10 of the Australian Internet Industry Spam code of practice: A code for Internet and E-mail Service Providers July 2004 version 1.0 accessed at <http://www.iia.net.au/nospam/Draft_IIA_Spam_Code.pdf> on 27 April 2005.

[90] Ibid., Arts. 6-7.

[91] See for example, Art. 1.3 of Western Australian Internet Association WAIA spam code accessed at <http://www.waia.asn.au/info/spamcode.shtml> on 26 April 2005. This code was developed in August 2002 before the enactment of the Australian 'Spam Act' in 2003. (accessed at <http://www.waia.asn.au/info/spamcode.shtml> on 27 April 2005).

[92] See for example Arts. 2-4 in Western Australian Internet Association Spam Code of Conduct accessed at <http://www.waia.asn.au/info/spamcode.shtml> on 27 April 2005.

4.2.4   Functions of self-regulation

The rules on content developed by the groups serve mostly: (i) to limit the sending of or access to content (in the absence of state law or as precursors of state law); (ii) to apply and implement state regulation; and (iii) to participate in the enforcement of state law.

Providing rules in absence of state legislation

Self-regulation rules can be the first rules to regulate the sending of or access to content. These rules may later be adopted by the state in the formulation of legislation. One important example of this function is the development of 'notice and take down' rules. They were first developed by ISPs in the regulation of (illegal) content and subsequently adopted in, for example, the EU e-Commerce Directive. Similarly, rules on the regulation of unwanted content pre-dating state legislation were used in the formulation of state law, for example in the formulation of the Australian Spam Act and the EU Directive on privacy and electronic communications. Even when the state law takes a different position from that earlier taken in self-regulation,[93] the self-regulation rules are still an important source for the state position that is taken. As a minimum, self-regulation rules provide an important point of departure for the route state regulation will (or will not) follow.

Self-regulation often pre-empts state regulation. Private groups are quick to identify the need for regulation, especially if the lack of legal certainty can have financial consequences for or affects interests of the group. Furthermore, private groups are often faster in reacting to the need for rules to regulate a particular activity. Unless the rules developed by self-regulating groups go against state laws or policies, states generally adopt the self-regulation rules in the legislation. One may argue that in the regulation of content, states recognise the 'usefulness' of the rules adopted by the groups and readily formally adopt them in legislation. This is not unique to the Internet. Many state laws regulating commercial transactions are based on customs and rules developed by traders long before the enactment of state law.

In two specific situations, self-regulation rules remain the only rules regulating content. One is when the identification of the content and related activities needing regulation depends directly on the individual group (and not on the state). The important example here is the regulation of harmful content, where what is considered harmful may depend on the particular shared values, traditions, morals and customs of the group. States, or more precisely democratic states, have only regulated harmful content in specific cases, such as the protection of minors.

---

[93] Such as, in the case of the EU Directive on privacy and electronic communications (2002/58/EC). The EU Directive on privacy and electronic communications took a different stand on consent of the recipient of unwanted content than the rules that were being followed until then by the Federation of European Direct Marketing Associations.

A second situation is the absence of international regulation, which leaves certain aspects of the regulation of content (e.g., spam) uncovered. Some self-regulation rules on spam developed by a group having an international membership, such as the list of best practices developed by LINX,[94] remain the only rules that apply uniformly to ISPs in different states.

Implementing and enforcing state legislation

Self-regulation rules often serve to implement state legislation on regulation of content. They clarify how state rules on the regulation of content are to be applied by the group. Furthermore, through self-regulation, state law rules are converted into technical rules for implementation. The function of self-regulation to apply state law is sometimes statutorily mandated, as in, for example, German law requiring ISPs to apply state rules for the protection of minors from harmful content. In other instances, the group is informally expected to apply state laws. Many times, the choice to apply state regulation is entirely in the hands of the group. One may argue that, in fact, whenever state law exists, groups have no other option but to apply the state rules. This is often the case for the application of national legislation. The involvement of groups in the application of international law is more limited, mainly because there is little international regulation apart from the Cybercrime Convention.

The rules of self-regulation often serve to assist in the enforcement of state regulation. One important example is the provision of a system of reporting and 'investigation' of alleged breaches of state law (in particular on child pornography) through the provision of hotlines. Another example is the blocking and takedown of content in breach of state law. The existence of state law legitimises the participation of the groups' 'policing' function.

The groups' participation in enforcement can be seen as a form of 'self-protection' from potential legal action (and undesired publicity) for obstructing the poten-

---

[94] The first version of the LINX Best Current Practice (BCP) for combating unsolicited bulk e-mail was adopted in May 1999. The current version was adopted on 17 August 2004. The BCP document identifies the 'industry's current collective opinion of the Best Practice in achieving minimising or eliminating the sending (or other use) of unsolicited bulk email' – that is, the BCP represents the current practices followed by members of the exchange. The rules aim at (i) limiting the sending of unsolicited e-mail from unidentified or false senders. Hence, an ISP must ensure that their e-mail system does not relay e-mail for unauthorised third parties; that all email generated within their network can be traced to its source; that the immediate source of e-mail which arrives from other networks can be determined; and that all e-mail generated within their own networks can be attributed to a particular customer or system. (ii) providing efficient systems to handle reports of spam received from the systems of a member. The member ISP must operate appropriate arrangements for the handling of reports of abuse by their customers; ensure that internet protocol allocation entries in regional registries contain appropriate abuse team e-mail addresses; and where abuse is proved, take effective action to prevent the customer from continuing that abuse. (see Arts. 2-10 of LINX Best Current Practice for combating Unsolicited Bulk E-mail (version 2.0 17th August 2004) accessed at <http://www.linx.net/noncore/bcp/ube-bcp-v2_0.html> on 19 April 2005).

tial prosecution of wrongdoers. In addition, groups have a (financial) interest in promoting a 'safe' and 'clean' Internet and hence enhancing user trust of the medium.

Essentially, self-regulation offers a customised regulatory solution to the regulation of Internet content. The rules are developed, applied and enforced at group level, that is, at the level of the particular private group. Self-regulation 'answers' the needs of the individual groups. Furthermore, through the wide patchwork of self-regulation arrangements, self-regulation reaches a broad array of activities and content. This extensive 'jurisdictional' reach of self-regulation often reaches across traditional territorial boundaries.

4.2.5   Self-regulation as a source of rules

Legitimacy

The legitimacy of groups as sources of rules on Internet content has been criticised in the literature.[95] The central criticism is that by regulating the flow of content, groups are taking decisions that are a matter of public law and the domain of state enforcement agencies or state courts. Questions on the legality of content (in particular child pornography), one can argue, are questions of public law, wrong application of which can result in breaches of fundamental rights of the content provider and users. Hence, only public authorities that are legitimate and that can be held accountable at law should decide such questions of public law.

There are two issues surrounding the legitimacy of the private groups to regulate Internet content: whether people accept the validity of a rule and whether they accept the authority of a governing regime.[96]

Members and users generally accept the validity of the rules of self-regulation and follow them. There are (perhaps) different reasons why members and users accept the validity of the rules and follow them. The members of the groups come together because of specific interests and needs to regulate the activities related to Internet content. Based on common interests the members are inclined to accept the rules made through common agreement. Following the rules secures some protection or ease of mind for the members and so they accept the validity of the rules and follow them.

The members trust the (technical) expertise and knowledge of the group. Thanks to this expertise, the groups can decide what regulation is required in the circumstances and the appropriate way to carry it out. They have the necessary familiarity and expertise to be able to design and apply appropriate rules and procedures on the

---

[95] For example, Kaspersen, et al. 1999.

[96] hese two issues are taken from a definition of 'legitimacy' in the political science literature. 'Legitimacy is whether or not people accept the validity of a law or ruling or the validity of a governing regime.' (see <http://en.wikipedia.org/wiki/Legitimacy> accessed 19 May 2006).

illegal, harmful or unwanted content. In the case of regulation of unwanted content (and similarly in the regulation of illegal and harmful content), for example, different groups are familiar with different aspects of unwanted content and create rules according to their expertise and familiarity. Hence, the focus in the rules of direct marketers is on the content of unwanted content while the rules of technical experts regulate the technical aspects of sending unwanted content.

Self-regulation rules also regulate the behaviour of users who were not part of the rule-making process like the members of the group. Users generally acquiesce to the validity of the rules and follow them. Most users acknowledge the critical technical position of ISPs and recognise that mostly users have a little choice but to follow the rules of the ISPs who ultimately grant them access to the Internet. At times, the service contract between a member of the group (for example, an ISP) and its customers is the basis for the validity and acceptance of the rules by the users. The service contract is a basis for a user's adhesion to the rules. This contract then gives authority to ISPs to take down the allegedly illegal, harmful or unwanted content. The acceptance of the rules and their authority by the members of the group and adhesion by users is often further reinforced through pressure by enforcement agencies and specific legislation mandating the involvement of the group in regulation.

The criticism found in the literature on the legitimacy of self-regulation of Internet content seems to be valid where users are bound by self-regulation rules in the absence of a contractual relationship between users and the self-regulating group or in the absence of specific legislation legitimising the self-regulation rules. Yet, one can argue that such criticism is to some extent irrelevant. In most of the regulation, the actual decisions to take down and block content rest ultimately on the authority of law enforcement agencies or are taken by users themselves (who decide what content to allow and what to block). In practice, for example, the providers of hotlines act only as recipients of reports on content and as initial sieves of these reports. As recipients of reports, they do not make any actual decision on the legality of the content and hence there is no real question as to their legitimacy. The ultimate decision on illegality and appropriate legal action remains in the hands of law enforcement agencies. The same sieving process benefits ISPs who, on the instructions of law enforcement officers, will then take down, or block content, and retain content for evidence in cases that the hotline providers highlight, without checking the legality of the content themselves.

In other situations, groups leave the decision on content to users. They offer the technical tools to the users and expect the users to take the actual decisions on what content to accept or block. A move towards user-empowerment can be viewed as a move to reduce questions of group legitimacy and to keep the involvement of states in the regulation of content to a minimum.

Ultimately, in the few cases where the decision on content is actually in the hands of the group, users can often choose whether to accept those rules or not. One example comes from users of 'safe portals': the users accept the decisions on content made by the portal provider. If they do not accept the rules of the group they can move away from the portal and use other portals to access content they choose. Another option is to question the validity of the rules (and action taken following the rules) before a court.[97]

Accountability of the group

While accountability is perhaps not the most important principle in the case of groups,[98] this does not mean, however, that groups cannot be held accountable for their rule-making. Most groups involved in the regulation of content are subject to both internal and external mechanisms of accountability. The actions, rule-making procedures and compliance with the rules are all subject, in differing degrees, to various mechanisms of accountability.

Internally, most groups have a hierarchical decision-making structure: such as a Board that takes day to day decisions with the rest of the members approving or voting against the actions of the Board. It may be rightly argued that this only applies to larger groups such as ISPAs or ICRA. In smaller groups based on shared common interests, the decision structure may not be so transparent. Even in groups where the structural hierarchy to keep the group in check is not evident (or not present) members have another option to keep the activities of the group in check – the option to leave the group and not follow its rules. The threat of diminished support can influence the direction of the rules formed by the group. Diminished support can also have an important financial consequence for the group, especially in groups where the funding of the rules and technical measures come solely from the members of the group.[99]

In most groups, the members are actively involved in the development of the rules and the technical implementation (where applicable). This can be seen in the case of the involvement of French ISPs in the creation of specific documents for the regulation of harmful content or on data retention. Similarly, in the Internet Content Rating Association (ICRA), members were also involved in the technical implementation and development of the content rating vocabulary list created by the group. By actively participating in the rules and their implementation and application, members keep the group on track with the reason for the existence of the group – to regulate content in the interest of the group.

---

[97] For example, the decisions of ISPs to take down allegedly illegal content have been taken to courts.

[98] From a private sector perspective, the procedural formalities of making rules are comparatively less important than they are in the case of the state. In private regulation, what is important is that the regulation is responsive to the needs of the group: that the self-regulation is efficient. The top priority for the private sector is that their needs are satisfied. Other institutional aspects (such as accountability) are of lesser importance. See Cutler, Haufler and Porter 1999: 4.

[99] In the portals listed as examples earlier – the portal is funded predominantly by the members of the group and at times by approved advertising revenue.

When the rules of the group are drafted by only a part of the group, the draft rules are subjected, in most cases, to the approval of all the members (in General Meeting) and are only adopted once approved by all (or the majority) of the members of the group.

Most groups, as seen in the case of ISPAs and the Australian Internet Industry Association, have a complaints mechanism in place to hear and investigate complaints against the ISPA members by customers or members of the public[100] and to sanction (if necessary) alleged non-compliance of a member with the rules of the group. Most ISPAs have established complaints boards apart from the right of redress being given to customers and members of the public, the publicity surrounding the claim is often sufficient to hold ISPs to account. ISPs, like other commercial enterprises, cannot afford a bad reputation. As has traditionally been claimed,[101] reputation is one of the most significant intangible resources any commercial enterprise can have.

In addition, when a group has a territorial/jurisdictional link with a particular state, those states act as a means of external accountability of the group. For example, in the regulation of unwanted content, the Australian Internet Industry Association and the Australian Direct Marketing Association are held to account by compliance procedures imposed by the state authorities.[102]

Private groups co-funded by the state are kept in check through the conditions associated with the financial funding of the initiative. States can use other measures too. The rules of all private groups are (at least theoretically) subject to the scrutiny of state courts. The actions of private groups can be challenged in court. Providers of hotlines are held in check for decisions taken on content by law enforcement agencies, the ISPs and content providers. They are in a position to question the decision of hotline providers and, in theory, to take legal action against a hotline provider if a decision is in breach of fundamental rights. In addition, where state

---

[100] For example, ISPA UK has a complaints procedure that comes into action when a specific complaint against a member is brought before the Council. A sub-group first investigates the complaint and then presents its conclusions to the Council. The final decision rests with the Council. The Council can apply a number of sanctions if it decides that a Member has violated the association's rules: it can require the member to remedy the breach; to give assurance for future behaviour; to reimburse a customer for service charges; and to reimburse the ISPA for administrative charges. In addition, the Council can suspend a member, convene an Extraordinary General Meeting to expel a member and make the final decision public. (see Art. 8 ISPA UK Code of Practice at <http://www.ispa.org.uk/html/index3.html?frame=http%3A//www.ispa.org.uk/html/about_ispa/index.html> accessed 19 April 2005).

[101] Zyglidopoulos 2002.

[102] Under Australian law for example the code on spam binding on ISPs and E-mail service providers (ESPs) in Australia who are members of the Australian Internet Industry Association needs to be registered with the Australian Communications Authority. Once registered, the Authority can call on any industry participant (including non-AIIA members) and require compliance with the code. (see p. 3 of Explanatory Statement to Australian Internet Industry Spam code of practice: A code for Internet and E-mail Service Providers July 2004 version 1.0 accessed at <http://www.iia.net.au/nospam/Draft_IIA_Spam_Code.pdf> on 27 April 2005).

funding supports the hotline, the state can hold the hotline in account for its activities and use of the state funds.

It can be argued that ISPs could in fact abuse their position of dominance granted through technology and act as a cartel and limiting the competitive differences between the ISPs. Services thereby become more uniform for customers and leaving customers with effectively no choice. Some states[103] have reacted to these situations by interfering in the market to ensure that a free market of ISPs exists.[104] This intervention ensures that consumers have an appropriate choice in the selection of services. States (and regional free markets such as the EU) are gradually taking on more responsibility in the maintenance of conditions allowing for a competitive free market. In addition, free market conditions are accompanied with (effective) consumer protection mechanisms that allow customers to seek redress for situations of abuse.

States also offer other systems that affect the accountability of ISPs. These range from the requirement of registration or licensing of ISPs from a central authority to the requirement to abide with the laws of the state that were not strictly enacted with the digital world in mind. Some countries,[105] for instance, require that an ISP be licensed to act as an ISP by some governmental authority or independent authority. Some Telecommunications Authorities have issued guidelines or regulations to ensure a minimum standard of service by ISPs to their customers. For instance, the regulatory scheme established by the Australian Broadcasting Services Amendment (On-line Services) Act 1999 applies specifically to the activities of ISPs and their liability in Internet content issues.[106] These guidelines limit arbitrary behaviour by an ISP.

The traditional principles of contractual liability, too, act as a safeguard against capricious behaviour. Since the basis of the relationship for doing business between ISPs and their clients is primarily contractual ISPs are expected to follow the law on contracts present in the particular state, whether that be based on the principles found in the civil code or other legislation or through common law principles of contract. This often includes rules on the liability of the parties to the contract and rules for the exclusion of liability of one of the parties. Some countries, for instance, do not allow complete exemption of liability of any of the parties. As Kaspersen, et al.,[107] argue, contract law alone is not enough to hold ISPs accountable. But taken together with other mechanisms it is an important source of accountability.

There is also some evidence of third party groups acting as auditors of the rules and measures developed by a self-regulation arrangement. For example, multiple

---

[103] Predominantly the US and the EU.

[104] For example, by liberalising the market. (See further Notice by the Commission Concerning the Status of Voice on the Internet Under Directive 90/388/EEC accessed at <http://europa.eu.int/ISPO/infosoc/legreg/docs/InetPhone.html> on 20 August 2002).

[105] For example, India and Mauritius.

[106] <http://www.aba.gov.au/internet/index.htm> accessed on 8 March 2002.

[107] Kaspersen, et al. 1999.

non-members use the tools developed by ICRA. These non-members review the tools and underlying rules developed by ICRA and report back to ICRA where the rules or tools are problematic.[108]

Legal effect of self-regulation rules

Another normative objection that can be levelled against self-regulation of content refers to the legality of the rules developed and applied by the groups. In spite of the objection, the self-regulation rules created are generally binding, transparent and certain – three qualities that influence the legal effect of the rules. The rules created by the group bind the members of the group. While membership is voluntary, once one becomes a member of the group he is bound by the rules of the group. Many times, the rules are implemented in technical measures, such as in filtering tools. Hence, once the member of the private group applies the technical measure, the member is automatically bound by the rules. This happens, for example, when using filtering tools created by a group. The rules are implemented in the technical settings of the filtering tools and once a member uses the tools he is automatically following the rules inbuilt in the tools.

When the rules are not implemented into a technical system but instead must be followed by the members, the groups generally have rules:

(a) to verify compliance with the self-regulation rules. The Internet Content Rating Association, for example, can verify whether content providers using the rating tools follow the ICRA ratings. There are generally a number of sanctions that can be applied by ICRA. These include the removal of the trust-mark for non-compliant users of the ICRA rating scheme.

(b) to sanction non-compliance and for the handling of complaints against an allegedly non-compliant member. For example, the UK ISPA Code of Practice contains a complaints procedure and possible sanction for members that do not follow or are in breach of the Code of Practice.[109]

In addition, in the regulation of unwanted content, a state authority can request compliance with the rules. For example, in the case of the Australian Internet Industry Association and the Australian Direct Marketing Association, the Australian Communications Authority can request that members of either of the associations comply with the rules developed by the respective association.[110]

---

[108] Cf., Programme in Comparative Media Law and Policy at Oxford University 2003.

[109] See for example Art. 8 ISPA UK Code of Practice at <http://www.ispa.org.uk/html/index3.html?frame=http%3A//www.ispa.org.uk/html/about_ispa/index.html> 19 April 2005.

[110] Under Australian Telecommunications Act 1997, the Australian Communications Authority is responsible to monitor whether the development of voluntary codes of practice and technical standards are in the public interest and do not impose undue financial and administrative burdens on industry

Even where no specific rules for the handling of non-compliance exist, the members are still bound by the rules of the group. Peer pressure ensures, in these cases, that members of the group comply with the rules. For example, while the London Internet Exchange (LINX) Best Current Practices (BCP) document on spam does not include a complaints' mechanism for a breach of the required practices, peer pressure played an important role in bringing a non-compliant member back in conformity with the BCP.[111]

Self-regulation rules are not only binding but they are generally transparent and certain. There is usually no difficulty identifying the rules of a group when these are written in a code of conduct. The codes are often public and easily accessible online. Often the group has an interest in having its rules publicly known. For example, most industry groups will benefit from being seen to take an active role in the regulation of certain categories of content, such as spam. Identifying rules that have been implemented in technical measures may be more problematic. An important issue raised by content filtering systems is that the lack of transparency in the rules makes it difficult to establish whether the blocking is overbroad or under-inclusive.[112] Were the criteria used more transparent, it would be easier to identify the exact legal effect of the rules. A member (or a user) would then be in a better position to choose whether to follow the rules or to move away to rules of other groups.

The importance of transparent rules is also a question of legal certainty. Members and users need to be in a position to know what the rules consist of, and to know that any amendment to the rules or enactment of new rules will follow a specific process. Knowing the content of the rule also implies knowing the effect of following or not complying with the rule.

One can question the legal certainty of self-regulation of content on the ground that the rules seem to develop in an *ad hoc* and haphazard manner. This impression comes primarily from the fact that the current picture of self-regulation on the Internet is one of a decentralised patchwork of self-regulatory initiatives. If what is meant by *ad hoc* is that the rules are often created for or concerned with one specific purpose then the *ad hoc* claim is correct. Groups create self-regulation rules to meet specific concerns.

The rules are developed at a localised level, customising the rules to meet the specific topical needs of the group. However, the 'customised solution' does not diminish the legal certainty of the rules to the members of the group.

---

participants. To be able to do so, all codes of conduct are to be registered with the Australian Communications Authority. Then, once an industry codes is registered, the Authority can require an industry actor to comply with a code.

[111] In the beginning of February 2005, it was brought to the attention of MCI Worldcom (a LINX member) that it was hosting a site (<www.send-safe.com>) that was selling and distributing stealth proxy spamware, which was in breach of the BCP. Initially, MCI Worldcom resisted removing or terminating service. However, after extensive pressure from peers, MCI finally relented and terminated service to the site. (cf., Krim 2005).

[112] OpenNet Initiative 2004.

If, conversely, the use of *ad hoc* implies that the rules are created arbitrarily, then the *ad hoc* claim is not accurate. Most groups follow a formal procedure in identifying the need for regulation, in creating the rules and in implementing the rules. The process followed in making the rules is generally transparent. In each example, the group identified the need for regulation of particular content. Then they considered the value of the need for regulation and chose the necessary action to be taken. A drafting team identified the relevant issues that needed regulation – whether to clarify the obligations under a specific legislation or to design obligations where no state direction existed. The draft rules were implemented into written rules and/or technical means. The members of the group in General Meeting adopted the draft. Once adopted the rules were applied and enforced for compliance.[113]

Another aspect of legal certainty involves the possibility that the rules conflict with rules of other groups or of the state. In practice, the rules usually do not conflict with the rules of the state as such, but with the application of those rules. This too can, to some extent, disturb the legal certainty traditionally expected of state law. For example, since blocking lists or filtering tools do not (always) distinguish issues of consent, in jurisdictions where prior consent for the sending of spam is not required, the blocking of e-mails sent in bulk can in practice block the 'legal' sending of bulk e-mail.[114] However, one can argue that this criticism, does not really impinge on the question whether self-regulation rules lack legal certainty but is more of a reflection on the fractured approaches to spam followed by states.

Similarly, in the regulation of harmful content, the different definitions of what is 'harmful' adopted by different groups can in effect lead to conflicting rules of the groups. One reason frequently given by states in favour of self-regulation of harmful content is that self-regulation can bridge the different cultural and social understandings of the term 'harmful content'. There seems to be an expectation by states that self-regulation will hold to a global definition of harmful content. How self-regulation can achieve this expectation is often not explained, though co-funding of projects creating a 'universal' content rating system[115] seems to point toward one solution. In practice, self-regulation offers partial, customised definitions of harmful content: definitions based primarily on the choices and beliefs of a particular group. This approach meets the certainty required by the members of the group – a certainty that the regulation is designed to ensure that each member's beliefs and values are respected in the content he receives.

---

[113] For example, in the UK ISPA example, the Council drew up the ISPA UK Code of Practice after having identified the need to formally draw up a set of rules of conduct for the members to follow in particular in the regulation of Internet content. The members in general meeting subsequently adopted the Code of Practice. See ISPA UK Code of Practice <http://www.ispa.org.uk/html/about_ispa/index.html> accessed 19 April 2005.

[114] OECD Directorate for Science, Technology and Industry (2004) Background paper for the OECD Workshop on Spam Doc Reference: DSTI/ICCP(2003)10/FINAL dated 22 January 2004 p. 14.

[115] Some funds of the EU Safer Internet Action Plan where earmarked for the creation of a 'universal' content rating system. Indirectly, it was thought that a common definition of harmful content can be achieved through the creation of 'universal' content rating tags.

In spite of a number of limitations and the wide variety of self-regulation arrangements involved in the regulation of Internet content, self-regulation arrangements, taken together with a variety of state rules provide a critical step in content regulation.

4.3   STATES AND THE REGULATION OF INTERNET CONTENT

Regulation of published content is not a new phenomenon unique to the Internet. Ever since the first means of making content public, public and private groups have sought to control what content is published and adequate means of punishment have been sought for persons publishing 'disapproved' content.[116] While states and the private sector are familiar with regulating flows of information in society, the changes brought by the Internet present a challenge to the traditional regulatory structures.

The traditional approach of each country regulating the flow of content in its territory is deficient when faced with the two significant shifts strongly bolstered by the Internet. First, a shift from the national space to a global space – hence a requirement of a global approach to the regulation of content instead of the customary national approach. The second shift is a move from a private audience of the content to a potentially global public audience – hence what would formerly have been regarded as the domain of private relations and regulated privately, is now potentially open to the public and according to existing assumptions subject to public (state) regulation.[117]

Furthermore, the same grounds for states to regulate or refrain from regulating content and difficulties in doing so that existed before the introduction of the Internet remain. The need to regulate the publication and distribution of 'illegal' content to protect national security, protection of the public interest or other reasons remains. The struggle to guarantee respect for freedom of expression while protecting certain groups in society from exposure to content or to the effect of 'harmful' content also remains. The difficulty in balancing the right of citizens to privacy against reasonable conditions for trade in regulating the flow of 'unsolicited/unwanted' content also remains.

---

[116] Just a mention to the time of the inquisition is enough to conjure the picture of what the publication (or mere stating in public) of 'disapproved' content could have led to in centuries well before the Internet!

[117] The Internet, in fact, blurs the distinction between public and private spaces. Indeed, one can argue that the Internet also boosts a shift in the contrary direction – a move for public (international) audiences gathering in private spaces. This shift makes it hence more difficult for states to intervene in the regulation as the space where the communities gather is 'private'.

Differences in regulatory approaches

The difference is that added to these reasons and difficulties, there are new reasons and difficulties linked to the global aspect of Internet content. There are multiple (individual) state regulatory approaches to the regulation of content. One can identify at least three different approaches. One approach followed by the United States and some other states, affords a citizen's right to freedom of expression a higher status than other rights. These countries are reluctant to regulate the publication or distribution of content except in 'exceptional' circumstances. The second approach, predominantly followed by most European countries, tries to reach a balance between the right to freedom of expression and other rights of individuals, such as the right to privacy, the right not to be importuned, the right to one's reputation, etc. The third approach, followed predominantly by China and other countries,[118] seeks to limit the publication, distribution and receipt of and access to all content that is not approved by the state.

Differences in what content to regulate

There is little agreement between states and individual communities on what content needs to be regulated. Different cultural traditions, religious or moral beliefs of communities imply that there are often conflicting interests and loyalties at stake. Research has shown that even though members of a group may more or less agree (with states) on the regulation of certain categories of content, there are particular categories of content where private groups disagree both among themselves and with the state(s).[119] For example, while states and copyright holders often agree that Internet content infringing existing copyright regulation (such as the 'illegal' distribution of music content) needs to be regulated, most users disagree with the state and other private interest groups on the need to regulate the activities related to copyrighted content.[120] The conflict between the legislative position and the views of users can lead to the development of 'customary non-application'[121] of the law, which can have significant consequences on the application of the law by the state.

Even in the best of circumstances, achieving global (or international) agreement between states on regulation is a painstaking endeavour. Given the multiple differ-

---

[118] Such as Saudi Arabia and Iran. See for example OpenNet Initiative 2005.

[119] For example, Svensson and Bannister 2004. They look into the possibility of using social control to control deviant behaviour in the distribution of Internet content (especially illegal or harmful content) within peer-to-peer networks. Their research shows that there are categories of content that users generally consider undesirable such as child pornography – thus agreeing with the categorisation by most or all states. But copyrighted material is not considered by users to be one of these categories. ['Copyright infringement is, however, a different issue. As this research shows, the acceptance of copyright law among users of p2p networks is indeed very low.' at p. 15].

[120] Cf., Svensson and Bannister 2004.

[121] *Consuetudo abrogatoria.*

ent traditions of regulating content, and the different cultural values and traditions of countries and users, achieving global inter-state agreement on the regulation of Internet is difficult. The drafting and negotiation of the Council of Europe's Convention on Cybercrime[122] showed clearly the (almost) insurmountable differences between the legal and cultural traditions of states on what content to prohibit. The drafting and negotiation process took more than five years. The Council of Europe's Convention on Cybercrime is the first and only international law instrument to include some specific regulation of Internet content. States involved in the drafting of the Convention, which included the forty-six Member States of the Council of Europe and five other states,[123] only secured consensus on content relating to child pornography. Content of a racist and xenophobic nature was relegated to an additional (optional) protocol of the Convention since a number of countries, predominantly the United States, would not have signed and ratified the Convention had the content of the protocol been included in the main text.[124] Governments endeavour to appease the public outcries on Internet content. Yet, given the experience in the drafting of the Council of Europe Cybercrime Convention,[125] states are well aware of the difficulties involved in securing consensus on what content may be restricted uniformly.

Technical access

Two other conditions make it difficult for individual states to regulate Internet content-related activities: technical access to the activities and the formation of private communities organised around specific interests on the Internet.

States may not always have technical access to the content that needs to be regulated, making the application and enforcement of state regulation, where regulation exists, difficult. However, in spite of the technical difficulties, states (and private groups) increasingly regulate Internet content through technical means. Some states, like China and Saudi Arabia, use technical means to control (as much as possible) all content within their jurisdiction, including content coming from outside their jurisdiction. Apart from the obvious undemocratic character of this approach, there are also technical problems – technical blocking does not always block all unauthorised content and often also blocks 'wanted content'. Other states limit their technical intervention to surveillance of the flow of Internet content and depend on technical gatekeepers (namely ISPs) to enforce existing regulation by blocking illegal content.

---

[122] Council of Europe Convention on Cybercrime (ETS No. 185).

[123] The Holy See, the US, Canada, Japan and Mexico.

[124] See Carr 2002.

[125] The Cybercrime Convention opened for signature in November 2001 but had been on the drafting and negotiating table for at least six years.

Private communities

The formation of private communities organised around specific interests rather than nationality or territorial presence challenges the regulation of content by states. Individual states have difficulty regulating activities of communities on the Internet that have no jurisdictional link (neither of territory nor of nationality) with the state. The Internet accommodates the creation and existence of groups/communities based on common interest(s) irrespective of the nationality or geographical presence of the parties. In spite of having no jurisdictional link over the participants, the content or the activities may be considered illegal by the state. An example can illustrate this: the Internet has facilitated the gathering of activists in favour of housing rights for the homeless in Zimbabwe. The activists are nationals and residents of a variety of countries but none of them reside in or is a national of Zimbabwe. The content they publish on their site (hosted in, say, Italy) denouncing the eviction of over a million residents of shantytowns is considered illegal by Zimbabwe. Yet, Zimbabwe's ability (independently of other states) to control the flow of content from this group of activists is very limited.

State initiatives to regulate Internet content

Recognising the difficulties in regulating Internet content and based on experience of the regulation of content published by other media, for example print media or broadcasting,[126] states[127] and inter-state organisations[128] have followed two approaches: using legislation and supporting self-regulation.

A.   Legislation regulating content

The first approach is to introduce new laws to regulate content on the Internet or amend laws traditionally intended for the regulation of content published or printed by means of other media.[129] Some content-related legislation pre-dates the introduction of the Internet, for example most libel and defamation legislation. This means that the laws are generally framed with a state-centred, media specific approach to the publication of content – an approach that does not fit the decentralised structure of the Internet. This has led some states to amend 'old' laws to fit the new

---

[126] For example, in the UK self-regulation of journalists has a long standing tradition. The Code of Conduct of the National Union of Journalists in Britain and Ireland has been in effect since 1936. (Code of Conduct accessed at <http://www.nuj.org.uk/inner.php?docid=59> on 15 December 2005).

[127] The UK and the Netherlands amongst other states have encourage and published studies and policy positions on self-regulation of Internet content (see for example, UK Office of Telecommunications (Oftel) 2003).

[128] Such as the EU and the OECD.

[129] Signatories to the Council of Europe Cybercrime Convention, for example, have amended their criminal laws to include child pornography as a crime.

reality.[130] In other states, it has been up to the Courts to interpret whether the 'old' laws can be applied to the Internet.

States have introduced new laws regulating content at an international – mainly the Cybercrime Convention – national and regional level – the introduction of new laws to regulate unwanted content is an important example. In the last three years,[131] states have been actively involved in the drafting of legislation on unwanted content. The European Union was one of the first to enact legislation against unsolicited commercial communications by adopting a Directive on privacy and electronic communications (2002/58/EC). Once the Directive is adopted in the twenty-five Member States, it leads (theoretically at least) to a pan-European 'ban on spam'.[132] An OECD report[133] in 2004 shows that eighteen OECD Member States have specific laws or decrees on spam. At least three other states[134] extend the application of existing laws and regulation to spam. Other countries are in the process of developing anti-spam legislation. The involvement of states in the regulation of unwanted content has primarily an economic motive. Unwanted content undermines users trust on the Internet and may result in less use. In addition, unwanted content has a significant impact on Internet businesses.[135]

There is a wide variety of legislation of individual states, each relying on different definitions of illegal, harmful and unwanted content.[136] For example, what is considered spam under one regulatory solution may not be considered spam at all under another.[137] These differences frustrate the effectiveness of state legislation regulating Internet content.

---

[130] See for example, UK Law Commission Report 2002.

[131] 2002-2005.

[132] The deadline for implementing the Directive was 31st October 2003. Infringement proceedings have been instituted against Member States who have not notified the Commission of the transposition of the Directive into national legislation.

[133] OECD Directorate for Science, Technology and Industry (2004) Background paper for the OECD Workshop on Spam Doc Reference: DSTI/ICCP(2003)10/FINAL dated 22 January 2004 p. 20.

[134] Canada, Czech Republic and Mexico.

[135] European businesses alone estimate that more than 2.1 billion euros are lost every year to lost productivity due to unwanted content. See Schenker 2004; Communication from the Commission to the European Parliament, The Council, The European Economic and Social Committee and the Committee of the Regions on unsolicited commercial communications or 'spam'. (COM(2004)28 Final 22 January 2004) (in particular p. 1-7).

[136] Unwanted content more known as 'Spam' refers to the sending of electronic mail in bulk to recipients who have not given their consent to receiving such electronic mail. There are many definitions of 'Spam'. Three elements are common in each definition: (a) the sending of electronic mail; (b) in large quantities; and (c) without the consent of the recipients. Each definition restricts or qualifies some aspect of these three characteristics. The definition given in the EU Directive (2002/58/EC) qualifies the purpose of the sending of the electronic mail. The Directive applies to electronic mail sent 'for the purposes of direct marketing'. In some definitions, the emphasis is on the sender of the electronic mail, for example, that the sender who disguises or forges his identity (see Gauthronet and Drouard 2001: 14).

[137] For example, under the EU Directive (2002/58/EC), electronic mail for the purposes of direct marketing is considered unwanted content if it is: (i) sent without obtaining the prior consent of the

- Enforcing state legislation

Inevitably, state legislation regulating Internet content is often hard to apply and enforce. State laws apply and are enforceable as long as the publication of the content takes place in the territory of a State banning the publication of the content once there is no jurisdictional link, it is difficult to apply national law. Furthermore, state law enforcement agencies do not (always) have[138] the necessary technical tools and access to control and enforce the legislation on the Internet. Neither do they always have the means to secure proof of the illegal activity.

In practice, states have to rely on groups for the enforcement of the legislation. For example, while a state may have legislation limiting the distribution of certain categories of adult content to minors, it is up to ISPs or other private entities (such as libraries) to actually implement rules that have an effect on the access of minors to the content.

Since most activities on the Internet take place in a transnational context, law enforcement agencies of one state need to collaborate with law enforcement agencies of other states. Increasingly, states are aware of the need for collaboration between law enforcement agencies of different states. They have started a process of international collaboration for the enforcement of laws regulating, primarily illegal content. The Council of Europe Cybercrime Convention is one example. The Cybercrime Convention addresses part of the difficulty by reaching consensus on collaboration on the enforcement and prosecution of crimes related to child pornography. However, the definition of the crime differs in the legislation of the different countries even within the European Union. In an attempt to harmonise the collaboration of law enforcement on combating the sexual exploitation of children and child pornography within the European Union, the European Union issued in late 2003 a European Council Framework Decision on combating the sexual exploitation of children and child pornography (2004/68/JHA).[139]

In other areas of illegal content, very little harmonisation of rules and collaboration in enforcement exist. The refusal of United States courts to recognise and enforce the decision of a French court in the *Yahoo!* case illustrates part of the difficulties that exist in the prosecution and enforcement of activities related to illegal content. In *Yahoo, Inc.* v. *La Ligue Contre Le Racisme et L'Antisémitisme, et al.*[140] a US District Court declared unenforceable the order of a of a French Court[141] ordering

---

recipients; or (ii) the sender details are disguised or concealed; or (iii) the electronic mail does not include a valid return address where the recipient can send an electronic mail to opt-out. The emphasis in the EU Directive is that the person receiving the electronic mail consents to the receipt of the mail. In contrast, the US CAN-SPAM Act of 2003 adopts an opt-out approach, that is, an unsolicited e-mail can be sent provided that the sender (a) provides a mechanism to opt-out from future listings; (b) is sent from a valid and function electronic mail address; and (c) clear lists in the subject line that the content is an advertisement.

[138] It is arguably preferable that they do not!

[139] The Member States had to comply with the Framework Decision no later than 20 January 2006.

[140] Case No. C-00-21275JF, 145 F. Supp. 2d 1168 (N.D. Ca., 24 September 2001).

[141] In *La Ligue Contre Le Racisme et L'Antisémitisme* v. *Yahoo! Inc.* High Court of Paris, May 22, 2000, Interim Court Order No. 00/05308, 00/05309, two French non-government organisations sued

Yahoo Inc. to block French citizens' access to websites hosting the sale of Nazi memorabilia. The US Court considered that the enforcement of this order would violate Yahoo's First Amendment rights.

B. Supporting and promoting self-regulation

A second approach that states and inter-state organisation take in the regulation of Internet content is to encourage the development of industry self-regulation. From official documents and debates, it appears that states expect that self-regulation, because of its allegedly flexible nature, can provide a global regulatory solution to the regulation of Internet content.

In view of the various difficulties facing state regulation, some states, particularly many European states and the European Union, defer the regulation to the private sector. The European Union, for example, financially supports and encourages private sector self-regulation in matters of harmful content. The European Union has long acknowledged that the only 'real' option for the regulation of harmful content is through self-regulation.[142] The EU choice in favour of self-regulation of 'harmful content' is based primarily on a general EU policy in favour of self-regulation[143] that can be traced backed to the early stages of EU policy on 'information highways', in 1993 and 1994. EU policy and practice in the telecommunications sector has been to provide legal frameworks within which the market can develop its own forms of control. This can be seen, for instance, in the Data Protection Directive (95/46/EC), where the European Union provides a legal framework for the protection of personal data but expects the private sector to create specific rules of practice.[144] The principle of subsidiarity is never far removed.

The same trend can be seen in the practice of individual states as well. Some countries, for example the United Kingdom, have a long tradition in favour of self-regulation of content even before the arrival of the Internet (e.g., in television broadcasting).[145] Other states still opt for direct regulation of the distribution of certain content to uphold the standards of the community. For example, Egypt bans the distribution of content on 'taboo issues' such as criticism of its President.[146]

Yahoo!, an ISP, for supporting anti-Semitism by hosting the sale of Nazi memorabilia, a criminal offence in France. The Court ordered Yahoo! to block French citizens' access to web sites hosting the sale of Nazi memorabilia under continuing penalties in case of default.

[142] See for example Opinion of the Economic and Social Committee on the 'Green Paper on the protection of minors and human dignity in audiovisual and information services' (*OJ* C287, 22 September 1997 p. 11) 'The deviation from the definition of harmful content will vary from country to country depending on the cultural and social norms of that country ... Because of the varying cultural and social norms self-regulation ... will provide the most suitable solution for the regulation of harmful content.'

[143] Feeley 1999.

[144] See Directive 95/46/EC at Art. 27 (and Simitis 1998).

[145] Leonardi 2004.

[146] OpenNet Initiative 2004: 6; Reporters without Borders, Egypt at <http://www.rsf.org/article.php3?id_article=10732> on 22 April 2005.

A reason for supporting self-regulation is that states are reluctant and often unable to reach the particular behaviour needing regulation without the involvement of self-regulation. Self-regulation is hence seen as better able to carry out regulation of Internet content. In particular, self-regulation is seen as especially applicable:

- in situations where states cannot easily be seen as involved in regulation such as in the regulation of harmful content;
- in situations where regulation by individual states cannot effectively regulate the transnational effects of the behaviour;
- in situations where states have been unable to build global consensus between states on what needs to be regulated.

- Examples of state encouragement of self-regulation

States and state regulation have some bearing on the functioning of self-regulation in the regulation of Internet content. They encourage and support self-regulation in fulfilling its functions. 'Encouragement' is carried out in a number of practical ways:

(a) by *financial assistance* for the development and implementation of self-regulation arrangements involved in the regulation of Internet content. The European Union has funded (and funds) multiple self-regulation initiatives in the regulation of Internet content area.[147] Under the Safer Internet Action Plan,[148] the European Union co-funded thirty-seven projects, amongst which thirteen projects related to filtering and rating of content, such as the SIFT project,[149] and an extensive study on ISP codes of conduct and a preliminary study on quality labelling. The funding programme continues to cover the period 2005-2008.[150] During this period this programme is providing,[151] 'funding for measures to facilitate and co-ordinate exchanges of information and best practices on effective enforcement against spam'[152] are envisaged. Other states too contribute to the funding of hotlines.[153]

---

[147] In 1999, the European Parliament and Council approved, the funding of a number of private sector efforts aimed at regulating Internet content (and ensuring user confidence), under the Multi-annual Community action plan on promoting safer use of the Internet by combating illegal and harmful content on global networks (Safer Internet Action Plan). (See Decision 276/1999EC 25 January 1999 *OJ* L33 6 February 1999 p. 1).

[148] The Action plan originally ran from 1999-2002. It was then extended to 2004.

[149] <http://www.sift-platform.org/>. However, the take-up of the filtering software products and the content rating criteria has been low. See Commission Evaluation Report at p. 3 doc reference (COM(2003)653 dated 3 November 2003).

[150] Commission proposal for a Decision of the European Parliament and of the Council on establishing a multi-annual Community programme on promoting safer use of the Internet and new on-line technologies (COM(2004)91 final (12 March 2004)).

[151] The European Union Safer Internet *plus* Action Plan was approved by the European Parliament on 2 December 2004 and by the EU Telecommunications Council on 9th December 2004.

[152] Proposal for a Decision of the European Parliament and of the Council on establishing a multi-annual Community programme on promoting safer use of the Internet and new on-line technologies (COM(2004)91 final 12 March 2004) at p. 8.

[153] For example Ireland. See Irish Child Pornography Hotline at <http://www.hotline.ie/>.

(b) *assisting in the drafting and enforcement* of the codes of conduct or other rules developed by the groups. For example, states or state agencies are involved in the drafting of rules of practices to be followed by hotline service providers. Since its inception in 1996, the Internet Watch Foundation (IWF) has had close ties with different UK government departments.[154] Similarly, the Irish Internet Advisory Board (a body set by the Irish government to 'make sure that self-regulation worked in practice')[155] is involved in the practices followed by the Irish ISPs responsible for the running of the Irish hotline. This assistance is at times statutorily mandated by specific state legislation. Some national broadcasting services legislation[156] and/or national telecommunications legislation give industry players the option to organise compliance with the legislation either through self-regulation or through direct statutory or government action. Some ISP associations were created in response to this 'invitation' and hence the drafting of their codes reflects principles dictated in framework legislation.

Another example comes from the Council of Europe (which also drafted the International Convention on Cybercrime). The Council issued a recommendation[157] to its Member States on self-regulation concerning Internet content proposing that member governments 'co-operate' with the Internet industry and its self-regulatory bodies in the regulation of harmful Internet content.

At times, state legislation sets minimum conditions that should be found in codes of conduct of industry groups. For example, in September 1998, the EU Council adopted a Recommendation (98/560/EC) promoting the development of national frameworks for self-regulation of content in the audiovisual and information services. The main aim is to achieve protection of minors and of human dignity. The Recommendation recommends that Member States take action to provide common guidelines for the implementation of self-regulation at the national level.[158]

(c) *supporting the training of staff.* In the case of most hotlines, law enforcement agencies and officers are involved in the training of hotline staff responsible for

---

[154] See <http://www.iwf.org.uk/government/page.6.htm> last accessed on 15 April 2005.

[155] Accessed at <http://www.iab.ie/AboutUs/Background/> on 15 April 2005.

[156] Like the Australian Broadcasting Services Act.

[157] Recommendation Rec(2001) 8 of the Committee of Ministers to Member States on Self-Regulation concerning cyber content (self-regulation and user protection against illegal or harmful content on new communications and information services. Adopted by the Committee of Ministers on 5 September 2001. Available at <http://www.coe.int/T/E/Human_Rights/media/4_Documentary_Resources/CM/Rec(2001)008&ExpMem_en.asp>.

[158] Annexed to the Recommendation are a set of guidelines for the implementation, at national level, of a self-regulation framework for the protection of minors and human dignity in audiovisual and on-line information services. (See Annex to COM(97)570 final 18 November 1997 – Commission Communication on the follow-up to the Green paper on the protection of minors and human dignity in audio visual and information services). Yet evaluation reports acknowledge that 'the Member States have applied the Recommendation in a heterogeneous way'. (See Conclusion COM(2001)106 final 27 February 2001 p. 14.) The aim of harmonisation has not been achieved.

assessing the illegality of content reported by users. For example, the police train the IWF hotline staff members.[159] Law enforcement agencies have an interest in the training of the staff members – trained staff is able to report to the law enforcement agency in a more precise and appropriate manner.

(d) *promoting the development of 'international' self-regulation projects* for the regulation of content. One example is the support shown by the Australian government to the signing of an agreement in February 2005 between the Australian Internet Industry Association and the Chinese Internet Society. In the agreement, the two organisations agree to co-operate, primarily through technical co-operation, to regulate trans-border spam activities.[160]

- Effects of state support of self-regulation
In practice, the action of states and state regulation lends added legitimacy to the rule-making power and rules of the groups. State support for self-regulation facilitates co-operation between groups, in particular ISPs, and law enforcement agencies in the taking down of content. For example, the Belgian ISP association and the Belgian Judicial Police have since May 1999 established a protocol of collaboration in the enforcement of claims of illegal content on the Internet.[161] Co-operation between law enforcement agencies and ISPs is occasionally, supported by specific legislation imposing a duty on ISPs to maintain the capacity to intercept activities on the Internet.[162]

At times states formalise positions taken earlier by self-regulation. Some of the rules developed through self-regulation, in particular the principle that ISPs are only responsible for content hosted on their servers or going through their servers if, once notified of an alleged illegal activity, they fail to stop/prevent the illegal activity from continuing, have been formalised in law. This position can be seen formalised in current legislation such as the US 1998 Digital Millennium Copyright Act[163] (DMCA) and the EU e-Commerce Directive (2000/31/EC).

In many situations, states and state regulation also acts as a form of external accountability process on the working of the different self-regulation arrangements. Groups can be held to account for the rules developed and being carried out. The process of keeping the working of private groups under scrutiny is more evident

---

[159] See 'The Hotline Service' in IWF Code of Practice accessed at <http://www.iwf.org.uk/funding/page.60.htm> on 15 April 2005.

[160] News Release: Australia and China sign historic agreement to help limit spam accessed at <http://www.iia.net.au/news/010305.html> on 27 April 2005.

[161] 'Cooperation Protocol in order to combat illegal acts on the Internet' signed on the 28th May 1999 between the Belgian ISPA and the Deputy Belgian Prime Minister and the Belgian Minister for Justice accessed at <http://www.ispa.be/en/c040202.html> on 12 March 2002.

[162] See UK Regulation of Investigatory Powers Act 2000.

[163] <http://thomas.loc.gov/cgi-bin/query/F?c105:1:./temp/~c1058HT6FY:e884>: accessed 15 April 2005.

where a specific legislative act or state policy mandates self-regulation. One example is the system under Australian law where industry self-regulation documents are to be registered with a specific Australian public authority. Another example is the assessment of compliance with German law protecting minors from harmful content.[164] However, state regulation can be used to hold groups to account even where no specific legislation defines the parameters within which self-regulation can develop. States can use general legal principles found within the state's body of laws regulating commercial behaviour. The rules of ISPs on harmful and unwanted content, for example, can be subject to consumer protection legislation or fair competition rules.

Furthermore, states and state regulation offer a general legal framework that groups can choose to plug into in carrying out the above functions. Self-regulation in the regulation of Internet content does not exist in a regulatory vacuum. It exists within a wider framework of general state and group rules. Some private groups, for example, formalise their internal organisation according to existing state law regulating commercial companies or non-profit organisations. Another example of self-regulation plugging into existing legal frameworks is the use of contract law in the formulation of service contracts (and 'acceptable use' policies) between, for example, ISPs and their customers.

There are, however, also important examples of self-regulation where state regulation is not directly involved in the self-regulation process, in particular where the self-regulation arrangement is not readily linked to a particular territorial arrangement. For example, the involvement of state regulation in the regulation of content by particular communities of interest is negligible.

4.4 CONCLUSION

Self-regulation in the regulation of Internet content is not a mere collection of social norms. The rule-makers are both legitimate and accountable. The rules created are binding, transparent and certain and are created following a pre-determined rule-making process. Self-regulation is an important and common form of regulation of Internet content. It forms a heterogeneous patchwork of decentralised arrangements accommodating the different needs of the various groups involved in the regulation of Internet content.

Self-regulation is not the only regulatory structure involved in the regulation of content. It co-exists with a patchwork of regulatory initiatives coming from indi-

---

[164] Since the entry into force of the *Jugendmedienschutz-Staatsvertrag* on 1 April 2003, while it is expected that ISPs ensure that minors do not have access to harmful material, the regulation used by the ISP must be assessed and tested by the authorities (p. 9 of Second Evaluation report on the application of Council Recommendation of 24 September 1998 concerning the protection of minors and human dignity (COM(2003)776 final 12 December 2003)).

vidual states and some international and regional organisation of states. State legislation typically regulates some aspects of 'illegal' and 'unwanted' content, while
state involvement in the regulation of 'harmful' content is limited to the protection
of minors or minorities.

Intertwining and complementary

How are the variety of private and public rules related to each other? The rules do
not merely co-exist. A mixture of rules coming from both states and groups regulate
Internet content. Self-regulation intertwines and complements state legislation in
three processes of regulation: in the creation of rules; in the application and implementation of rules; and in the enforcement of rules.

Often, self-regulation is the first to provide a set of rules to regulate content.
These sets of rules may later be included in state legislation (at both international
and national level). One important example was the development of 'notice and
take down' rules first defined by ISPs in the regulation of content and subsequently
adopted in national legislation and EU directives, such as the e-Commerce Directive. Internet users are then subject to both group rules and state regulation.

At times, states take an opposite position to the rules formulated by self-regulation. The self-regulation rules still serve as an important point of departure for states.
They help in clarifying the aims of the state legislation. One example, the EU Directive on privacy and electronic communications took a different stand on consent
of the recipient of unwanted content from the rules that were being followed until
then by the Federation of European Direct Marketing Associations.

In other instances, self-regulation fills in for the absence of state legislation particularly where states are reluctant or unable to regulate. The most important example here is the regulation of harmful content, that is, the situation where what is
considered harmful depends on the shared values, traditions, morals and customs of
the particular group. Yet states and general legislative frameworks of states also
come into play here. States assist in the drafting of the rules. General legal principles, such as those of contract law, are used as a basis for self-regulation. Self-
regulation rules do not exist in a vacuum. They exist in the shadow of generic state
legal systems.

Groups and states participate in the application of each other's rules. Self-regulation rules often implement state legislation on regulation of content. They define
how state rules regulating the publication of illegal content and the sending of unwanted content can be applied in practice. They convert the state rules into technical rules, which are then implemented by the groups (especially groups having
technical access to the content). Self-regulation assists in overcoming the limitations of state legislation – filling in missing details (especially when the laws to be
applied were originally drafted for other media and do not deal with the difficulties
posed by Internet) and supplying the means to ensure the (technical) application
and implementation of the laws.

States also assist in the application of group rules, mostly by providing mechanisms to keep the group in check. State law mechanisms of accountability also confirm the legitimacy of the groups to participate in the regulation of content, strengthening the position of the groups in regulation.

The intertwining of self-regulation and state law can also be seen in the enforcement process of the rules. Self-regulation participates in the enforcement of state regulation. One important example is the provision of a system of reporting and *prima facie* 'investigation' of alleged breaches of state law (in particular on child pornography) through the rules of hotlines. Another example is the blocking and take-down of content in breach of state law, or the blocking of the sending or receipt of spam when this is in breach of state law. The self-regulation rules carry out the enforcement of state law at a technical level – at the level where the actual content is stored and can be accessed.

Some self-regulation rules are self-enforcing, that is, once they are technically implemented they will enforce the rule automatically. For example, if a rule providing that once a system detects the sending of unwanted content the system should block the sending is technically implemented, then the enforcement of the rule will take place automatically each time the system detects the sending of spam. When the rules are not technically implemented, the same problems of enforcement that confront state law exist. State legal systems are some times involved in checking compliance with such rules.

The complementarity between self-regulation and states does not stop here. States encourage, even by financial assistance, the development and implementation of self-regulation arrangements. In turn, self-regulation satisfies the political and regulatory needs of states. While all states feel the need to regulate the flow of content on the Internet, they are not always keen to regulate or be seen to be regulating Internet content. Self-regulation lends itself to regulation where states cannot readily regulate, as in the regulation of illegal and harmful content, and where states are still unable to achieve global consensus, such as in the regulation of harmful or unwanted content.

A developing interdependence

One sees an interdependence developing between self-regulation and state regulation. States rely on the 'insider' information of groups, that they are often not privy too, for the identification of what needs to be regulated and for the smooth application and enforcement of state rules. Thanks to the groups' access to what is actually happening on the Internet, self-regulation can offer a customised regulatory solution that fits the policies of the state and the needs of the group and meets the demands imposed by the technical reality of the Internet. One can clearly identify a trend towards 'customisation' of regulation in the current regulation of Internet content. To solve the difficulty of achieving a common international/global agreement on what content needs regulation, Internet content regulation is shifting to the group level. Rules are developed, applied and enforced addressing the needs of the particular group. This is a shift from a 'one measure fits all' approach to 'to each the necessary measure' approach.

This trend is complemented by a move towards supporting user empowerment. In regulating Internet content, the risk of being 'accused' of censorship is a powerful restraint on regulation. Increasingly, both states and groups seem to prefer to leave the ultimate decision on what content to block and receive to the end user. The trend is to offer technical tools and measures that allow the user to make the choice himself. Empowering users to take decisions on content is thought to achieve a better balancing of rights than direct regulation – the right to publish any content remains untainted and the recipient's right to determine what content to receive is sustained. What remains, is the technical problem of providing appropriate tools fast and accurate enough to make the rights of recipients effective.

The technical dominance of certain groups, such as ISPs, on the Internet critically contributes to the developing interdependence between states and self-regulation. States recognise the position of dominance of some groups, such as ISPs. They acknowledge the need to collaborate with these groups in identifying the rules to be applied and in carrying out the application and enforcement of rules. This position of technical dominance exposes groups to potential legal liability unless their legal position is clearly defined (and supported by state legislation). The groups are dependent on states and state courts for such protection.

State legislation has reacted to this need for protection by specifically legislating on the responsibility of ISPs in the regulation of content. States increasingly rely on the technical expertise present in groups to develop (technical) tools that can control the flow of Internet content. The development of technical tools, such as content filtering tools, that implement rules on the receipt and blocking of Internet content, have proved to be effective means to control the receipt or sending of content. While states can invest in the development of technical tools to control content (and indeed some countries do),[165] many choose to encourage groups to develop the technical tools. Moreover, while private groups have the expertise to develop the tools, they are mostly dependent on the financial support of states to invest in developing them. The consequence sometimes is that states dictate the direction to be taken by self-regulation.

In any sphere, the Internet included, the development and carrying out of regulation has a pecuniary cost. States seem increasingly keen to shift part of the costs of application and enforcement of regulation on to the private sector and are dependent on the private sector's collaboration. The cost attached, for example, to the retention of content is the responsibility of ISPs even if the data is retained because it may eventually help in the prosecution of a wrong-doer by the state. States are dependent on groups to carry out regulation where states cannot regulate. Hence, the financial backing of self-regulation by states comes particularly in areas where

---

[165] China, Iran, Saudi Arabia perhaps invest in technical tools more openly than other countries.

states cannot effectively regulate the behaviour but is still under pressure from different constituencies to provide a solution.[166] (And) since developing (financially) self-sustainable self-arrangements is often a challenge, some groups are dependent on state funding.

These underlying relationships of interdependence between state regulation and self-regulation explain the current complementary intertwining in the regulation of content. While neither state regulation nor self-regulation completely regulates all the different concerns and needs of the diverse groups on the Internet, together they provide an important measure of regulation in a difficult field.

---

[166] An example is the EU co-funding Action Plan of self-regulation in the enforcement of illegal content (in particular child pornography) and in the regulation of harmful content.

Chapter 5
SELF-REGULATION OF THE DOMAIN NAME SYSTEM

5.1 INTRODUCTION

The Domain Name System (DNS) is the central system of identification on the Internet. It is a critical technical resource. All of the Internet's users depend on the DNS to find content or services they are looking for or to attract other users to the content and services they provide.[1] Through a set of technical arrangements, the DNS uses 'domain names', such as 'google.com', as signposts of locations of content on the Internet. Every domain name is associated with a numerical Internet Protocol (IP) address assigned to machines on the network. On the Internet, computers recognise and communicate with each other by means of numerical IP addresses. Each computer on the network is assigned, temporarily or permanently, an IP address by which it can be identified and located through the domain to which it belongs.

The DNS enables users to use domain names to locate and access information at particular sites[2] using user-friendly names instead of hard to remember IP numbers. Each domain name is unique and hence a permanent identifier of a location, whereas IP numbers, since they can be assigned temporarily to a machine/location, are not fixed identifiers of a location. The uniqueness of each domain name facilitates the tracing of the desired location. Applications, such as Internet browsers and e-mail software, use domain names as part of the process to identify and locate a desired information source or recipient.[3]

While the original purpose of developing and designing the DNS in the 1980s was to provide a clear and easily remembered system of locating activities on the Internet, domain names today also satisfy other purposes not originally intended or thought of. With the growth of the Internet as a commercial space, domain names are associated with products or services rather than just location names on the Internet. The domain name has developed into a means of identifying an organisation or service on-line.[4] In this context, domain names fulfil a purpose similar to trademarks and service marks in the off-line world. Hence, apart from their critical purpose in identifying locations on the Internet, domain names also have an economic/commercial value. This has lead to disputes over the ownership of specific 'valuable' names.

---

[1] Cf., US National Research Council of the National Academies 2005: ES-1.
[2] Id. 2005: vii.
[3] Id.2005: 2-4.
[4] Manheim and Solum 2003: 367.

J.P. Mifsud Bonnici, Self-Regulation in Cyberspace
© 2008, *T·M·C·ASSER PRESS, The Hague, and the author*

In view of the critical importance of the DNS, 'control' over the DNS has been generally equated in the literature with 'control' over the Internet. Frequently, debates on the governance of the Internet are reduced to debates on the control and regulation of the technical infrastructure, predominantly the DNS.[5] As a consequence of the historical development of the DNS, the United States has an important role in the regulation of the DNS even if self-regulation is the predominant source of regulation. The same persons that designed and developed the DNS technically were (initially) associated with the US government and responsible for its regulation.

It is clear and uncontested in the literature that the regulation of DNS depends on private regulation. Nevertheless, in the literature on the regulation of the DNS, the role of self-regulation is generally overshadowed by discussions that emphasise the role of states in the regulation and control of the DNS. Indeed, there is an imbalance in the literature: the actual reality of private regulation of the DNS is far less represented than arguments for desired predominance of states over the DNS. Authors argue that the importance of the DNS as a central resource on the Internet merits an active role of all states in the governance of the resource. There is, they claim, a public interest argument that supports the involvement of states.[6]

In this chapter, I review and explain the self-regulation carried out by the three major groups involved in the administration of the DNS – the Internet Corporation for Assigned Names and Numbers (ICANN), domain name registries and domain name registrars. Self-regulation serves two fundamental functions. It is the main regulatory system of the DNS, regulating matters on which, apart from some sporadic regulation by states,[7] no regulation from other sources exists. It serves a political function – it fills in the middle ground between the need for regulation and the slowness and inability of states to agree to common regulatory positions. These purposes are achieved through a set of centralised and concatenated self-regulation arrangements. The centralisation and concatenation of rules is particular to self-regulation of the DNS. It is a contrast to the decentralised patchwork of arrangements found in the self-regulation of other Internet activities.

Despite the agreed less dominant involvement of state legislation in the regulation of the DNS, as in the case of the self-regulation of other Internet activities, self-regulation of the DNS intertwines with and is complementary to state legislation. This chapter shows how the functions served by self-regulation complement and are complemented by the involvement of states in the regulation of the DNS, espe-

---

[5] The Working Group on Internet Governance (2005) Background Report accessed at <http://www. wgig.org> on 5 August 2005 (see p. 10).

[6] Froomkin (2000a), for example, argues that it is specifically because of the public interest involved that the transfer of management by the US government of the DNS to ICANN was unconstitutional.

[7] Such as the US Anti-cybersquatting consumer protection act and other specific legislation regulating particular country code Top Level Domains.

cially now that states are increasingly interested in participating in the regulation of the DNS.

In the conclusion, I argue that regulation of the DNS is still in a process of development. Maintaining the *status quo* on the regulation of the DNS, agreed to in Tunis in November 2005,[8] is not the final word. Gradually states and the private sector will need to work out their respective functions in the future regulation. The current intertwining and complementary relations, I argue, can form the basis of future governance of the DNS.

Before embarking on the description of self-regulation of the DNS, in the next sub-section, I give a brief description of the technical structure of the DNS. Some knowledge of the technical structure will ease the understanding of the regulation needed and actually taking place, especially since the technical structure and the regulation of the DNS are very closely related.

5.1.1   The technical structure of the DNS

There are three essential elements in the DNS design – (a) a domain namespace; (b) a hierarchical structure to store domain name lists and resolve queries; and (c) software that specifies operations within the name space and the hierarchical structure. There are essentially two main software components: software that converts domain names to the IP numbers on various computers, and technical standards that define the formats of the communication between programmes, as well as the logical structure of the files in a domain name server.[9] This chapter looks predominantly at the regulation related to domain namespaces.

5.1.1.1   *The Domain Name*

A *domain name* is usually made up of a number of parts (levels) (each called domain names) separated by dots (or full-stops), for example, <www.amazon.com>.

A top-level domain part can be identified at the end of a string of characters when reading from left to right, '.com' in the example. The top-level domain name can either be a generic Top-level Domain Name (gTLD), for example '.org' or a country code Top-level Domain Name (ccTLD), for example, '.nl' or an infrastructure Top-level Domain Name (iTLD), for example, '.arpa'. There are currently 14 gTLDs.[10] Domain names may be registered in seven categories without restrictions[11] and in the other seven categories only if the registrant belongs to a particular

---

[8] World Summit on the Information Society (2005) Tunis Agenda for the Information Society. Agreed on 18 November 2005 Doc. Ref. WSIS-05/TUNIS/DOC/6(Rev.1)-E <http://www/itu.int/wsis/docs2/tunis/off/6rev1.htm>.

[9] Cf., US National Research Council of the National Academies 2005: 3-6.

[10] .aero; .biz; .com; .coop; .edu; .gov; .info; .int; .mil; .museum; .name; .net; .org; .pro.

[11] .com; .net; .org; .biz; .info; .name and .pro are unrestricted.

community.[12] For example, only musea can register a '.museum' domain name. There are 253[13] ccTLDs, each consisting of two letters corresponding to two-letter abbreviations for countries or territories (for example '.nl' for the Netherlands) according to the standard set by the International Standards Organisation.[14] There is only one iTLD: the '.arpa' domain. The '.arpa' is the Address and Routing Parameter Area domain. It is used exclusively for Internet-infrastructure purposes.[15]

A second level domain part can be any set of characters (letters and numbers) often descriptive of the activities of the organisation, business, group or individual registering the domain name. The second level domain name is the portion of the domain name that appears immediately to the left of the top-level domain, 'amazon' in the example.

A third (or more) level domain part is the portion of the domain name that appears two segments to the left of the top-level domain, 'www' in the example. The hierarchy of levels/parts can be extended indefinitely, but most domain names use only three levels,[16] especially from a commercial marketing perspective the shorter the domain name the easier it is to remember.

5.1.1.2   *The hierarchical structure*

The DNS stores lists of domain names in a *hierarchical structure* that reflects the hierarchical structure of the domain name space. The hierarchical structure facilitates the resolution of domain name queries. The DNS could have been designed to work with a flat structure (for example, having one domain level structure with tens of millions of names).[17] Each domain name query would have had to run through all the domain names each time instead of a selected number of files according to the top-level domain and second level domains in the current hierarchical structure.

The name resolution side of the DNS is based on an interdependent, distributed and hierarchical database.[18] At the top of the hierarchy lies a single data file that contains the list of servers that have the master lists of domain name registrations in each top-level domain. This is the 'root zone' or 'root'.[19] Only the TLDs listed in the root zone file can be queried through the DNS system.[20] The root zone file is maintained in parallel on thirteen different computers.

---

[12] .aero; .coop; .edu; .gov; .int; .mil; .museum are restricted.

[13] According to CENTR 2003.

[14] ISO 3166 list.

[15] The Internet Assigned Numbers Authority (IANA) administers this domain in co-operation with the Internet technical community under the guidance of the Internet Architecture Board (<http://www.iana.org/arpa-dom/> accessed 2 December 2004).

[16] Manheim and Solum 2003: 365.

[17] Cf., US National Research Council of the National Academies 2005: 2-6.

[18] Froomkin 2000a: 42.

[19] Sometimes also known as the 'legacy root'.

[20] Froomkin (2000a: 42) comments 'Although there is no technical obstacle to anyone maintaining a TLD that is not listed in the legacy root, these "alternate" TLDs can only be resolved by users whose

The current root name server operators were not selected through a formal evaluation and qualification process. Rather, the group is the cumulative result of a sequence of separate decisions taken over the years since the establishment of the DNS. It is a loosely organised collection of autonomous institutions. Ten of them are based in the United States. Of those, three are associated with the US government,[21] two are universities,[22] two are corporations[23] and two are not-for-profits.[24] Three are based outside the United States: in Sweden, the United Kingdom and Japan.[25]

These thirteen machines, currently identified by letters from A-M, contain a copy of the list of the TLD servers that have full databases of the registered names and their associated IP numbers within their respective top-level domains. Until recently, the 'A' root server was the first among equals with the other root servers taking their cue from it. The role of the primary server from which the other 12 servers took their cue was transferred to a 'hidden primary' server. The hidden primary server is a server that is used to update the 13 root servers.[26] Root servers are ultimately authoritative in that they hold the definitive information about which other domain name servers are authoritative for which domains.[27]

Each top-level domain registry has an authoritative list of second-level domains registered for that top-level domain. The authoritative list is held on a 'zone server'. There are multiple 'zone servers' distributed across many computers hosting lists of domain names according to the top-level domain.[28]

Conceptually, the root servers are at the top of the hierarchy. The zone servers form the next level of the hierarchy. A third level of the hierarchy are domain servers. Queries concerning the location of a domain are resolved by sending queries to hierarchically linked databases. The query starts at the bottom, at the domain server selected by the user's ISP. If the data is not in the domain server, the query works its way up the hierarchy until it can be resolved.[29]

---

machines, or Internet service providers (ISPs) as the case may be, use a domain name server that includes this additional data or knows where to find it. A combination of consensus, lack of knowledge and inertia among the people running the machines that administer domain name lookups means that domain names in TLDs outside the legacy root cannot be accessed by the large majority of people who use the Internet, unless they do some tinkering with obscure parts of their browser settings.'

[21] At the National Aeronautics and Space Administration, Department of Defence and the US Army.

[22] University of Maryland and University of Southern California.

[23] Verisign and Cogent Communications.

[24] ISC, Inc. and ICANN.

[25] Cf., US National Research Council of the National Academies 2005: 3-21.

[26] Id. 2005: 3-16.

[27] Smith 2002: 79.

[28] Id. 2002: 78.

[29] Froomkin 2000a: 43.

5.2   THE PREVALENCE OF SELF-REGULATION IN THE ADMINISTRATION OF
       THE DNS

5.2.1   The different self-regulation groups

Self-regulation is the predominant form of regulation of the DNS. The DNS is
regulated by multiple rules developed by groups. Three sets of groups are principally involved in the regulation of the DNS: ICANN, top-level domain registries or
operators, and registrars. There is a hierarchical link between the groups. This can
be visualised as pyramidal.[30] (See figure 1) Each group level carries along the rules
of the higher level. The linking and centralisation are essential. Without the linking
and centralisation, the key feature of the domain name space – the uniqueness of
every address – cannot be maintained.

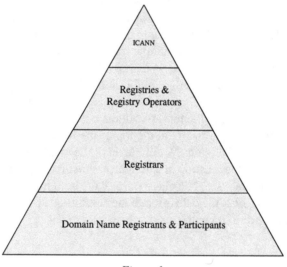

Figure 1

At the top of the hierarchy is the central body, **ICANN**, responsible for the management of the DNS (and arguably lending authority to the other groups down the
hierarchy). ICANN is a non-profit, private corporation registered in California since
1998. It has a complex organisational structure reflecting the multiple interest groups
affected by domain name policy.

ICANN has a President and Board of Directors and three Supporting
Organisations (ultimately responsible to the President and Board of Directors). Each
of the supporting organisations corresponds to one of ICANN's primary areas of
responsibility identified in the Memorandum of Understanding signed with the US

---

[30] Frankel (2004: 449) uses the different layers of the pyramid to show the different technical
levels of the DNS. Figure 1 in this study uses the shape and levels to describe the corresponding
regulatory arrangement at each level.

government.[31] The Address Supporting Organization within ICANN is responsible for developing recommendations for the IP addressing system. The Country Code Names Supporting Organization is responsible for developing recommendations for the ccTLDs. The Generic Names Supporting Organization is responsible for developing recommendations for the gTLDs.[32]

In addition, ICANN has four advisory committees: the At-Large Advisory Committee for the Internet community at-large; the DNS Root Server System Advisory Committee for root server operators; the Governmental Advisory Committee (GAC) for governments; and the Security and Stability Advisory Committee for security. There is also the Technical Liaison Group for standards-setting organisations and an Internet Engineering Task Force that provides technical advice to ICANN. The supporting organisations and advisory committees together represent a broad cross section of the Internet's commercial, technical, academic, non-commercial and user communities. They advise the board on matters lying within their areas of expertise and interest.[33] Participation in ICANN is open to any interested user, business or organisation. It holds several meetings a year at locations around the world.

ICANN was set-up in response to increasing political pressure on the United States from other states to relinquish some of the responsibility for the DNS. The US government transferred the management of the administration of the DNS to ICANN[34] through a Memorandum of Understanding (MoU) between the US Department of Commerce (DOC) and ICANN. The link between the US government and the DNS goes back a long way. It was US Department of Defence grants that originally funded the current structure of the DNS developed by Jon Postel and Paul Mockapetris in the early 1980s.[35] Initially, Postel implemented the rules on the allocation of top-level domains, registries and registrars. Then between the late 1980s and 1998, responsibility for domain name registration under particular top-level domains was transferred from Postel to the Internet Assigned Numbers Authority (IANA) – a specifically created project group of the University of California's Information Science Institute led by Postel. The US Department of Defence[36] continued to fund the work of IANA. Until 1995, the US government had played a low-key position in the regulation of the allocation of the top-level domains and the

---

[31] The Memorandum of Understanding entrusted ICANN with: a. the establishment of policy and direction of the allocation of IP number blocks; b. the oversight of the operation of the authoritative root server system; c. the oversight of the policy for determining the circumstances under which new top level domains would be added to the root system; d. the co-ordination of the assignment of other Internet technical parameters as needed to maintain universal connectivity on the Internet; and e. other activities necessary to co-ordinate the specified DNS management functions. (see Manheim and Solum 2003: 375).

[32] See ICANN, Bylaws for Internet Corporation for Assigned Names and Numbers accessed at <http://www.icann.org/general/bylaws.htm> on 6 December 2004.

[33] Cf., US National Research Council of the National Academies 2005: 3-20.

[34] The legal nature of this 'transfer' of management to ICANN has been criticised in literature. See for example Froomkin (2000a: 20).

[35] Yu 2003: 2.

[36] Together with the National Science Foundation.

general monitoring and development of the DNS. Its role remained predominantly that of funding and of some policy decisions via IANA and the National Science Foundation.[37] In 1998, the US government transferred the management of the administration of the DNS to ICANN.[38]

This transfer has not succeeded in toning down the opposition especially since there are still existing links between the DOC and ICANN. In particular, the US government acts as an overseer. The main involvement of the United States is through the relationship formulated in the MoU with ICANN. In terms of the MoU, the DOC, ultimately, has the right not to renew the terms of the MoU whenever it comes up for review. The current arrangement terminates at the end of September 2006. The (implicit/contractual) threat that the DoC may terminate the MoU with ICANN unless it carries out steps considered necessary by the US government, acts as a check on ICANN's activities.[39]

In 1998, the US government stated that if ICANN fulfils a number of conditions the US government would withdraw from the regulation of the DNS completely. However, not only has this not happened yet, but in June 2005,[40] the US government issued a statement declaring that it had no intention of withdrawing from the regulation of the DNS. The June 2005 statement, seeing that it was issued before the report of the Working Group on Internet Governance (WGIG) and the then upcoming World Summit on Information Society (WSIS) in November 2005, may have actually been simply a political ploy by the United States to defend its position of control in debates on the future regulation of the DNS. Understandably, the United States is reluctant to withdraw from its 'comfortable' position in relation to regulation the DNS unless the alternative offered proposes a better option from a US perspective. Indeed, the recent announcement[41] of the US government that it has

---

[37] Froomkin 2000a: 57.

[38] The legal nature of this 'transfer' of management to ICANN (made by means of a Memorandum of Understanding and not a formal delegation by law) has been criticised in literature. Froomkin (2000a: 20), for example, argues that the handling of the US government is in violation of the US Administrative Procedures Act and the Constitution. 'ICANN is formally a private nonprofit California corporation created, in response to a summoning by U.S. government officials, to take regulatory action that the DoC was unable or unwilling to take directly. If the U.S. government is laundering its policymaking through ICANN, it violates the APA; if ICANN is, in fact, independent, then the federal government's decision to have ICANN manage a resource of such importance and to allow – indeed, require – it to enforce regulatory conditions on users of that resource violates the nondelegation doctrine of the U.S. Constitution. In either case, the relationship violates basic norms of due process and public policy designed to ensure that federal power is exercised responsibly.'

[39] The Working Group on Internet Governance 2005a: 20.

[40] The US Department of Commerce National Telecommunications and Information Administration (NTIA) released a document on 30 June 2005 entitled 'US Statement of Principles on the Internet's Domain Name and Addressing System' accessed at <http://www.ntia.doc.gov/ntiahome/domainname/USDNSprinciples> on 5 August 2005.

[41] US Department of Commerce National Telecommunications and Information Administration (NTIA) (2005) (US Statement of Principles on the Internet's Domain Name and Addressing System (published 30 June 2005)). This document gathered considerable reaction see for example Internet Governance Project 2005a; 2005b and Froomkin 2005.

no intention to withdraw from its position of control over the DNS confirms that politically none of the alternatives proposed have (as yet) any benefits from a US perspective.[42]

The links with the US DOC have raised doubts (in the literature) concerning the independence of ICANN and hence whether its rules can be considered 'private'.[43] Indeed one could question whether an examination of ICANN fits in the study of examples of self-regulation in the Internet. In including ICANN in this examination I am guided by Moore's definition of a 'semi-autonomous social field'[44] (which I take as the basis for the working definition of 'the self' in this study). In this definition, influence of the state is not inconsistent with the concept of self-regulation. The group is 'semi-autonomous' regulating its affairs to the extent 'allowed' by regulation of other sources or, as in the ICANN situation, by a state.

The 'membership' of the ICANN (as a social field) too has been criticised. Some authors[45] argue that ICANN – as an administrator of a 'global' resource – does not adequately represent all the groups involved on the Internet. As set-up, they argue, ICANN allows greater power to some strong economic players than to private users or states. Other authors[46] disagree, claiming that ICANN is an important model of an institutional framework that avoids the dominance of one group over another in self-regulation by ensuring adequate representation.

At the next level in the hierarchy are **domain name registries** are entrusted (by ICANN or its predecessors) with the registration of generic and country code top-level domain names and the operation of the related zone name registries.[47] The organisation running the registry may at times be called a 'designated manager' (particularly in the case of ccTLDs). A registry need not operate the required name server and domain name registration functions itself. It can contract the services/functions out to specialist organisations.[48] The organisation contracted to run the name server is often called a registry operator. Registration of certain gTLDs is restricted to certain groups or categories. In this case, the rules for registration of domain names are organised by a 'sponsor'. The term 'registry' is being used in this chapter as a collective term to refer also to operators, sponsors and designated managers.

Registries are predominantly private organisations. Ten private registries administer gTLDs.[49] One operator, VeriSign Inc., operates two registries (the '.com'

---

[42] US Department of State Bureau of Economic and Business Affairs (2005) Comments of the United States of America on Internet Governance (15 August 2005); Cukier 2005.

[43] Manheim and Solum (2003: 334) argue further that 'the precise nature of the relationship between the DOC [Department of Commerce] and ICANN is murky at the level of legal theory.'

[44] Moore 1973. This is discussed in Chapter 3 of this study.

[45] Cf., Clerc 2001.

[46] Brousseau 2001.

[47] Cf., US National Research Council of the National Academies 2005: 3-35.

[48] Id. 2005: 3-33.

[49] Out of the remaining other three gTLDs, one is run directly by ICANN and the two others are run by the US government.

and the '.net' registries). Most of the 253 ccTLDS are privately run. Some ccTLDs are administered by non-profit organisations[50] usually formed by ISPs and Internet-related organisations. Other ccTLDs are administered by private (for-profit) companies (such as the '.us' (United States) and '.jp' (Japan) ccTLDs), academic institutions (such as the '.mt' (Malta) and '.mx' (Mexico) ccTLDs) or government agencies (such as the '.ie' (Ireland) and '.fi' (Finland) ccTLDs).[51] State run registries are a small minority (around 10 ccTLDs).[52]

With the growth and commercial importance of domain names, some of the not-for-profit ccTLD registries have delegated the registration of domain names to commercial companies.[53] Some commentators[54] have noted two new trends in the operational arrangements of ccTLDs in some countries. The first is that there seems to be a tendency to replace informal arrangements (such as academic institutions) with more formal arrangements that provide clearer legal rules and engage a wider national community in the setting of rules. The second is to contract the actual operations to commercial organisations more motivated to undertake the associated responsibilities than are academic institutions.

In turn, registries delegate the domain name registration functions to **registrars** – the next level in the hierarchy. Registrars register second level domain names within a particular top-level domain. Registrars are private organisations that offer domain name registration to users. In practice, the registrars implement the rules for domain name registration created by ICANN and by the respective registry.

All registrars are private companies/organisations. The relationship between the registrars and the registrants is a contractual one. The registrar offers registration services to the public. The public can register domain names based on the terms and conditions offered by the registrars.

There are many registrars for gTLD domains. More than 150 registrars alone are involved in the registration of the three most popular gTLDs – .com, .org. and .net.[55] Only ICANN-accredited registrars can offer registration services under gTLDs. For a private organisation to be able to act as a gTLD registrar it must have (a) agreed to the conditions imposed by ICANN under an ICANN Registrar Accreditation Agreement and (b) agree to the conditions imposed by the particular gTLD registry. The ICANN Registrar Accreditation Agreement imposes certain requirements on registrars. Amongst these requirements, a registrar is expected to

---

[50] Sometimes called Network Information Centres (NIC).

[51] OECD Working Party on Telecommunication and Information Services Policies (2003) Comparing Domain Name Administration in OECD Countries Report dated 8 April 2003 Doc. Ref. DSTI/ICCP/TISP(2002)11/FINAL at p. 7.

[52] See Yu 2003: 6.

[53] For example, the Austrian name registration is carried out by Nic.AT is a limited-liability company that since 2000 has been wholly owned by a charitable foundation, the Internet Private Foundation Austria. The University of Vienna computer centre runs the .at name server. See US National Research Council of the National Academies 2005: 3-35.

[54] Cf., US National Research Council of the National Academies 2005: 3-35.

[55] Id. 2005: 3-41.

(a) submit specified information for each registrant to the registry; (b) enable public Internet access to a file of information about registrants – the Whois file – both in query and bulk access form; (c) maintain a file of all registrant information submitted to the registry; (d) regularly submit a copy of the file to ICANN or to an escrow agent; (e) comply with consensus policies established by ICANN; and (f) comply with ICANN's Uniform Domain Name Dispute Resolution Policy.[56]

Registrars under ccTLDs do not need to be ICANN accredited registrars. Any registrar – in practice mainly Internet Service Providers – entering into a contract with the ccTLD registry can act as registrar.[57]

5.2.2 Reasons for self-regulation

Why do these three sets of groups self-regulate? The simple need *to enforce the uniqueness* of domain names, that is, the need to prevent two or more people from using the exact same domain name (at the various levels of the domain name space) creates a need for regulation and for some sort of body to monitor and allocate naming.[58]

The importance of the role of the DNS in *enabling access* to the Internet triggers a need for rules on the distribution of domain names. In essence, these rules determine who can have access, can be accessed and can be located on-line.

The use of domain names as *'commercial' identifiers* launched a conflict with prevalent trademark and service mark practice and law in the off-line world. There are at least three types of clashes: (i) conflicts on who can use the same string of characters. Conflicts may also involve multiple owners of a trademark in the same string of characters. For example, the same string 'queens inn' may be owned by different trademark owners in separate countries or in different lines of business, and at the same time be a registered domain name of another person; (ii) conflicts where a domain name is similar to a trade-mark and is meant to pass for the other; (iii) situations of cyber squatting – cybersquatters register domain names before the trade mark owners have done so, with a view to exacting a price for transferring the domain name to the trade mark owner.[59]

Conflicts between trademark holders and domain name registrants give rise to a need for regulation to prevent and regulate disputes. Such conflicts triggered the need for, *inter alia*, three types of regulation: (i) rules on who and what can be

---

[56] A copy of accreditation agreement accessed at <http://www.icann.org/registrars/ra-agreement-17may01.htm> on 9 January 2005. See also US National Research Council of the National Academies 2005: 3-40.

[57] For example, Nominet UK policy accessed at <http://www.nic.uk/RegisteringYourDomainName/ChoosingARegistrationAgentisp/> on 4 January 2005.

[58] Froomkin 2000a: 20. This is similar to the situation of unique identification numbers for persons, such as the Social Security Number in the US, the Sofi Nummer in the Netherlands and Identity Card Number in Malta. In each case, a central body regulates the issuing of numbers.

[59] Smith 2002:78.

registered as a domain name; (ii) rules for the resolution of conflicts that arise between trademark owners and domain name registrants; and (iii) rules preventing or
limiting cybersquatting when new top domain levels are launched.

The need to have *accurate information* at each level of the hierarchical structure
necessitates rules and bodies to maintain the name files and to regulate the accessibility of the content. Interruption in the domain name querying system in essence
means that users cannot locate the desired locations on the network. One central
issue in the regulation of the DNS relates to the regulation of the root zone file.
Verisign, Inc., on contract from the US government, manages the root zone file (on
the hidden primary server). The contract includes explicitly that the US Department
of Commerce has the power to decide what gets listed in the root file. The authority
to make changes lies with the US Department of Commerce. This means, in effect,
that the United States has ultimate authority over the DNS.

Different organisations carry out the responsibilities maintaining the root servers, zone servers and name servers. The multiplicity of groups arguably gives rise
to a need for oversight. Currently, the handling of the root name servers lacks any
formal oversight. One of the responsibilities that ICANN assumed under its agreement with the DOC is to co-ordinate the stable operation of the root server system.
To do so, it established the DNS Root Server System Advisory Committee.[60] The
Committee has drafted a Memorandum of Understanding between ICANN and the
server operators. This Memorandum of Understanding spells out the root name
server performance requirements.[61] However, as of June 2006, no Memorandum of
Understanding had yet been signed between ICANN and any of the server operators.

It has been argued that

> 'not everyone would agree that formal oversight is desirable. Should one or more of
> the current root name server operators withdraw from the responsibility, or fail to ex-
> ercise it reliably, effectively, or securely, there would be no responsible organization
> or formal process for removing the failed operator or for recruiting and selecting a re-
> placement. In their absence, the informal, collegial processes that led to the current
> group of operators would likely continue to be used.'[62]

5.2.3   What is regulated by self-regulation?

The self-regulating groups regulate four sets of activities related with the DNS.
They regulate (a) the way top-level domains are set-up and increased; (b) the allocation of the top-level domains to registries and operators; (c) the registration of
domain names; and (d) the resolution of domain name conflicts.

---

[60] See ICANN Bylaws Art. XI, Section 3 accessed at <http://www.icann.org/general/bylaws.htm#XI-
2.3> on 5 August 2005.

[61] See <http://www.icann.org/committees/dns-root/model-root-server-mou-21jan02.htm> accessed
5 August 2005.

[62] Cf., US National Research Council of the National Academies 2005: 3-23.

The setting-up and increase of top-level domains

While ultimate authority to add a new top-level domain to the root zone file lies, as noted, with the US Department of Commerce, the rules and procedures recommending that a top-level domain be added and who shall operate the new domain are created by ICANN. The rules and decision process are different for gTLDs and ccTLDs.

The original eight gTLDs, still in use today, '.com', '.edu', '.gov', '.int', '.mil', '.net', '.org' and 'arpa' were created before the setting-up of ICANN in 1998. In 2000, ICANN introduced seven gTLDs – '.aero', '.biz', '.coop', '.info', '.museum', '.name' and '.pro'. It is currently in the process of evaluating the addition of a series of new gTLDS, such as '.jobs', '.travel',[63] '.cat', '.post', '.mobi', '.asia', '.mail', '.tel' and '.xxx'.

In 2000, in considering what new gTLDs could be added to the DNS root, ICANN established a broad list of selection criteria. These criteria include considerations concerning the utility of the new gTLD to the functioning of the DNS, and the extent to which the new gTLD would meet previously unmet needs of communities, or types of needs.[64]

In addition, in the introduction of the new gTLDs in 2000, ICANN distinguished between sponsored and unsponsored TLDs. The gTLDs that are sponsored have an organisation representing the community of potential registrants. The charters of the sponsored TLDs specify that registrants are restricted to those satisfying criteria appropriate to the community. For example, the '.aero' is restricted to people, entities and government agencies that provide for and support the efficient, safe, and secure transport of people and cargo by air.[65]

Following an evaluation process to assess the need for new sponsored gTLDs, consumer protection issues with the introduction of new gTLDs and the impact on the technical stability of the DNS with the introduction of new gTLDs,[66] a call for

---

[63] .jobs and .travel were approved at 22nd ICANN International Conference held in Argentina in April 2005 accessed at <http://www.icann.org/announcements/announcement-08apr05.htm> on 6 August 2005.

[64] There were nine criteria: 'The need to maintaon the Internet's stability. The extent to which selection of the proposal would lead to an effective proof of concept concerning the introduction of top-level domains in the future. The enhancement of competition for registration services. The enhancement of the utility of the DNS. The extent to which the proposal would meet previously unmet types of needs. The extent to which the proposal would enhance the diversity of the DNS and of registration services generally. The evaluation of delegation of policy-formulation functions for special-purpose TLDs to appropriate organizations. Appropriate protections of rights of others in connection with the operation of the TLD. The completeness of the proposals submitted and the extent to which they demonstrate realistic business, financial, technical and operational plans and sound analysis of market needs.' Cf., US National Research Council of the National Academies 2005: 3-36.

[65] Cf., US National Research Council of the National Academies 2005: 3-25.

[66] On 31 August 2004 ICANN published a report prepared for it by Summit Strategies International, entitled 'Evaluation of the New gTLDs: Policy and Legal Issues'. (See Summit Strategies International 2004). Studies for the evaluation process were carried out by independent outside organisations.

new sponsored TLDs was launched in December 2003.[67] The selection criteria were published in the 'Request for Proposals' document.[68] These criteria include that the new gTLDs satisfy specified technical requirements, that the new TLD address the needs and interests of a clearly defined community, and that the new TLD offer a new value to the domain name space. The ICANN Board established these criteria. Ten proposals for new sponsored TLDs were received in March 2004.[69]

The rules for the introduction of new ccTLDs are simple. ccTLDs are available to countries and territories represented by country codes in the standard list established by the International Standards Organisation (ISO) – ISO 3166-1. This list has been used as the authoritative source for country codes since the late 1980s.[70] When new entities are assigned a two-letter identifier by the ISO, that entity is automatically entitled to have a ccTLD.

Since ICANN became responsible for the DNS, few new ccTLD allocations were made ('.ps' – Occupied Palestinian Territory; '.ng' – Nigeria; '.af' – Afganistan; '.bi' – Burundi; '.mw' – Malawi; and '.la' – Lao People's Democratic Republic). The '.zr'-Zaire ccTLD was deleted in light of the country's change of name.

In 2000, the European Union requested the inclusion of the '.eu' domain name in the DNS root file. The 'eu' code was not in the ISO 3166-1 but the ISO had agreed to include the 'eu' in an 'exceptional reserved status' enabling its use for specific ISO-approved purposes. The ICANN Board approved a resolution to accept all codes on the 'reserved status' list and hence approved the inclusion of the 'eu' in the DNS root.[71]

In 2002, the Country-Code Names Supporting Organization (ccNSO) was set-up as a 'policy-development body' within ICANN.[72] The ccNSO is made up of ccTLD managers. The terms of reference of ccNSO include the developing of global policies relating to name-related activities of country-code top-level domains.[73]

The allocation of top-level domains to registry operators

- gTLDs

The rules on the allocation of gTLD operators are set by ICANN. Registry operators are assigned two important responsibilities. The first is to establish and operate the name servers for a particular TLD following specific technical requirements.

---

[67] Accessed at <http://icann.org/announcements/announcement-15dec03.htm> on 6 August 2005.

[68] Can be in part A of the Request for Proposals Document accessed at <http://icann.org/tlds/new-stld-rfp/new-stld-application-parta-15dec03.htm> accessed on 6 August 2005.

[69] Accessed at <http://icann.org/announcements/announcement-19mar04.htm> on 6 August 2005.

[70] It was agreed in RFC1591 in the early 1990s. See Postel 1994.

[71] The '.eu' was approved in March 2005. See <http://www.icann.org/announcements/announcement-23mar05.htm> accessed on 6 August 2005.

[72] See ICANN bye-laws at <http://www.icann.org/general/bylaws.htm> (accessed on 29 November 2004) Art. IX: Country-Code Names Supporting Organization.

[73] Id. Art. IX Section 1.

The second is to establish and operate the domain name registration process in a way that meets the needs of the international or local community.

The first wave of gTLDs, in particular '.com', '.net' and '.org',[74] were allocated by the National Science Foundation[75] (and IANA) before the setting-up of ICANN. In 1998 when ICANN came into the picture, VeriSign Inc was the operator for '.com' and '.org'.[76] Network Solutions Inc. managed the '.net' TLD.[77] ICANN has in the meantime re-negotiated new contracts with VeriSign Inc for '.com' and '.net' and with the Public Internet Registry for '.org'.

The sponsors and operators of the seven gTLDs introduced by ICANN in November 2000 were chosen after a long process of discussion, solicitation of applications and staff evaluation. At the end of the process, ICANN entered into written contracts with the seven operators or sponsors[78] of the new gTLDs.[79] The process followed in 2000 was criticised as lacking transparency and fairness. In the current process of allocating new sponsored TLDs, ICANN has made a clear effort to improve the transparency and fairness of the process. The selection of the potential registry operators is based on the evaluation criteria established and published in the 'Request for Proposals' for new sponsored TLDs issued in December 2003.[80] Those proposals that met all the criteria were followed by contract negotiations. Those proposals that did not meet all the criteria were sent back to the sponsors with suggestions for improvement and were resubmitted.

An alternative method/rule for the allocation of operators is mentioned in the literature – the use of auctions. Prospective operators bid for the managed of particular TLDs. In a recent report, the OECD[81] favoured the use of an open-auction system for the introduction and allocation of new gTLDs and their operators.

The rules binding gTLD operators are found in written contracts between ICANN and a gTLD sponsor/registry operator. On delegation from ICANN, the registry will act as the sole operator for the applicable gTLD.[82] The rules outline the general

---

[74] The first wave of gTLDs included also four other gTLDs: (i) .edu – registration to this domain is restricted to US degree-granting educational institutions. It is now operated by Educause. (ii) .gov – a US government only domain operated by the US General Services Administration; (iii) .mil – a US armed forces only domain operated by the Department of Defense Information Center; (iv) .int – a domain restricted to organizations established by International treaties. This is currently run by ICANN.

[75] Under the auspices of the US Department of Commerce.

[76] Since January 2003, the Public Internet Registry manages the 'org'.

[77] VeriSign Inc. took over Network Solutions Inc. in 2000.

[78] Operators or sponsors (the latter are the operators when the domain is restricted to a certain class of activity only) carry out the same roles as registries in the ccTLD arrangement.

[79] Hence, ICANN has a written contract with the Société Internationale de Télécommunications Aéronautique S.C. for the .aero domain; with NeuLevel Inc. for the .biz domain; with Dot Cooperation LLC for the .coop; with Afilias Inc. for the .info domain; with Museum Domain Management Association (MuseDoma) for the .museum domain; with Global Name Registry, Ltd. for the .name domain; and with the Registry Pro for the .pro domain.

[80] Accessed at <http://icann.org/announcements/announcement-15dec03.htm> on 6 August 2005.

[81] Paltridge and Matsui 2004.

[82] Id. 2004: 11.

obligations of the registry. These include, *inter alia*, the obligation[83] to carry out the provision of registry services; to follow the minimum functional and performance specifications for registry services dictated by ICANN; to use ICANN-accredited registrars and not offer direct registration services to users itself; to ensure that registered name holders enter into agreement with registrars; and that the contracts contain the minimum conditions dictated by ICANN.[84] The contract also contains a commitment to comply with new or revised ICANN specifications and policies (such as the Uniform Domain Name Dispute Resolution Policy).

ICANN binds itself to include the gTLD in the authoritative root-server system; to permit the registry to be recognised in the root-zone contact database; and to maintain the Authoritative Root server system in an accurate and authoritative manner.[85]

The contracts usually include provision for administrative issues, such as dispute resolution processes and the fees to be paid to ICANN and charged to registrars.

- ccTLDs

The rules for the allocation of ccTLDs are different from those for gTLDs. In a contract with the US government, Postel and later IANA was entrusted with the allocation of the ccTLDs. From 1985 (when the first allocations where done: first '.us' (United States) then '.uk' (United Kingdom) and '.il' (Israel)) to 1993, Postel allocated the ccTLDs on a 'first come, first served' basis to any person or organisation willing and wanting to run the ccTLD of a particular country. Especially in the early years, since many countries were not connected to the Internet backbone, the number of allocations of ccTLDs was small. Most allocations of ccTLDs were made to universities, educational and research networking organisations – organisations that had the necessary technical expertise, technical capabilities and interest on the Internet.

By 1993, more and more countries, seeing the potential of the Internet, joined the network. This increased the demand for ccTLDs. In 1994, Postel/IANA issued RFC 1591[86] describing the delegation and administration policy that would thereafter be followed in the allocation of ccTLDs. Each ccTLD should be run by a 'designated manager' who acts as a 'trustee of the top-level domain for both the nation, in the case of a country code, and the global Internet community.'[87]

---

[83] Taken from agreement and annexes between ICANN and SITA for .aero registry accessed at <http://www.icann.org/tlds/agreements/sponsored/sponsorship-agmt-16oct01.htm> on 9 January 2005.

[84] These conditions are found in attachment 10 to the contract. Accessed at <http://www.icann.org/tlds/agreements/sponsored/sponsorship-agmt-att10-20aug01.htm> on 9 January 2005.

[85] Taken from agreement and annexes between ICANN and SITA for .aero registry accessed at <http://www.icann.org/tlds/agreements/sponsored/sponsorship-agmt-16oct01.htm> on 9 January 2005.

[86] Postel 1994.

[87] See at <http://www.isi.edu/in-notes/rfc1591.txt> p. 3.

The potential of a country ccTLD attracted the interest of national governments and their concern, mostly undeclared, that the United States was controlling (in some manner) the potential asset of the individual country. In the 1994 document, the managers had a wide discretion in carrying out their management functions. They could further delegate the management of portions of the name tree especially since the setting of rules on the hierarchical structure to be followed in domain names registered under the ccTLD was left in the hands of the designated manager.[88]

In view of this growing concern, the relationship between the IANA and the national governments was discussed in a ccTLD News Memo issued by IANA in 1997.[89] In essence, IANA declared that 'The IANA takes the desires of the government of the country very seriously, and will take them as a major consideration in any transition discussion.'[90] The Memo did not include, however, any recommendations on the relationship between 'designated managers' and particular national governments.

In 1998, when the US government transferred the management of the DNS to ICANN, most ccTLDs had been allocated (on the basis largely of oral contracts) to designated managers predominantly in the private (for profit or not-for-profit) sector.

In 1999, ICANN reiterated the position declared by IANA, that in the delegation of ccTLDs 'The desires of the government of a country with regard to delegation of a ccTLD are taken very seriously. The IANA will make them a major consideration in any TLD delegation/transfer discussions.'[91] The ICANN ICP-1[92] document confirmed the requirements expected of designated managers outline in RFC 1591 and put an emphasis on the designated manager's duty 'to serve the community'.[93]

---

[88] The document also listed a number of requirements that the designated managers as 'trustees for the delegated domain' (Art. 3 Postel 1994: 3) needed to fulfil: (a) the designated manager needs to carry out the job in an equitable, just, honest and competent manner; (Art. 3 Postel 1994: 3) (b) the designated manager must have connectivity to the Internet; (c) must provide an administrative and a technical contact for each domain; (Art. 3 Postel 1994: 3) (d) must assign domain names delegating subdomains and operate nameservers and be done with technical competence; (e) respond to requests in a timely manner; (Art. 5 Postel 1994: 4) and (f) operate the database with accuracy, robustness, and resilience.

[89] See <http://www.iana.org/cctld/cctld-news1.htm> accessed 6 December 2004.

[90] Ibid.

[91] In document ICP-1 (ICANN Corporate Policy) – 'Internet Domain Name System Structure and Delegation (ccTLD Administration and Delegation)' accessed at <http://www.icann.org/icp/icp-1.htm> on 6 December 2004.

[92] Accessed at <http://www.icann.org/icp/icp-1.htm> on 6 December 2004.

[93] Abstract of ICP-1 document accessed at <http://www.icann.org/icp/icp-1.htm> on 6 December 2004. The ICP-1 document also added some other requirements, for example, (a) that the policies and procedures followed by the designated manager be documented and publicly available; (sub-paragraph (c)) (b) that the allocation of domain names is carried out without preferential treatment and with no stipulation that a particular application, protocol or product be used; (sub-paragraph (c)) and (c) that the designated manager operates the technical side of the domain well, that is, for example by keeping the zone database accurate at all times and technically operational. (sub-paragraph (d)).

In 2000, ICANN's Governmental Advisory Committee (GAC) issued a set of 'Principles for Delegation and Administration of ccTLDs'.[94] While initially the GAC was solely an advisory body it now has more direct involvement in ccTLD matters. The 'development' of relations between the national governments and the designated managers was one of the objectives of the GAC document. The document argued that since the national government 'ultimately represents the interests of the people of the country or territory for which the ccTLD has been delegated', the national government 'is to ensure that the ccTLD is being administered in the public interest'.[95] One can argue that through this declaration of principles, the GAC is trying to claim authority over ccTLDs and hence over the private groups administering the ccTLDs. Strictly speaking, a 'designated manager' has no direct responsibility or attachment to the state but rather to IANA/ICANN from whom the powers of administration have been received. The GAC declaration of principles tries to vary this situation. Using the 'public interest' argument, states are trying to claim 'ownership' or 'possession' of the ccTLD and hence 'regulatory power' over the designated manager.

The GAC set of principles also gives a list of requirements that a designated manager/country registry (in the Principles called 'delegee') should follow. The requirements reiterate the 'public interest' mantra of the document. The designated manager 'has a duty to serve the residents of the relevant country or territory'[96] and perhaps more importantly, 'recognised that ultimate public policy authority over the relevant ccTLD rests with the relevant government or public authority.'[97] National governments seem to want to formalise a relationship with the privately run country-code domains.

Since the taking over of the DNS by ICANN, few new ccTLD allocations were made. A number ccTLDs were re-delegated[98] (such as .au; .ke; .jp; .tw;). The GAC set of principles have been used extensively[99] in the re-delegation efforts. All re-delegations (except Canada) are now covered by a written contractual agreement. A Memorandum of Understanding between ICANN and the ccTLD registry covers the new delegations. It covers cover the same conditions as the contract between gTLD registries and ICANN.

Despite ICANN's efforts to get ccTLDs to enter into agreements with it, by December 2004 it had completed only 12 such agreements. A number of ccTLDs object to accepting ICANN's formal authority over their operation.[100]

---

[94] Accessed at <http://194.78.218.67/web/docs/cctld/cctld.pdf> accessed on 3 December 2004.

[95] See point 5.1 in GAC Principles for the delegation and administration of country code top level domains accessed at <http://194.78.218.67/web/docs/cctld/cctld.pdf> accessed on 3 December 2004.

[96] Id. point 4.1.

[97] Id. point 4.4.

[98] At the end of term of delegation, a new term can be negotiated with the 'old' designated manager or with a new manager. The GAC set of principles was used extensively in the negotiation of the new contracts.

[99] According to Yu (2003:5).

[100] Cf., US National Research Council of the National Academies 2005: 3-34.

- The registration of domain names

The groups in each hierarchical level contribute to the rules that need to be followed in the registration of domain names. ICANN sets the minimum conditions that need to be followed by registry operators and designated managers (and by registrars) when registering domain names under generic top-level domains. Primarily these require that the allocation of domain names be carried out without preferential treatment and with no stipulation that a particular application, protocol or product be used.[101] The rules also include that the registry operators keep (i) accurate contact details of registered name holders; (ii) names of the primary and secondary nameserver(s) for the registered name; (iii) detailed technical and administrative contacts.[102]

The practical (day-to-day) rules on the registration of the domain names come from registry operators and designate managers. gTLD registries can only delegate name registration services to ICANN-accredited registrars (that is, only registrars who have a contractual agreement with ICANN[103] can act as gTLD registrars). The relationship between the registry and the registrars is a contractual one.

The rules include that the Registrar (registering a domain name for a user) must enter into a written registration agreement with the domain name registrants. They also include the terms that need to be included in registration agreement, e.g., that domain name will be used for *bona fide* business or commercial purposes; bound by the domain name dispute resolution policy and the restrictions dispute resolution policy.[104]

Some registries include a rule that the registry reserves the right to deny, cancel or transfer any registration of a domain name that it deems necessary.[105] Or rules on the Registry's right to freeze a domain name during the resolution of a dispute and rules on fees payable by the registrar to the registry.

Often designate managers of ccTLDs provide more detailed rules. Each ccTLD is operated separately under the rules of each ccTLD registry. These rules and policies may vary significantly between ccTLDs. Each registry makes rules that need

---

[101] See sub-paragraph (c) in The Management of Delegated Domains paragraph in ICP-1 document accessed at <http://www.icann.org/icp/icp-1.htm> on 6 December 2004.

[102] These minimum conditions are found in attachment 10 to the contract between ICANN and registry operators. Accessed at <http://www.icann.org/tlds/agreements/sponsored/sponsorship-agmt-att10-20aug01.htm> on 9 January 2005 and Postel 1994: 3.

[103] A copy of accreditation agreement accessed at <http://www.icann.org/registrars/ra-agreement-17may01.htm> on 9 January 2005. The ICANN Registrar Accreditation Agreement imposes certain requirements on registrars.

[104] As an example I have looked at NeuLevel Inc. – the .biz registry agreement with registrars accessed at <http://www.neulevel.biz/faqs/registrar/other_faqs.html> on 9 January 2005.

[105] For example, for the following reasons: (i) to protect the integrity and stability of the Registry; (ii) to comply with any applicable laws, government rules or requirements, requests of law enforcement, in compliance with any dispute resolution process; (iii) to avoid any liability, civil or criminal, on the part of Registry, as well as its affiliates, subsidiaries, officers, directors, and employees; (iv) for violations of the Registry-Registrar Agreement and its Exhibits; or to correct mistakes made by Registry or any Registrar in connection with a domain name registration.

to be followed for the registration of second (for example, rules on '.co.uk') and third (for example rules on 'amazon.co.uk') level domain names under their ccTLD.

Some ccTLD registries offer direct domain name registration to the public.[106] Others accept registration of domain names only through one or multiple registrars that are accredited by the registry. The relationship between the ccTLD registry and registrar is usually of a contractual nature.

These rules generally include rules:

- on fixed second-level domains: Some ccTLD registries have established fixed second-level domains, for example under the '.uk' TLD there are a number of fixed second-level domains such as '.co.uk' for the registration of domain names describing commercial enterprises; '.ltd and .plc' for registered commercial companies, '.ac.uk' for academic institutions.[107]
- on location: some registries require that the domain name registrant has a local presence in the country and/or be a national of the country to be able to register under the particular ccTLD. Other registration authorities require no local presence requirement.
- on the number of domain names that can be registered: some registries regulate the number of domain names that be can be registered by individual or corporate applicants. For example, at one point the Netherlands registration authority, Stichting Internet Domeinregistratie Nederland, had no limits to the number of names registered by a corporate entity but individuals could only register one domain name.[108] It has since been changed.
- on the registration of trademarks as domain names: Most registries follow a 'first come, first served' rule for domain name registration. Hence, most registration authorities include a rule that registrants must take all responsibilities related to trademarks and other rights of third parties in domain name registrations.[109] Other registration authorities provide detailed conditions for domain name registrations, for example that the domain name must match the name of the registrant; or be an acronym or abbreviation of the name of the registrant or be otherwise closely connected to the registrant (such as the rules under the Australian ccTLD).[110]

---

[106] See OECD Working Party on Telecommunication and Information Services Policies 2003:11 Table 3.

[107] A complete list of second-level domains registered under the '.uk' TLD is: '.co.uk' for commercial enterprises; '.org.uk' for non-commercial organizations; '.ltd or .plc' for registered company names; '.net.uk' for Internet Service Providers; '.sch.uk' for schools; '.ac.uk' for academic institutions; '.gov.uk' for government bodies; '.nhs.uk' for National Health Service Organisations; '.mod.uk' for Ministry of Defence agencies and '.police.uk' for UK Police Forces. Accessed at <http://www.nominet.org.uk/SecondLevelDomains/AboutSecondLevelDomains/> on 5 August 2005.

[108] See OECD Working Party on Telecommunication and Information Services Policies 2003:11 Table 5.

[109] Id. 2003: 12.

[110] Id. 2003: 12.

- on the keeping of a 'WHOIS?' service: a 'WHOIS?' service "enables inquirers to find contact information on registered domain names."[111] This can include information on, *inter alia*, the name of the registrant, administrative contacts for the domain name and technical contacts for the domain name.
- on the resolution of disputes: The World Intellectual Property Organisation (WIPO) developed in 2001 the WIPO ccTLD Best Practices for the Prevention and Resolution of Property Disputes.[112] These best practices together with the UDRP are adopted in the rules of some registration authorities, as for example buy Nominet UK for conflicts under the '.uk' ccTLD.

Some of these rules were developed together with ICANN, particular states and WIPO. Even though the relationship between ICANN and ccTLDs registration authorities is not clearly defined, some ccTLD registration authorities include in their rules ICANN policies like the Uniform Domain Name Dispute Resolution Policy (UDRP) to be used in cases where a conflict is alleged between a trade mark holder and a domain name holder (of the particular ccTLD). Rules developed in collaboration with states include rules on the collection and processing of personal data of domain name registrants; rules that conform to the requirements of consumer protection legislation;[113] and rules that the actions of registrars should not go against public order.[114]

Mostly the rules set by registrars identify the contractual relationship between the registrar and the person registering a particular second (or third) level domain name. These include rules on the fees to be paid for the registration of the domain name.

- The resolution of domain name conflicts

By the time ICANN came into operation in 1998, disputes between trademark holders and domain name registrations and disputes of cybersquatting, especially under the .com domain, were at their strongest. The resolution of these disputes was not very clear at the time. Since the use of the domain name is not limited to any geographical or territorial location conflicts with trademarks registered in any country could allegedly arise anywhere. While many disputes were brought before state courts, state courts were at the time unequipped to handle these cases. Court decisions though forthcoming were often slow, contradictory and expensive. Some countries,

---

[111] Id. 2003: 14.

[112] See <http://arbiter.wipo.int/domains/cctld/bestpractices/bestpractices.pdf> accessed 3 December 2004.

[113] For example, Nominet, the .uk registry includes references to both the UK Data Protection Act and the UK Consumer Protection (Distance Selling) regulations of 2000 accessed at <http://www.nic.uk/ReferenceDocuments/TermsAndConditions/TermsAndConditions.html> on 4 January 2005.

[114] For example rules of the Stichting Internet Domeinregistratie Nederland, the .nl registry accessed at <http://www.domain-registry.nl/sidn> on 4 January 2005.

such as the United States,[115] enacted specific legislation to attempt to curb cybersquatting practices. ICANN was under pressure to develop a uniform domain name dispute resolution policy that would be applied in the resolution of trademark-domain name disputes of gTLD domains.

ICANN adopted the Uniform Domain Name Dispute Resolution Policy (UDRP) in August 1999. The policy was formulated in collaboration with the World Intellectual Property Organisation (WIPO).[116] WIPO had previously been asked to report on the procedural method that should be adopted in the resolution of conflicts between legitimate trademark holders and domain name registrants.[117] The recommendations drawn up by WIPO where included in the ICANN dispute resolution policy.

The UDRP was originally developed for the resolution of three gTLDs: .com, .net and .org. With the introduction of the new gTLDs in 2000,[118] the dispute resolution policy was included in the agreement with the new registries and is now used in the resolution of disputes involving the new gTLDs.

Furthermore, by agreeing to follow ICANN policies, registries agree to mandatory administrative/alternative dispute proceedings for any disputes that may arise and agree to include the same provisions in the contracts with registrars and the registrants.

The UDRP policy has two important effects. Firstly, it establishes an actual system to resolve disputes between trademark holders and domain name registrants. ICANN has approved dispute resolution providers to actually provide the service.[119] (A description of the provision of dispute resolution services is found later in Chapter 7.)

Secondly, it gives an effective remedy when the panel finds in favour of the complainant – the Registry will automatically implement the decision (after ten business days from the decision) to cancel or transfer the domain name accordingly.

The UDRP rules outline the procedure to be followed in the lodging of a complaint before a panel of one or three experts. It determines the grounds on which a complaint can be submitted, namely where

---

[115] US Anticybersquatting Consumer Protection Act (1999) (amending the Trademark Act of 1946 also known as the Lanham Act).

[116] Selby 2003:133.

[117] The report was requested in July 1998 by WIPO Member States. The Report of the WIPO Internet Domain Name Process was published in April 1999. WIPO Report (1999) and Gibson 2001: 34.

[118] (.aero, .biz, .coop, .info, .museum, .name, .pro).

[119] There are five approved dispute-resolution providers: (a) Asian Domain Name Dispute Resolution Centre (ADNDRC) (approved since 28th February 2002); (b) CPR Institute for Dispute resolution (approved since 22nd May 2000); (c) eResolution (approved 1st January 2000 and not accepting proceedings since 30 November 2001); (d) The National Arbitration Forum (approved since 23rd December 1999); and (e) World Intellectual Property Organisation (WIPO) (approved since 1 December 1999).

(1)   the domain name is identical or confusingly similar to a trademark or service mark in which the complainant has rights; and

(2)   the registrant has no rights or legitimate interests in respect of the domain name; and

(3)   the domain name has been registered and is being used in bad faith.[120]

Though these rules have been criticised, they have been used extensively and have served an important purpose in deterring spurious registrations.[121] Domain Name disputes are now in decline.[122] Arguably, the existence and use of the UDRP is part of the reason of for the decline.[123]

UDRP rules are criticised on the basis that they do not provide a mechanism to supervise the work of the panellists with respect to both their neutrality and impartiality and to decisions' conformance with UDRP provisions.[124] Another criticism is that the rules do not provide for a fair system for appointing panellists.[125] Furthermore, the rules do not provide for a penalty to be imposed for overreaching complaints.[126] Neither do they provide for a system of administrative appeal from the panel decision.[127]

Apart from the UDRP rules, ICANN has subsequently adopted other dispute resolution policies to apply to various types of disputes between registrants and third parties over the registration and use of domain names.[128]

---

[120] Art. 4a of the UDRP accessed at <http://www.icann.org/dndr/udrp/policy.htm> 4 August 2004.

[121] As of 10 May 2004 (that is, in a period of four years) 9377 proceedings involving 15,710 domain names had been brought under the UDRP (see <http://www.icann.org/udrp/proceedings-stat.htm> accessed 6 August 2004) 6262 proceedings resulted in a transfer of the disputed domain name to the complainant or in a cancellation of the domain name. 1892 decisions found in favour of the respondent.

[122] Cf., US National Research Council of the National Academies 2005: 3-46.

[123] See for example WIPO Press Release PR/2002/303 (26th February 2002) 'WIPO continues efforts to curb cybersquatting' accessed at <http://www.wipo.org/pressroom/en/release/2002/p303.htm> on 6 December 2004 – 'an expedited on-line dispute resolution service has been effective in dissuading Internet pirates from hijacking names.'

[124] Lehmkuhl 2002.

[125] See Geist 2000a.

[126] Lemley and Reese 2004: 4 and footnote 10.

[127] Froomkin 2002b. Lametti (2002:5-6) argues to the contrary.

[128] These include: a. the Charter Eligibility Dispute Resolution Policy – This is followed by the sponsored TLDs '.aero', '.coop', and '.museum' for challenges to registration of a domain name on the grounds that the registrant does not meet the eligibility requirements (set forth in the sponsored TLD charter) for registration of a domain name in the given TLD. b. Eligibility requirements dispute resolution policy – This is followed in the '.name' TLD. It provides for challenges to a registration on the grounds that it does not meet the eligibility requirements. c. Intellectual Property Defensive Registration Challenge Policy – This applies to intellectual property defensive registrations in the '.pro' TLD, which is restricted to use by certified practicing members of certain professions (currently the medical, legal, and accounting professions). d. Restrictions Dispute Resolution Policy – This applies to the '.biz' TLD and can be used to challenge a registration or use of a domain name on the grounds that it is not being used primarily for a *bona fide* business or commercial purpose. e. Sunrise Challenge Policy – this

Neither ccTLD operators nor, consequently, registrants of domain names under ccTLDs are bound by the ICANN rules for domain name dispute resolution. The individual ccTLD operators have at times chosen to adopt the UDRP rules or have created their own set of dispute resolution rules.

5.2.4   Functions served by self-regulation

Self-regulation (a) regulates the DNS (almost all rules regulating the DNS are created by groups). It fills in for the (almost) complete absence of state rules regulating the DNS. (b) satisfies a political need.

The groups are involved in the creation of rules for the creation and allocation of TLDs, for the creation and allocation of second level domains and for the provision of domain name dispute resolution. They carry out the application and implementation of the rules created by them (or by the groups in a higher level of the pyramidal hierarchy). Where necessary, the groups carry out the enforcement of the rules. Some of the implementation and enforcement of rules is carried out through technical means.

The different processes of regulation are often carried out by different self-regulatory arrangements. For example, while the rules of the domain name dispute resolution policy were created by ICANN (for gTLD disputes) or by registries (for country code TLD disputes), other groups implement the rules – registrars in contracts with the registrant and the dispute resolution providers.

Self-regulation bridges two important difficulties in the regulation of the DNS: technical and transnational difficulties. It offers a regulatory solution to a predominantly technical environment that is difficult to regulate without a proper understanding of how the technical side of the DNS is structured and functions. But self-regulation does not stop with the regulation of the technical aspects of self-regulation. It regulates the relationship between the groups responsible for the technical structure and domain name registrants. In addition, it regulates the consequences of the commercial aspect of the DNS.

Self-regulation bridges the transnational aspects of the DNS resulting from the global use of the DNS on the Internet. It simultaneously maintains the global accessibility of all domain names and allows the development of localised rules for the creation and allocation of second (and third) level domain names. As a result, a domain name registered under a particular country code TLD is accessible globally despite the fact that the rules that regulate the registration of the second and third levels within the particular domain can be specific to the particular local context

---

was used in the sunrise period (= first 120 days when TLD is opened for registration) for the '.info' TLD. f. Transfer Dispute Resolution Policy – this applies to transactions in which a domain-name holder transfers or attempts to transfer a domain name to a new registrar. Apart from dispute resolution policies, ICANN also provided other measures during the launch of the new gTLDs to reduce the possibilities of cyber-squatting, for example by giving trademark holders a head start in registration. For complete list <http://www.icann.org/udrp/> accessed 9 January 2005.

providing, for example that only nationals of the particular country can register a second (and third) level domain name under the particular ccTLD.

In addition, many of the rules (especially those for generic TLDs) are applicable irrespective of territorial jurisdictions. One example is the dispute resolution rules developed by ICANN. They can be applied across (and irrespective of) national boundaries.

At times, the regulatory process carried out by self-regulation parallels a similar function carried out by state institutions. This is true in particular of domain name dispute resolution. In many cases, state courts offer an alternative forum for dealing with such disputes.

Self-regulation also serves a political function. While self-regulation of the DNS predates the creation of ICANN, self-regulation carried out by ICANN and by the other groups in the pyramidal hierarchy is for the time being an acceptable solution to a political stalemate. The stalemate is created on the one hand by the reluctance of the US government to renounce a position of relative authority over the DNS. On the other hand, by the increasing opposition of other states for the power of one state over the DNS especially when states recognise the DNS as a critical resource in the technical and economic development of the Internet. Self-regulation of the DNS offers a possible middle ground.

The stalemate could be vividly seen in the 2005 summit on the Information Society.[129] Here, a number of states strongly contested the distinctive involvement of the US government in the DNS. They strongly oppose the claim of 'ownership' and power over a (small but) critical part of the DNS hierarchical structure – the root zone file[130] – and the role of 'oversight' of the administration carried out by ICANN. Some states feel that since the DNS is a critical resource in the current structure of the Internet, used by millions of users around the world, the oversight of its administration should not be carried out by one single state. The stability (and availability) of the Internet is put under threat by the position of dominance of one state. Understandably, the United States strongly resisted any change in the current system. Ultimately, the states agreed to maintain the current *status quo*, indirectly confirming the important political function of self-regulation in the regulation of the DNS. Self-regulation fills in a situation of political uncertainty. Even as commentators and states argue for possible different arrangements for the regulation of the DNS,[131] self-regulation provides an important regulatory solution that allows the DNS and consequently the Internet to continue to develop.

---

[129] World Summit on the Information Society (2005) Tunis Agenda for the Information Society. Agreed on 18 November 2005 Doc. Ref. WSIS-05/TUNIS/DOC/6(Rev.1)-E <http://www/itu.int/wsis/docs2/tunis/off/6rev1.htm>.

[130] The root file is important in that only the top-level domains included in the root zone file are accessible via the DNS structure. Any top-level domain not in the file is, in practice, not available to the majority of users on the Internet. The 'legal' basis for the US position is that originally persons and resources funded by the US government created the DNS.

[131] For example, delegating the regulation of the DNS to an intergovernmental body like the International Telecommunications Union or the creation of a framework convention similar to the United

5.2.5   Self-regulation as a source of rules

The legitimacy of the group

ICANN's authority to manage the DNS has been questioned in the literature. The discussion concerns the question whether the 'delegation' of authority to manage the DNS by the US government was a valid delegation of power. Some authors[132] argue that the transfer of the management of the DNS was not made in a legitimate manner. Essentially, it is argued that ICANN lacks the legislative authority to regulate.

Some authors and some states[133] have argued that any regulation of the DNS should take into consideration the public service responsibilities of the DNS, which are comparable to the public service responsibilities of an electricity or a telecommunications service. It is suggested that ICANN (or any other self-regulation arrangement) does not sufficiently protect the public interest nature of the DNS. What ICANN protects, it is argued, are the interests and concerns of its different constituencies. Greater involvement of states would, it is claimed, introduce some balance.

Some other authors[134] suggest that the DNS should be treated in the same way as outer space in public international law, that is, as an area not bound to one territory or private group but belonging to all mankind in common. The creation of an international treaty on the regulation of the DNS would offer a legislative framework within which ICANN (or another private body) can regulate the DNS.[135]

In looking at the legitimacy of ICANN, one further issue needs to be discussed: whether ICANN represents all the interests involved in the regulation of the DNS. ICANN involves the participation of multiple actors – states and private (business and non-commercial) groups in the rule-making process. However, each group argues that it is not sufficiently represented. The states in the Governmental Advisory Committee (GAC), for example, argue that their influence in the decision taking and rule formation is in fact very small. Similarly, user and other private groups argue that their influence is minimal. Being such an important body in the current regulation and set-up of the DNS, ICANN attracts the attention of a wide number of participants, each with its different concerns and interests. All the interests and concerns of all ICANN's different constituencies cannot be equally considered in the decisions and regulation carried out by ICANN. The regulation carried out by

---

Nations Framework Convention on Climate Change (adopted in 1992). Cf., The Internet Governance Project 2004.

[132] Froomkin (2000a) in particular argues the transfer of management by the US government of the DNS to ICANN was unconstitutional.

[133] Sitompoel. et al. 2001; for public interest and states see Geist 2004.

[134] For example Koops and Lips 2003: 309.

[135] Other international treaties, such as the United Nations Framework Convention on Climate Change (adopted in 1992) is also given as a model in literature. See for example, The Internet Governance Project 2004.

ICANN (like state regulation) is the result of compromise and negotiation with multiple groups. The criticism stems principally from different views about what ICANN's role is or should be. Groups that perceive ICANN as primarily a technical-administrative body would consider ICANN not sufficiently representative unless members of the technical community dominate. Groups who look at ICANN as a major element of Internet governance would consider ICANN not sufficiently representative unless states and civil society are strongly represented in the decision-making process.[136]

Nevertheless, the rules developed by ICANN are followed by its members and by the organisations with which it has contractual relations. One can argue that the different members and organisation in practice accept the authority of ICANN. There are at least two areas in which its authority has been challenged. One involves root server operators, who have to date been slow in signing a Memorandum of Understanding (by the DNS Root Server Advisory Committee) between each root server operator and ICANN. The second example is the resistance of ccTLD registry operators to enter into new agreements with ICANN. But despite such frictions, ICANN's position is increasingly accepted. In the debates at the United Nations World Summit on the Information Society,[137] one can trace a shift from debates questioning the legitimacy of ICANN to debates on ways to ensure accountability without substituting another entity for ICANN.[138]

The legitimacy of registries and registrars in DNS rule-making has attracted no attention in the literature. The rules created by registries and registrars are somewhat anomalous as a form of self-regulation. The registries do not collectively regulate as a group. Each individual registry and registrar acts on its own, entering into a contractual relationship with a registrar and domain name registrants. The registrars and domain name registrants accept that registries (and registrars) are legitimate parties to enter into contractual relations with them. This trust comes because of their technical and operational position in the DNS hierarchy and, in particular in the case of gTLDs and some ccTLDs, from the knowledge that the registries and registrars are in that position because of their contractual arrangements with ICANN.

Furthermore, in the case of some country code registries, the state involved has directly or indirectly given support to the country code registry – confirming the authority of the registry to operate and regulate the particular country TLD. The system of accreditation of registrars by ICANN also serves to confirm the authority of gTLD registrars to implement the rules on the domain name registration developed by ICANN and the respective gTLD registry. Notwithstanding the fact that country code registrars are not bound by the same system of accreditation as gTLD

---

[136] US National Research Council of the National Academies 2005: 5-9/10.

[137] Tunis, November 2005 see <http://www.itu.int/wsis/>.

[138] See for example the Working Group on Internet Governance 2005b. In nearly all the models proposed in the report the issue is no longer the legitimacy of ICANN but the accountability of ICANN – in particular, securing a transparent process and being subject to external audits of its activities.

registrars, each registry has an interest in ensuring that the registrars endorsed by it have the expertise and technical knowledge necessary to implement the applicable domain name registration rules satisfactorily. This endorsement (even if undeclared) confirms the authority of the registrars.

The accountability of the groups

It has been argued in the literature,[139] that there are no structures that can hold ICANN's Board of Directors accountable for any of the decisions taken. But despite the absence of a formal structure through which an individual or a group can hold ICANN responsible for its actions, ICANN has arguably been kept in check through internal and external sources of accountability[140] as seen below.

The Governmental Advisory Committee's (GAC) transformation into a committee that reviews all the decisions to be taken by the Board has introduced a degree of internal scrutiny of the actions of ICANN's Board.[141] ICANN's Board is expected to warn the GAC 'of any proposal raising public policy issues on which it or any of ICANN's supporting organizations or advisory committee seeks public comment'[142] and to inform (and give reasons to) the GAC if the Board rejects a GAC recommendation.

External sources also hold ICANN to account. The need to fulfil the commitments listed in the Memorandum of Understanding signed with the US Department of Commerce indirectly keeps ICANN in check. Criticism from external commentators, public bodies and private groups on the different activities of ICANN act as another form of external check on the actions taken by ICANN. In many circumstances, ICANN has reacted to the criticism and sought to improve or change positions taken. For example, ICANN has tried to improve the way it carries out the allocation of TLDs following suggestions made in a OECD report.[143] There are also other mechanisms, available to the state if it wishes to hold ICANN accountable. For example, Froomkin and Lemley argue that ICANN could be subjected to anti-trust scrutiny. [144]

In the hierarchical structure, each registry is accountable, to a certain extent, to ICANN, especially where a clear contractual relationship exists between ICANN and the individual registry. However, individual registries have questioned ICANN's authority to check on their activities. For example, in 2003 VeriSign introduced a

---

[139] By Froomkin and Lemley 2003; Mueller 1999; The Internet Governance Project 2005c and others.

[140] Cf., De Vey Mestdagh, C.N.J. and R.W. Rijgersberg 2006.

[141] Froomkin (2003) argues that the 2002 changes are really only cosmetic.

[142] ICANN, Bylaws for Internet Corporation for Assigned Names and Numbers Art. VI at 9.1 accessed at <http://www.icann.org/general/bylaws.htm> on 6 December 2004; see also Froomkin 2004: 863 and Kleinwoechter, Wolfgang 2003: 1122.

[143] Paltridge, Sam and Masayuki, Matsui (2004)

[144] They claim that not only could ICANN be subjected to anti-trust scrutiny but that ICANN would fail the scrutiny. (See Froomkin and Lemley 2003)

Site Finder service that raised a number of technical and institutional issues. ICANN formally demanded the suspension of the service. VeriSign suspended the service (under protest) and challenged ICANN's authority in court.[145]

The individual registries are principally held in check through their contractual relationships with registrars and registrants. The actions and authority of some country code registries have been challenged in court.[146] Some individual registries have established a complaints-procedure to register and look into complaints by registrars and registrants on the actions of the registry.[147]

A number of European country code registries have formed a group – the Council of European National TLD registries (CENTR) – to promote collaboration between registries including rules and registration procedures followed by the different member ccTLD registries. In practice, the group also acts as a source of external accountability on the activities of the members of the group (especially when the activities of an individual member may have an affect on the activities of the other members).[148]

The contractual relationship between the registry and the registrar acts as an external check on the relationship between the registrar and the registrant. Each registrant can (at least in theory) bring legal action against the registrar for breach of contract. It can be argued that while access to state courts is relatively easy in the case of registrants and registrars of country code top-level domains, it might be more difficult in the case of gTLD where the registrar and registrant are not (necessarily) in the same jurisdiction.

By no means, however, does all this mean that there is no scope for further development of measures of accountability. Indeed, the current debates on accountability of the different groups – for example the debate on oversight of root server operators, the debates on accountability of ICANN and debates on oversight of ccTLD registries – reflect the need for further improvement. The current debate on ICANN accountability is aimed in part at the removal of or change in the (theoretically) 'enviable' role of the United States in the oversight of ICANN. The models proposed in the Report of the Working Group on Internet Governance identify different possible arrangements – including multiple states and private stakeholders – to act as auditors of the regulation of the Internet (and ICANN in particular).

---

[145] In February 2004, VeriSign filed a federal lawsuit in the US District Court, Central District of California against ICANN claiming that ICANN had overstepped its contractual authority and was in breach of anti-trust legislation. The anti-trust claims were dismissed in August 2004. The claims on the contractual authority were re-filed in a state court in August 2004. The suit was still pending as of August 2005. All litigation documents of VeriSign Inc. vs. ICANN can be accessed at <http://www.icann.org/general/litigation-verisign.htm> last accessed 15 August 2005.

[146] For example, suits were filed against the '.uk' registry Nominet UK claiming breach of contractual terms, e.g., Diane Wraith -v- Nominet UK see <http://www.nominet.org.uk/ReferenceDocuments/CaseLaw/DianeWraith-v-NominetUk.html> accessed on 5 August 2005.

[147] For example Nominet UK accessed at <http://www.nominet.org.uk/ReferenceDocuments/ComplaintsProcedure/> on 5 August 2005.

[148] <http://www.centr.org/about/> accessed on 5 August 2005.

The legal effect of the self-regulation rules and the rule-making process

The rules created by the groups are binding on the parties to the rule-making, on the groups in a lower level of the hierarchy and on the domain name registrants. The rules created by ICANN, for example, are binding on the other parties involved in regulation: on ICANN itself, on gTLD operators and ccTLD registry operators and ultimately on domain name registrants.

The choice to implement the various rules primarily through contracts entails that the rules are binding on the parties to the contract. The enforcement of these binding rules is at times technical, at times accomplished by internal mechanisms (such as dispute resolution) and at times based on legal mechanisms offered by the states.

The rules are transparent to the parties involved in the regulation and publicly available. For the most part the contractual terms, even though they determine a 'private' relationship between the parties of the contract, are also publicly available. All the rules created by ICANN are publicly available. The ICANN's rule-making process is transparent. Article III of the ICANN byelaws provides that

> 'ICANN and its constituent bodies shall operate to the maximum extent feasible in an open and transparent manner and consistent with procedures designed to ensure fairness.'[149]

All the documents prepared by and decisions taken by the different groups in ICANN are publicly available at the ICANN web site. Nevertheless ICANN has been criticised for not following a transparent rule forming process. One example is in the creation of new gTLDs and the allocation of the gTLD registries. An OECE report[150] and some authors[151] argue that the lack of transparency in the most recent increase of gTLDs is one that could have been avoided.

The legal certainty attached to the rules is enhanced by the fact that rules developed by ICANN are not changed unilaterally or haphazardly by the ICANN Board. As ICANN is aware, the stability of the regulation affects the stability of the technical structure of the DNS. The rules are certain and there is a follow a formal process for changing or amending them. Furthermore, given the pyramidal/hierarchical relationship between ICANN, registries and registrars, the rules found in the contracts between registrars and registrants are not easily changed. Each change would have to be renegotiated with the different individual parties to the contracts at each level.

---

[149] Accessed at <http://www.icann.org/general/archive-bylaws/bylaws-08apr05.htm#III> on 5 August 2005.

[150] Paltridge and Matsui 2004.

[151] For example, Manheim and Solum 2003.

5.3   STATES AND THE REGULATION OF THE DNS

States and state legislation serve a number of functions in the self-regulation of the DNS as discussed below.

Accountability and oversight

The position of apparent privilege of the US government in the regulation of the DNS is a source of tension between the United States and a number of other states (such as China, Russia, the European Union, South Africa and Brazil),[152] which argue that the DNS should not be under the control of one state alone. In the regulation of other important 'global' resources – the international telephone numbering system – for example, is regulated by an intergovernmental organisation, the International Telecommunications Union (ITU), and not as in the case of the DNS by private groups and only one state. Indeed, some suggest that the ITU should shoulder the oversight responsibility.[153]

Others prefer an international body that includes not only governments but also civil society and private (commercial) groups, and established through an international treaty. Establishing the body through an international treaty would in their eyes give the body 'authority' to oversee the regulation of the DNS.[154]

However, one can also argue that the unique position of the DOC, while a matter of political concern to some nations, has not impeded ICANN from carrying out the necessary regulation of the DNS and affords an important source of oversight over the activities of ICANN.

While the United States seems to have a 'theoretical' final say over ICANN's decisions, other states are involved in the ICANN process. Originally devised as solely an advisory body, ICANN's Governmental Advisory Committee (GAC) since 2002 has become directly involved in the management of ICANN.[155] Representatives of over 30 national governments, and multinational governmental organisations, such as the ITU and the World Intellectual Property Organisation (WIPO), regu-

---

[152] See US National Research Council of the National Academies 2005: 5-3.

[153] The membership and experience of the ITU with the adoption and implementation of international telecommunications standards followed in much of the world gives the ITU the necessary legitimacy and credibility to carry out the necessary oversight of the DNS regulation. Indeed, the members of the ITU have given a mandate to the ITU to work at suggesting proposals on the role of (ITU) Member States in the management of domain names and addresses (and in particular the management of internationalised (multilingual) domain names). See ITU Plenipotentiary Resolution 102 on Management of Internet Domain names and Addresses (adopted in 1998 and revised in 2002) and Resolution 133 on the Role of administrations of Member States in the management of internationalized (multilingual) domain names. Accessed at <http://www.itu.int/osg/spu/resolutions/2002/res102.html> and <http://www.itu.int/osg/spu/resolutions/2002/resplen5.html> on 5 August 2005.

[154] See The Working Group on Internet Governance 2005a; 2005b:13-16; The Internet Governance Project 2005c; 2004.

[155] See Froomkin 2004: 863.

larly attend the GAC. Membership of the GAC is open to all national governments recognised in international fora, and multinational governmental organisations and treaty organisations.[156] The GAC is particularly active in formulating rules to be followed in the allocation of new ccTLDs and in re-delegation of ccTLDs. It is also occasionally involved in issues relating to generic TLDs. For example, after the December 2003 call for proposals for new sponsored TLDs, one of the proposals was for a new TLD '.xxx' intended to be used for adult content. The GAC has expressed its concern about the implications and effects of this new TLD.[157] The effect of the GAC concern on the final decision on the '.xxx' domain is still to be seen.

A number of intergovernmental organisations, such as WIPO, OECD and ITU, are also interested in the regulation of the DNS. WIPO and OECD participate actively in the ICANN process. For example, WIPO was involved in the preparation of the Uniform Domain Names Dispute Resolution Policy. Furthermore, the WIPO Arbitration Centre is one of the domain name dispute resolution providers approved by ICANN. The OECD has produced a report on the allocation of generic TLDs.[158] This report suggests possible improvements in the regulation of the allocation of TLD to registry operators. ICANN has followed up a number of the suggestions.

Apart from the function of States in the oversight of ICANN, state anti-trust regulation, consumer protection legislation and other general legal principles, can be used to keep the various private groups involved in regulating the DNS in check.

A general legal background

While minimal state legislation[159] regulates the technical and economic aspects of the DNS, states and state regulation have influenced the working of self-regulation. States provide a general legal background within which self-regulation could and can develop. Self-regulation of the DNS does not exist in a separate legal space from that of state regulation or in a legal vacuum. It relies on the general principles of contract law offered by the legal systems of states. While in the self-regulation of other areas of Internet activities the main instrument of regulation is a code of conduct, the rules in DNS self-regulation are found in contracts, for example in contracts between ICANN and gTLD registries, between registries and registrars, between registrars and registrants and so forth. The main reason for preferring contracts over other instruments of self-regulation such as codes of conduct in the regulation of the DNS seem to be that contract law is a familiar instrument for regulating what are seen as private-relationships. Had the regulation of the DNS

---

[156] See <www.gac.icann.org>.

[157] See letter from GAC Chairman to ICANN Board on new 'xxx' TLD dated 12 August 2005 accessed <http://www.icann.org/correspondence/tarmizi-to-board-12aug05.htm> on 12 August 2005.

[158] Paltridge and Matsui 2004.

[159] There is some state legislation regulating the allocation of second and third level domain names under country code TLDs and some sporadic legislation against cybersquatting (like the US Anti-cybersquatting Consumer Protection Act of 1999).

involved groups, for example had all ccTLD registries needed to act collectively – their chosen self-regulatory instrument would probably have been an agreed code of conduct.

The aim of the DNS regulation is not to create a legal system but to regulate the relations of the different parties involved in the running and registration of domain names. The choice in favour of contracts confirms this aim: regulation of the DNS has developed in a framework of existing legal structures – contract law and private international law – suitable for regulating relations between parties in the same territorial jurisdiction or in different jurisdictions. Self-regulation of the DNS relies extensively on the remedies and interpretation of obligations offered by contract law and private international law developed by states. Indeed, private contracts have been used to regulate relations between parties in most private transnational transactions long before the creation of the DNS. Solving conflicts that arise under international contracts has been the subject of private international law for centuries. The experience gained in the regulation and resolution of disputes arising from contracts regulating off-line activities has proved invaluable in the regulation of DNS.

Apart from contract law in the regulation of country code TLDs, registries, registrars and registrants are reliant on other state legislation, such as data protection rules that determine the way personal data related to particular domain name registration are to collected and processed, and trademark law.

Ultimate fallback remedy

Furthermore, state institutions, such as courts, provide a means to enforce self-regulation rules where any of the parties fall short. State courts also provide an ultimate fallback remedy for the resolution of disputes between trademark holders and domain name registrants, in particular since state courts are ultimately the only *fora* where financial damages can be sought. The domain name dispute resolution policy developed by ICANN and by individual country code registries do not provide for the allocation of financial damages by the resolution panel.

Advisory function

States have an important advisory function in the development of self-regulation of the DNS. The running of gTLDs has been left predominantly[160] to the 'market' and to ICANN. States have limited their participation in the running of gTLDs to an advisory role. There are two important examples of this advisory role. One comes from the Governmental Advisory Committee (GAC). A second is played by inter-governmental organisations, such as WIPO. The OECD also plays an important advisory role, for example, by suggesting possible improvements to the regulation of the allocation of TLDs to registry operators.[161]

---

[160] Of course apart from the '.gov'; '.mil' and '.edu' domains.
[161] Paltridge and Matsui 2004.

Active participation in ccTLDs

It has been argued[162] that in the last five years, especially since the introduction of ICANN in the administration of the DNS, states have shown a keen interest to be involved in the governance of the DNS at a global level and more specifically in the running of the ccTLD associated with their respective state. To some extent, the clear link with state territory in ccTLDs facilitates the presence and involvement of the state in the regulation of the respective ccTLD. Individual states are involved in the regulation of their country's ccTLD. In an extensive report on the operation of ccTLDs, Geist[163] identifies four forms of government participation:

(a)   by directly operating the national ccTLD as part of a government ministry or agency;
(b)   by establishing a subsidiary company to manage the national ccTLD;
(c)   by enacting legislation granting some branch of government final authority over the national ccTLD; and
(d)   by entering into operational contracts with the ccTLD manager in which ultimate authority lies with the government and day-to-day operations with the private manager.[164]

Ultimately, each ccTLD registry, since it is located in the jurisdiction of a particular state is subject to the laws of that state. In theory (as well as in practice), a state may enact laws to limit or determine the fate of a particular ccTLD associated with the state.[165] A case in point is the government of South Africa, which recently introduced legislation to reclaim control of the .za name space from the incumbent ccTLD manager. Similarly, during the controversial re-delegation of the .au domain, the Australian government reminded ICANN that 'as a last resort the Australian Government could invoke legislation relating to the self-regulation of the domain name system.'[166] Some states, such as the United States, have also enacted anti-cybersquatting legislation. [167]

5.4   CONCLUSION

The DNS is a key technical resource in the current Internet set-up. It supports a system of domain names that function irrespective of the geographical and physical location of the user using the domain name or of the server linked to the domain

---

[162] Geist 2004 and Froomkin 2004.

[163] Geist 2004: 4.

[164] Geist, Michael 2004: 4.

[165] Froomkin 2004: 864.

[166] Yu 2003: 7.

[167] US Anticybersquatting Consumer Protection Act (1999) (amending the Trademark Act of 1946 also known as the Lanham Act).

name. The function of domain names on the Internet resembles the function of identification numbers, such as social security numbers or identity card numbers, in the off-line world.[168] Apart from the essential function of identifying (technical) locations on the Internet, users frequently associate domain names with an organisation or service on-line.[169] Domain names have acquired a commercial function.

Given the importance of the DNS some form of regulation is critical. By contrast with other important technical infrastructures, such as the International Telephone Numbering System, states are not the main actors in the formulation, application, implementation and enforcement of rules regulating the DNS. The actual regulation of the DNS is predominantly a matter of self-regulation. It offers a system of regulation where only sporadic state regulation exists. The centralisation and concatenation of rules (absent in self-regulation of other Internet activities) gives the self-regulation robustness, making self-regulation the main legal ordering system of the DNS. Yet, as we have seen in the previous section, states and state regulation are never far from the scene. The two sources of rules intertwine and complement each other.

Intertwining and complementary relationship

While self-regulation provides the rules regulating the DNS, it does so by using general legal principles supported by state legal systems. It relies extensively on contract law. Self-regulation rules and state-supported legal principles law offer together the necessary powers, obligations, and enforcement needed in the regulation of the DNS. The intertwining is most evident in the regulation of the commercial and financial aspects of domain names. Self-regulation regulates the way domain names are registered and the resolution of domain name disputes. State dispute resolution institutions then use these self-regulation rules in resolving trademark-domain name disputes that are brought before them.

The two sources complement each other. On the one hand, self-regulation fills in for an almost complete absence of state legislation directed specifically towards the DNS. It provides rules that are applied transnationally, an accomplishment that state regulation would find very difficult to achieve (at least in a reasonably short time). Furthermore, self-regulation serves an important political function for states. In the work leading to the Tunis Summit on the Information Society, one can see how the existing self-regulation of the DNS helped to attain a middle ground between the two 'extreme' positions – that of the United States and that of those states wishing to move away from the US dominance.

On the other hand, states complement self-regulation. By acknowledging the existence and authority of the self-regulation rules regulating the DNS, states confirm the legitimacy of the private groups and the rules. Furthermore, states, pre-

---

[168] Cf., Scott 1999 for a description of the function of identification systems.
[169] Manheim and Solum 2003: 367.

dominantly the United States, are always available as external mechanisms to ensure accountability. Furthermore, self-regulation relies on the advisory support of
states and international organisations for the development of the necessary regulation. The experience of states and international organisation in rule-making complement the technical knowledge of the groups involved in self-regulation of the DNS.

Historical baggage

The complex relationship has not developed out of a pre-determined plan. To some
degree, it is a remnant of the technical and regulatory development of the DNS, of
its early relationship with the US government, and of political choices made by the
US government. Self-regulation has developed in parallel with the technical development. Considering the DNS a predominantly technical arrangement, states (particularly the US government) in the beginning left the regulation of the DNS to the
same persons developing the technical structure. The gradual increase in the commercial aspects of domain names saw self-regulation adopting new rules to fit the
new exigencies. The substantive regulation at each level of the pyramidal hierarchy, though today more detailed and developed, is based on the initial rules developed earlier on in the regulation of the DNS.

The increasing popularity of Internet and attention to the commercial aspects of
domain names attracted the attention of states. States have chosen to taken an advisory role in the regulation of the DNS or a more active role (as in the case of
country code TLDs). States are selectively motivated into getting involved in the
regulation of the DNS. The motivation is based on the perception that participation
would be either directly (financially) beneficial to the state or necessary to protect
the rights of its citizens. For example, since the link between registrations under the
ccTLD and the possible interests of the state or its citizens are clearer than in the
registration of generic TLDs states have been more motivated to participate in their
regulation. Arguably, some states are keen on being involved in the respective ccTLD
allocation and regulation as a way to counter US control (even if only theoretically
perceived) over the ccTLD and indirectly the state territory.

The current increased involvement of some states in the respective ccTLD domain name regulation is likely to increase now that the commercial/financial sig-
nificance of key domain names is clear. Some states may be tempted to see their
respective ccTLD as a 'brand' – a representation of the state – that they can market
exclusively. Froomkin,[170] for example, argues that the EU's active insistence for
the creation of a '.eu' TLD is an example of treating the TLD as a brand. A statement of the European Commission stating that '[t]he creation of a .eu suffix would
certainly increase the power of the EU "brand"'[171] reinforces Froomkin's argument. While no state has formally claimed an exclusive right over the ccTLD assigned to it, states are not blind to the possible financial gain for them where they

---

[170] Froomkin 2004.
[171] As quoted by Froomkin 2004: 843.

are more involved in the domain name regulation. Furthermore, some states may be interested in reserving specific domain names for themselves[172] especially because of the growing emphasis on governments being able to deliver their service electronically.

Transnational nature

The transnational nature of the DNS is another element that contributes to the intertwining and complementary relationship between self-regulation and state regulation. The application of the DNS is not restricted to any territorial boundary. Domain names, even if belonging to particular country code TLD, are accessible across territories. Furthermore, generic TLDs (and some country code TLDs) are available for registration irrespective of the nationality and physical location of the registrant. Similarly, rules that regulate the DNS must apply and be enforced across territorial boundaries. Given the need to maintain the transnational nature of the DNS, in the absence of an international treaty, legislation of one or a few states alone could not be sufficient. The inability of states to co-ordinate their positions on the regulation of the DNS and draw up an agreed inter-state position has left states dependent on self-regulation to regulate the DNS. One can look at the disputes between trademark holders and domain name registrants as an illustration of this point. State legislation in individual countries, such as the US Anti-cybersquatting Consumer Protection Act 1999, was not enough to solve the then wave of disputes over registrations made by alleged cybersquatters. Neither were court decisions from a variety of countries a suitable enough deterrent, even if recourse to state courts is still an available remedy for trademark holders claiming that a domain name registrant is infringing their rights or passing off their trademark. The UDRP policy, developed by ICANN in collaboration with the WIPO, eventually offered an effective remedy (even if the system has been criticised) to trademark-domain name disputes. It offers an effective solution to disputes between trademark holders and domain name registrants irrespective of the physical location and territorial jurisdiction of the parties.

In addition, technical enforcement of some of the rules in the DNS contracts further strengthens the transnational application of the rules regulating the DNS. For example, one of the rules in the ICANN – gTLD registries' contract is that the gTLDs are to follow the technical specifications issued by ICANN. Unless the registry follows these technical specifications, none of the registrations under the gTLD can be accessed on the Internet – in effect, the domain name does not exist on the Internet. This technical enforcement applies irrespective of any territorial considerations.

---

[172] Sitompoel, et al. (2001:106) claim that the Dutch government, for example, was interested (at the time of the publication of their book) in reserving specific domain names for itself.

Public interest

It is important to remember that the DNS was created and developed to address the needs of the then expanding Internet community – essentially the need to be able to communicate with each other in a fast and accessible way. Private groups (had and) have an interest that the regulation of DNS does not limit their use of the DNS. But the protection of group interests alone would neglect the wider picture of considering the 'public interest' or value of the DNS for the whole Internet community. States are increasingly inclined to view the DNS as a public resource comparable to, for example, telecom services.[173] States are, therefore, more inclined to propose a public law framework within which the private sector can offer domain name related services.[174]

Looking ahead

The complex intertwining and complementary relationships between state and self-regulation are not static. New technical developments, such as the introduction of more multilingual and internationalised domain names,[175] require adequate regulation to balance the different interests involved.

Furthermore, while in Tunis in November 2005, the *status quo* was maintained, the discussion on the regulation of the DNS is not yet over. The struggle for more multi-state power over the DNS will continue. Yet, the trend in current discussions on the governance of the DNS to accept the role of ICANN in the regulation of the DNS[176] if accountability and transparency structures are improved,[177] indicates that the current intertwining and complementary relationship between self-regulation and state regulation can be used to form the basis of future governance of the DNS. Ultimately, as this Chapter shows, equilibrium between the different interests involved in the running of the DNS can only be achieved by a more complete intertwining and complementary relationship between self-regulation and states.

---

[173] Sitompoel, et al. (2001) compare the assignment of domain names with the assignment of telephone numbers; for public interest and states. See also Geist 2004.

[174] For example, The US Department of Commerce National Telecommunications and Information Administration (NTIA) released a document on 30 June 2005 entitled 'US Statement of Principles on the Internet's Domain Name and Addressing System' accessed at <http://www.ntia.doc.gov/ntiahome/domainname/USDNSprinciples> on 5 August 2005. '… Given the Internet's importance to the world's economy, it is essential that the underlying DNS of the Internet remain stable and secure. As such the United States is committed to taking no action that would have the potential to adversely impact the effective and efficient operation of the DNS and will therefore maintain its historic role in authorizing changes or modification to the authoritative root zone file.'

[175] That is, the creation of domain names using different language and script character sets.

[176] Cf., the different models proposed in the Working Group on Internet Governance 2005b.

[177] Cf., De Vey Mestdagh, C.N.J. and R.W. Rijgersberg 2006.

Chapter 6
SELF-REGULATION BY TECHNICAL STANDARDS

6.1 INTRODUCTION – CODE AS LAW

Just as the architectural shape of a building enables and encourages people to move and congregate in certain ways so does the technical architecture of the Internet.[1] The technical structure,[2] called 'code' by Lessig,[3] determines how certain activities can be followed or discouraged. Each technical (design) decision can have implications for the behaviour of Internet users. For example, the simple technical choice to assign a fixed IP address for access to the Internet rather than a randomly assigned IP address, may have implications on other legal rights of the user, such as the user's right to privacy.[4]

The effect of technology on behaviour is similar to that of law and can at times, arguably, go further, especially when the user has no choice but to follow the rules imposed by technology.[5] Reidenberg calls regulation by technology, *lex informatica*.[6] Lessig[7] uses a more emphatic way to point at the regulatory effect of technology. He claims that 'code is law'. Code, that is the technical architecture of the Internet, is an instrument of social and political control. He argues that technical code in cyberspace has a very important role in controlling activities as it can control more perfectly and completely than traditional state rules and sanctions.[8] The freedom once associated with the Internet can be either supported or limited depending on the choice of technical code that supports the Internet.

It is principally private groups that create the technical structures that regulate Internet activities and the rights of individuals. Increasingly however, as Reidenberg[9] argues, regulation by technology is not only a matter of private regulation. States

---

[1] Cf., Solum and Minn Chung 2004: 828.

[2] That is, the hardware and the software that support (and allow) activities to take place. Cf., Lessig 1999a: 6 and 20.

[3] Lessig 1999.

[4] The assumption being that a given user can be more easily identified with a fixed IP address than with a random one.

[5] Cf., Karl Llewellyn's observation that the cloverleaf highway interchange was the 'greatest legal invention of the Twentieth Century'. (quoted in Griffiths 2003: 64-65) Griffiths (2003) calls this 'secondary mobilization'.

[6] *Lex Informatica*, in summary, is a collection of rules controlling, *inter alia*, information flows, which are imposed by technology and not by classical systems of regulation such as legislation by the state. (see Reidenberg 1998)

[7] Lessig 1999a, 1999b, 1996.

[8] Spinello 2001: 139.

[9] Reidenberg 2005, 2004a.

J.P. Mifsud Bonnici, Self-Regulation in Cyberspace
© 2008, T·M·C·ASSER PRESS, *The Hague, and the author*

have increasingly become aware of the power of technical architecture and use technology to pursue the aims of state policy. For example, the e-commerce product, '.NET Passport,' developed by Microsoft, was structured more carefully to ensure compliance with European data protection rules after European regulators persuaded Microsoft to modify the product design.[10]

While there is no denial that code has behavioural effects, the main criticism of the position of Reidenberg[11] and Lessig,[12] in the literature, is whether code as a form of regulation can be called 'law' and classified as 'law'. Other authors[13] are sceptical about the idea that technology is a main means of rule-making and question the legitimacy of code as a substitute for formal law. In particular, according to critics, code is neither created nor developed in the same way as legislation and code does not satisfy a number of formal criteria for 'law', such as Lon Fuller's criteria for legal systems.[14] However, irrespective of whether code is 'law' or not, private persons (including non-lawyers) see code as a way of regulating virtual spaces without the intervention of states.

An interesting example of the interplay between rule-making and emerging technical architecture from a participant's perspective can be seen in the recent development of the Croquet Project. At first, the Croquet Project was an attempt to replicate/simulate in an on-line context the participative environment of campus life. That is, the creators tried to simulate on-line an environment where students and academics gain relevant information and other resources from the physical interaction with other scholars.[15] Quickly this led to the realisation that the technical structure of the Internet may influence the nature of the rules and rule-making that would govern the on-line campus interaction. Indeed, the developers of the Croquet Project were 'forced' to reflect upon the 'Meta Rules of Cyber Space'

---

[10] See Reidenberg 2005 and Art. 29 (EU Data Protection Working Party) (2003) Working Document on On-line Authentication Services Doc. Dated 29 January 2003 Doc. Ref. 10054/03/EN WP68 <http://www.europa.eu.int/comm/justice_home/fsj/privacy/docs/wpdocs/2003/wp68_en.pdf> accessed 5 October 2005 in particular at p. 4.

[11] Reidenberg 1998.

[12] Lessig 1999.

[13] For example in the work of the 'Code as Code' research group at IViR at the University of Amsterdam, the Netherlands.

[14] Fuller (1964) identifies eight criteria crucial to law: it must be of general application; public; prospective; comprehensible; consistent and stable; possible; and real. Fuller's main claim is that a legal system that does not satisfy any one of the eight criteria 'does not simply result in a bad system of law; it results in something that is not properly called a legal system at all'. Critics argue that the failure of code to satisfy each of the criteria means that 'code' cannot properly be called 'law'. It is argued in this chapter, that these criteria are a list of normative criteria and not a list of descriptive and empirical characteristics of law and legal systems. Like state legal systems, code can, in some instances, fail to satisfy each of the eight normative criteria. Failure to satisfy any of the normative criteria does not exclude either state or private regulation including code from being referred to as 'law' and of having a legal effect on citizens and participants.

[15] In seeking a philosophical basis to the approach, Marilyn Lombardi (2005) claims that 'The unique value of campus life, then is a matter of proximity-the ability to position oneself in direct relation to relevant people and resources.'

following a comment in a blog[16] – by a person who was clearly seeing new scope for forms of self-regulation. The comment read:

> 'there's something even more fundamentally different about this technology [the Internet] and that is the ability for users – simple users, not corporations or governments – to create virtual worlds and exist within those virtual worlds and invite others into those virtual worlds and have those virtual worlds be only subject to the limitations of the technology and the RULES created by that owner. In other words, a fully privatized virtual space for every single user wherein every single user could establish the rules for social interaction within his or her world.'[17]

In this chapter, I look at a subset of 'code' as law: technical standards as means to regulate Internet activities. Technical standards[18] are an essential feature of the Internet. Indeed, without technical standards, the current form of the Internet would not exist at all. It is based on multiple technical standards that include standards for the addressing of machines, standards for the way data is routed, standards for accessing data and so forth. For example, based on uniform standards, machines can find and communicate with each other and content hosted on one machine can be accessed and recognised by other machines. Any machine not following the agreed technical standards is simply technically non-existent on the Internet since it would not be able to communicate or be reached by other machines.

Often, apart from the technical use of the standard, the technical standard also has a regulatory effect on Internet activities. Like codes of conduct (or other formal

---

[16] Cf., Julian Lombardi (one of the architects of the Croquet Project) 'Meta Rules of Cyber Space' accessed at <http://jlombardi.blogspot.com/2004/10/meta-rules-in-cyberspace.html> on 6 September 2005.

[17] The comment goes further in considering the potential of new standards in technology that Croquet sets: 'At a basic level, this technology allows us to test out rules of just conduct to find out which sets of institutions, norms, and rules operate most effectively online AND, by extension, in the real world. I can imagine social science, for instance, being made much more rigorous by testing out certain propositions about human interaction on humans, or at least, representations of them. But at a more concrete level it makes the world(s) far more efficient. Let's imagine we have 10,000 worlds each created by 10,000 users (there could be many more). I create my own world which features very strict rules against blaspheming god. These rules require Avatars when they enter my world to pray to Jesus and to watch a video extolling the virtues of Southern Baptism. I forbid swearing, do not allow sex-oriented behavior or talk, and forbid the posting of advertisements in my world that are pro-choice. My world, it turns out, is very popular for Christian homeschoolers because, in addition to having those rules, I also have featured lots of resources (much of it authored by other people, but filtered by me) for that audience. Other Christians in the real world find out about my world and, through some identifier akin to a domain name, know how to find it among the 10,000 other worlds out there. It's very popular among that audience. But curiously, metrosexuals find it all off-putting (incidentally, I realize metrosexual is so 2003). Fortunately for them, there are other worlds tailored to their tastes, preferences of social interaction, and so forth. If you can imagine such a world – all graphically sophisticated and easily modifiable by a fairly novice user – you can begin to see the power of Croquet.'

[18] That is, 'a published specification that establishes a common language and contains a technical specification or other precise criteria and is designed to be used consistently as a rule, guideline or definition', British Standards Institute as quoted in Bellagio Conference 2003: 82.

rules), technical standards can set the parameters of acceptable 'behaviour' (functioning) in a particular activity. Furthermore, the standards represent what a particular community (creating and developing the technical standard) considers
acceptable 'behaviour' (functioning) of the activity. Consequently, by conforming
to technical standards users ('subjects of the regulation') conform to the acceptable
behaviour.[19] Once accepted and adopted, technical standards have an absolute and
automatic binding effect on the parties using the standards.

While the process of developing technical standards is often seen as a technical
discipline, since all the technical standards described in this chapter have important
behavioural implications, the process of developing technical standards is also a
process of regulation. Since the group creating the standard will then abide by it
and use it, the process of developing technical standards can also be a process of
self-regulation. I examine the use of technical standards as instruments of self-
regulation by private groups in the regulation of four Internet activities:

(i)   in the regulation of privacy issues on-line. In this chapter I describe the cre-
      ation and development of the Platform for Privacy Preferences (P3P) techni-
      cal standard;
(ii) to increase the availability of Internet addresses: the Internet Protocol version
      6 (IPv6);
(iii) in regulating 'authentication' and 'integrity' of transactions on the Internet;
      and
(iv) in the regulation of intellectual property rights on the Internet.

In line with the main research question of this study, I examine the function of self-
regulation by technical standards in the regulation of these four Internet activities.
The research shows that in spite of the technical character of the standards, this
form of self-regulation is an important source of rules customized to satisfy particular needs. The standards implement rules coming both from states or private groups.
Importantly, for an Internet context, the standards apply across territorial borders
reaching activities that states are unable or reluctant to reach. In this way, self-
regulation complements state regulation. In turn, state regulation complements the
rules of self-regulation by encouraging groups to adopt technical standards and
providing a legal framework that influences the development of technical standards. The two sources of regulation intertwine, complementing each other.

I argue in conclusion that the effect of self-regulation by technical standards is
not different from that of self-regulation by contracts or codes of conduct. Similar
to Reidenberg's argument that '*lex informatica* allows customized rules to suit particular network situations and preserve choices for individual participants',[20] technical standards allow for customised measures suited to address specific needs.

[19] Cargill 1989: 13.
[20] Reidenberg 1998: 574.

6.2   SETTING TECHNICAL STANDARDS

In the off-line world, the setting of technical standards is often done by state-led organisations such as the International Standards Organisation. On the Internet, in contrast, private groups, be they industry participants, academic institutions or engineers, create technical standards. Their technical expertise and knowledge of the activities that need regulation allows them to provide appropriate technical means to regulate the activity. The involvement of private groups in the formation of technical standards can be explained both historically and through the nature of the technical standards concerned. Historically, the development of technical standards for cyberspace has been primarily the ambit of academic communities, supervised to an extent by the US government. With the evolution of the Internet to the international and commercial community that it now is, technical standards aroused the attention of various private sector groups. Furthermore, states have often deferred to private organisations, especially since it is considered likely that industry or private participants are likely to have 'superior knowledge of the subject compared to a government agency'.[21]

6.2.1   The different self-regulation groups

The development of technical standards on the Internet is thus, in many instances, a process of self-regulation by private groups. Different private groups are involved in the development of technical standards. There is no one centralised group creating all technical standards in all areas. It would be practically impossible and in any case impractical to have one centralised group organising all standards. Some groups like the Internet Engineering Task Force (IETF) and the World Wide Web Consortium (W3C) are involved in the creation of several technical standards regulating various practices. Others, like the European Electronic Signature Standardization Initiative (EESSI) are involved in the creation of one particular standard or standards.

The bond between the members in each group is one of technical expertise, interest and need for regulation. The groups are not based on territorial links. Membership is often worldwide. The IETF and the W3C are two important examples of this. The IETF is one of the more important standard-making bodies for the Internet. It is also one of the oldest. Its roots go back to the late 1960s. Originally, academics and researchers gathered informally to create interconnection standards, which are still the basis of the modern Internet.[22] Today the creation of a technical standard follows a formal process. Participation in IETF is open to any person who has the

---

[21] Weiser 2001: 824 quoting Douglas C. Michael (1995), 'Federal Agency Use of Audited Self-Regulation as a Regulatory Technique', *Administrative Law Review*, Vol. 47, pp. 171, 181-182.

[22] See the description of IETF given by the Center for Democracy & Technology accessed at <http://www.cdt.org/standards/ietf.shtml> on 9 May 2003.

necessary level of expertise and who can commit a considerable amount of time to the development and creation of technical standards. IETF does not have any formal membership. This chapter looks at the IPv6 technical standard developed by IETF.

The W3C is a private consortium of paying member organisations.[23] The members include sellers of technology products and services, content providers, corporate users, research laboratories, standards bodies, and governments.[24] Membership to W3C is open to all organisations under a number of conditions, including the payment of a membership fee.[25] It was created in 1994 with the aim of developing technical standards that could be used for the long-term development of the World Wide Web (www).[26] Since its creation, it has developed more than fifty technical standards for the Web's infrastructure.[27] In this chapter, I examine the setting of the Platform for Privacy Preferences (P3P) standard developed by the W3C.

Involvement in a standard setting group depends on the need the group is trying to address. Hence, for example, when the need is to protect the use of 'protected' content the rule-making group represents the interests of owners or holders of 'protected' content. One such industry consortium is the 'Secure Digital Music Initiative' (SDMI). SDMI is a consortium of recording companies, technology companies and manufacturers of consumer electronic devices formed in 1998.[28] It was set-up specifically in response to the need felt by the music industry for protection of intellectual property rights that are being 'abused' in the digital context. Similarly, the 'Copy Protection Technical Working Group' (CPTWG) is an informal association of motion picture studios, consumer electronics manufacturers and the computer industry. The aim of CPTWG is to support the creation and development of technical systems to protect content.[29] Individual companies have also assumed the task of developing technical systems to implement intellectual property rights. Microsoft and the software company Adobe[30] are examples of such companies.

Some private groups like the European Electronic Signature Standardization Initiative (EESSI) have particular co-operation with public authorities in the standard setting process. EESSI is made up of industry members but with public au-

---

[23] There were 412 members as of 8 July 2006 accessed at <http://www.w3.org/Consortium/#membership> on 8 July 2006.

[24] The W3C site claims 'These organizations are typically investing significant resources into the web, in developing software products, in developing information products, or most commonly in its use as an enabling medium for their business or activity', accessed at <http://www.w3.org/Consortium/#membership> on 29 September 2004.

[25] There is a distinction in fees to be paid according to whether the organisation is a not-for-profit or a for-profit organisation. There are no differences in privileges between the two membership classes.

[26] See the description of the W3C given by the Center for Democracy & Technology accessed at <http://www.cdt.org/standards/w3c.shtml> on 9 May 2003.

[27] Accessed at <http://www.w3.org/Consortium/> on 29 September 2004.

[28] Besek 2004: 453.

[29] Id. 2004: 457 and 461.

[30] Accessed at <http://www.adobe.com/aboutadobe/main.html> 12 October 2004.

thorities having an important input in the process.[31] The standards are discussed in workshops that are open to all interested parties. Decisions on standards are taken by consensus. Once the EU Commission approved the standards developed by the EESSI, the EESSI Work Group disbanded.[32]

6.2.2 Reasons to set technical standards

Mainly technical standards are set to address particular regulatory (or technical) needs that can be best (and at times only) be satisfied by technical standards. The standards examined in this chapter show that standards are set: (a) to satisfy legislative requirements; (b) to pre-empt possible state legislation; (c) to extend the reach of legislation; (d) to assuage specific interests of the private groups; and (e) to satisfy technical requests.

In response to specific state legislation

One important example here is the setting of standards for digital signatures. The increased use of electronic signatures in electronic transactions led a number of states (including the United States and the European Union) to introduce legislation in which digital signatures were given the legal equivalence to written signatures in contracts. Indeed in 2000-2001, digital signatures legislation was introduced in several jurisdictions. One example is the EU Directive 1999/93/EC of the European Parliament and of the Council of 13 December 1999 on a Community framework for electronic signatures.[33] The US Electronic Signatures in Global and National Commerce Act 2000 is another example. The need for technical standards to meet

---

[31] See EESSI home page at <http://www.ictsb.org/EESSI_introduction.htm> accessed on 2 November 2004.

[32] A Commission Decision (2003/511/EC) officially recognised the standards in July 2003 (*OJ* L175 15 July 2003) EESSI stopped functioning in October 2004. See <http://www.ict.etsi.org/ EESSI_home.htm> accessed 5 October 2005.

[33] *OJ* L13 19 January 2000 p. 12. The drafting of the Directive started in 1997. The Commission, seeing that some Member States were in the process of introducing new legislation on encryption and on electronic signatures and that the different approaches adopted by the Member States could have a negative impact on trade within the Union, presented a Communication to Council and the European Parliament proposing a European framework for digital signatures and encryption. (See Commission Communication to the Council, the European Parliament, the Economic and Social Committee and the Committee of the Regions. Ensuring security and trust in Electronic Communication: Towards a European Framework for Digital Signatures and Encryption (COM(1997)503 final 8 October 1997)). Commission was then instructed by the Council and European Parliament to propose a draft directive 'to take the necessary step to remove obstacle to the use of digital signatures in the legal system, industry and public administration'. (See para. 3 of Parliament's resolution on Commission Communication in the Minutes of 17 July 1998, Part II, p. 14). Commission submitted a proposed draft Directive in May 1998. (See Proposal for a European Parliament and Council directive on a common framework for electronic signatures (COM(1998)0297 (*OJ* C325 23 October 1998 p. 5)). The final text of the Directive was approved in December 1999.

the legal requirements adopted in the EU Electronic Signatures Directive, for example, triggered the development of technical standards for digital signatures.

To pre-empt state legislation

Pre-empting possible legislation on privacy was one of the reasons the lead the W3C to set the P3P standard. The EU Directive 95/46/EC on data protection adopted in 1995 brought to the fore the wide divergence on the treatment of personal data in the United States and the European Union and the ensuing difficulties attending the transfer of personal data from Europe to the United States. The P3P standard was planned to pre-empt possible new US legislation on the protection of data privacy in electronic commerce. It was created as a non-legislative alternative to the requirements posed by the EU directive on US organisations (including some of the W3C members).[34] This was not the first attempt by the W3C to formulate technical standards as a reaction to legislation. Around the same time, W3C had adopted the PICS rating system for web sites.[35] As Cranor notes 'the PICS effort had been launched primarily as a non-legislative alternative to the US Communications Decency Act and other similar legislation.'[36]

To extend the reach of legislation

The primary example here is the creation of the technical protection measures (TPM) to protect intellectual property rights on the Internet. Traditionally, intellectual property legislation has been the major source of 'law' in the regulation of intellectual property rights. Legislation, particularly protecting copyright, exists in almost all states. Intellectual property is not only protected at the national level but also internationally through a number of international treaties.[37] New technical developments converting content into digital form, making possible duplication without loss of quality of the original and the possibility of widespread 'transmission' of that information inexpensively over the Internet, offer a challenge to the 'traditional' systems of applying and implementing intellectual property protection.[38]

From a state and rights-holder perspective, traditional state law alone does not efficiently protect the rights of the rights holders. The application, implementation

---

[34] Cranor 2002a.

[35] The Platform for Internet Content Selection (PICS) was mostly used to rate web pages according to their suitability for children.

[36] Cranor 2002a.

[37] For example the World Intellectual Property Organisation (WIPO) Copyright Treaty which opened for signature on 20 December 1996 and entered into force the depositing of the 30th ratification on 6 March 2000 (<http://www.wipo.int/treaties/ip/copyright/wipo-copyright.pdf> accessed on 11 October 2004) and WIPO Performances and Phonograms Treaty which opened for signature on 20 December 1996 and entered into force on 20 May 2002 (<http://www.wipo.int/treaties/ip/performances/wipo-performances.pdf> accessed on 11 October 2004).

[38] Kerr, Maurushat and Tacit 2002: 1-2.

and enforcement of rights as envisaged by legislation are difficult to maintain on the Internet context. Rights holders allege that the non-application and difficulties of enforcement on the Internet result in alleged loss of revenues for the rights holders.[39] In response to these difficulties, some rights holders in three content areas traditionally covered by copyright legislation – music, motion picture and book publishing – have chosen to develop technical rules[40] that implement and enforce traditional copyright legislation on the Internet. Prompted by the need to extend protection to their works on the Internet industry consortia have worked together to create and develop systems to implement rights given through copyright legislation. There is no agreed technical standard yet, though it is standard practice to include technical protection measures on the release of new content. The different initiatives are still in the process of achieving some agreement.

To address particular interests of the group

A concern for consumer privacy on-line was another reason that triggered the development of the P3P standard. While states have long recognised the need to regulate the collection and use of personal information the choice of regulation has not been uniform. On the one hand, the European approach has been primarily one of direct state legislation balancing the right to information with the right to private life and to the protection of personal data. European legislation has for the past decades delimited the parameters of the collection and use of personal data. On the other hand, the US policy approach to the protection of personal information has been to leave the regulation of the use of personal data to self-regulation.

W3C members recognised the need for the regulation of privacy practices on-line. Contrary to the off-line context where technical measures for the protection of privacy may not be useful, technical standards can offer means of protection in the on-line context. As Cranor[41] records, both the W3C work group and a number of technical and academic experts recognised the possibility that technology could be use to regulate privacy practices on-line.

At the same time, there was increasing concern by public interest groups and governments (including European governments) that the development in technology was increasing the ease with which personal user data could be abused or misused and that the commercial sector should take some responsibility for the uses it was making of personal user information. The inclusion of privacy policies in web sites (by the late nineties) is one indication that the commercial sector were feeling the pressure being put in favour of regulation of the collection and use of personal information.

---

[39] This is claimed in all the cases files by the Recording Industry Association of America (RIAA) in the US and similar organisations worldwide against alleged copyright infringers.

[40] Often referred to as 'technical protection measures'.

[41] Cranor 2002a, 2002b

To satisfy technical requests

The driving motivation for the development of the IPv6 standard is to solve an address space exhaustion problem.[42] The current Internet Protocol address, that is IP version 4, is made up of four bytes of information (totalling 32 bits) expressed as four numbers between 0 and 255 shown separated by periods, for example, 129.125.113.196. Following the IPv4 standard, only a finite number of IPv4 addresses can be allocated.[43] With the growing number of computers participating on the Internet, the exhaustion of the possible numbers was foreseeable. The new protocol, IPv6 was created to satisfy this technical problem.

While the Internet Engineering Task Force (IETF) had known since the creation of IPv4 that IPv4 offers a finite number of address numbers. It was thought, at the time of its creation, that these would be sufficient to cover the needs of the Internet. It was not anticipated that developments in technology would allow such an increase in individual computers connecting to the Internet. The need to deal with the exhaustion of finite numbers became apparent in the early 1990s with the surge of participants on the Internet. Recognising the need, there were only two plausible choices: (a) to keep to the current IPv4 finite number of addresses and limit the participation on the Internet only to the current assignment of numbers;[44] (b) to create a standard that allows unlimited numbers of machines on the Internet. The Internet community choose in favour of the latter position. To satisfy this choice, the standard to be developed needed to be one that would

(a) carry on the role of IP address – that is a system that allowed the source and destination computers to be identified or identifiable so that data could be sent from one machine to the other over the Internet;
(b) satisfy all future demand for address numbers.

6.2.3   What is regulated by technical standards?

The technical standards under examination in this Chapter are created and used to regulate: (a) privacy issues on the Internet; (b) access to and identification on the Internet; (c) authentication and integrity in digital signatures; and (d) on-line intellectual property issues.

Privacy issues

The P3P technical standard allows users to decide whether to allow web sites to collect personal information about them or not. Simply described, the technical

---

[42] Klensin 2002: 3.

[43] Each of the four numbers can be any number between zero and 255. Therefore, there are 4,294,967,296 possible IP addresses (256*256*256*256).

[44] See RFC1752 at para. 2 accessed at <http://www.ietf.org/rfc/rfc1752.txt?number=1752> on 23 August 2004.

standard defines a way web sites can technically use personal information to match the preferences of the user whose personal information is obtained while the user is visiting and using services on the site. This includes a way a user's computer can communicate with the web site and check whether the uses of the personal information of the site coincide with the preferences of the user.

The P3P technical specifications include three important standards:

(a) a 'standard' vocabulary for describing a web site's data practices – that is, a list of data practices that sites can refer to in privacy policy. A site's privacy policy is encoded in a machine-readable XML format using the P3P standard vocabulary.[45] 'The vocabulary creates a comprehensive, standardized, machine-readable language to describe both personal data and data-handling practices.'[46]

(b) a technical protocol for requesting and transmitting web site privacy policies to users' machines. Technically, the P3P protocol is a simple extension to the HTTP protocol used for fetching web pages. [47]

(c) a technical standard for a 'user agent' – that is, the code that will be used by the user's machine to access the web site's privacy policy and check whether the site's uses match the user's privacy preferences. As Cranor[48] explains

> 'P3P user agents use standard HTTP requests to fetch a P3P policy reference file from a well-known location on the web site to which a user is making a request. The policy reference file indicates the location of the P3P policy file that applies to each part of the web site. There might be one policy for the entire site, or several different policies that each covers a different part of the site. The user agent can then fetch the appropriate policy, parse it, and take action according to the user's preferences.'

The initial idea (in 1996-1997) was to develop a rating system for privacy together with a tool allowing the users to negotiate with web sites over information practices.[49] A 'vocabulary sub-committee' was set-up to develop a draft privacy vocabulary that web sites could use to describe their privacy practices. In the meantime, the P3P work group focused on the development of 'negotiating agreements' about web site privacy practices. Between 1998-2000, the work groups worked with invited experts from the academic and governmental sectors and from data protection authorities on the development of the standard.[50] The initial idea was modified a number of times.

---

[45] Cranor 2002a [From a European perspective the use of the term 'identified data' instead of 'personally identifiable data' limits the scope of P3P as a complimentary system of regulation to EU Data Protection Directive as the term does not cover all the nuances linked to the phrase 'personally identifiable data' in the Directive.]

[46] McGeveran 2001.

[47] Cranor 2002a.

[48] Ibid.

[49] Ibid.

[50] Ibid.

The P3P vocabulary list for the web sites privacy policies too was elaborated upon many times. The European Union[51] and a number of European Data Protection authorities contributed significantly to the process to ensure that the vocabulary list would, as far as possible, be in line with the long established definitions found in the European Data Protection Directive and European data protection legislation.

During the process of developing the technical standard, public working drafts were issued every few months. The public, W3C members and governments submitted their responses to the working drafts. Meetings with data protection authorities were also held periodically.[52] Software developers, some companies and technical experts built prototypes of the user agents and vocabulary editors based on the draft standards and raised a number of concerns. In 2001 and 2002, Microsoft and AT&T each released a 'user agent' and IBM released a privacy policy editor tool based on the P3P standard. The working group took some of the responses and suggestions on board in the further development of the standard.

In 2002, the P3P specification work group issued a 'Proposed Recommendation' draft of the P3P technical standard. The P3P 1.0 technical standard developed by W3C work groups was published as a 'Recommendation' on 16 April 2002. W3C Members and other interested parties reviewed the 'Recommendation' and the W3C Director (in accordance with the accepted procedure within W3C)[53] endorsed it. A 'recommendation' is considered a final and 'stable document and may be used as reference material or cited as a normative reference from another document.'[54]

The effectiveness of the P3P standard is dependent on whether software developers and web site owners use the P3P 1.0 standard to reflect the data practices of the site. Adoption of the standard by web sites is crucial: without the machine readable format of the privacy standard the 'user agent' would be unable to check the site's conformity with the user's preferences. In recent researches,[55] it has been shown that P3P adoption is increasing over time and that adoption is highest for the most popular web sites.[56]

The effectiveness of the P3P standard also depends on the development of user agents based on the P3P1.0 standard. Currently, Microsoft's Internet Explorer 6

---

[51] Art. 29 (EU Data Protection Working Party) (1998) Opinion 1/98 Platform for Privacy Preferences (P3P) and the Open profiling standard Adopted by the Working Party 16 June 1998 (Doc. Ref. XV D5032/98 WP11).

[52] For example, in 1999 the working group established under Art. 29 of the EU Data Protection Directive (95/46/EC) met with representatives from the P3P working groups. See Cranor 2002a.

[53] See para. 5.2.5 of W3C Process Document dated 19 July 2001 (Paragraph 5 outlines the stages and procedure to be followed by W3C and its working groups in the development of a technical standard. Paragraph 5.2.5 refers to the final stage of the process-the approval of a technical standard to be considered as a recommendation) accessed at <http://www.w3.org/Consortium/Process-20010719/> on 30 September 2004.

[54] See <http://www.w3.org/TR/P3P/> accessed on 30 September 2004.

[55] Such as Cranor, Byers and Kormann 2003.

[56] Cranor, Byers and Kormann 2003: 2.

(IE6) browser and Netscape's Navigator 7 include a 'user agent'. The IE6 'user agent' is restricted to following the user's instructions in the context of cookies. The user is allowed to decide whether to block or restrict cookies by web sites. Using the browser's general privacy settings, the user chooses one of six possible privacy levels. The lowest level is 'Accept all cookies', and the highest is 'Block all cookies'. The levels in between restrict data collection to various degrees depending on whether a site has a P3P policy, whether third parties are collecting data while the user is at that site, and whether the use of information is without the user's implied or express consent. 'Medium', which is the default setting for IE6, restricts first-party cookies that collect personally identifiable information without the user's explicit consent and restricts certain cookies from third parties.[57]

The lesser-known AT&T Privacy Bird gives the user more options. The user can determine which categories of personal information (health and medical information; financial and purchase information; personally 'identified' information and non-personally identified information) he/she will allow the web site to collect.[58]

Finally, the effectiveness of the P3P standards also depends on users to 'instruct' the user agent to carry out the user's choices on the use of his/her personal data. Ultimately, the P3P technical standard is a 'user empowerment' tool, empowering the user to make appropriate decisions on the use of his/her own personal information by web sites that he/she may access. The IE6 'user agent' is set at default setting automatically until the user proceeds to change the settings. Unless the user is aware of the possibility of changing the settings, the effective protection is arguably of only 'medium' value.

The adoption of the technical standard by web site owners, 'user agent' developers and users is voluntary. There is no mechanism to check whether the standard has been adopted as specified in the P3P 1.0 technical specifications. If, for example, the web site machine readable privacy policy does not fully comply with the P3P standard there is no mechanism that ensures that it be brought into compliance. Since the adoption of the recommendation of the P3P 1.0 specification the Working Group are amending parts of the technical standard in part to address some of the concerns raised in the criticism of the P3P 1.0 standard. The modifications are still under review. The latest Working draft was published in July 2005.[59]

Access to and identification on the Internet

One way of regulating access to the Internet is by setting a standard that machines wanting to access the Internet must follow. Any machines not following the standard are automatically unable to access the Internet. The Internet Protocol version 6

---

[57] Goldberg 2003.

[58] Cranor, Guduru and Arjula 2004: 10-11.

[59] P3P 1.1 Specification W3C Working draft dated 1 July 2005 at point 1 accessed at <http://www. w3.org/TR/P3P11/> on 5 October 2005.

(IPv6) standard, though essentially created to meet a technical demand for unique addresses, has this regulatory effect. The IPv6 is a set of technical specifications on how each machine can be assigned a unique address.[60]

The IPv6 standard specification includes specifications for the standardisation of Internet addresses and standardisation of IPv6 protocols (that is, the technical means that determine how data packets are to be moved between machines). The IPv6 specification describes three types of Internet addressing.[61] Each type of IPv6 addressing is made up of two specifications:

(a) One defines the (numerical) address. Each IPv6 address is made up of 128-bit identifiers. There are three conventional forms for representing an IPv6 address as text strings. The most popular (and preferred way) is x:x:x:x:x:x:x:x, where 'x' is the hexadecimal value of the eight 16-bit pieces of the address.[62]

(b) The other defines the header of the address. A header describes the contents of the data packet to be transmitted. An IPv6 header has six information fields together with the source and destination address.[63]

Allowing access and increasing possibilities of access to the Internet has an effect on activities (and regulation) at the content level. The indirect effect is that participation in Internet activities is open to a larger community of users than would have been the case it the IP standard chosen had been one restricting access to existing numbers and machines. Due to IPv4 number allocation restrictions users of some continents had less access than others. The wider distribution of numbers under IPv6 will necessarily imply more users from previously less represented users. This will have an effect on content.[64]

• Identification
The IPv6 standard specifies how sending and receiving machines are identified and are able to identify each other. Any machine having another technical set-up is unable to receive or send data packets on the network. This element of identification, while a technical *sine qua non*, is also influenced by the need to be able to

---

[60] Packets of data are moved around on the network by means of an Internet Protocol. The Internet Protocol specifies the technical standards needed to be followed in the encoding of IP addresses and the routing of the data packets on the network. Solum and Minn Chung 2004: 840.

[61] (a) Unicast – that is, addressing needs for communication between one host to one other host; (b) anycast – that is, addressing needs for communication between one host to the nearest multiple hosts; and (c) multicast – that is addressing needs for communication between one host to multiple hosts. See RFC 3513 accessed at <http://www.ietf.org/rfc/rfc3513.txt?number=3513> on 1 October 2004.

[62] For example, FEDC:BA98:7654:3210:FEDC:BA98:7654:3210 For a more complete description see RFC 3513 at para. 2.2; and Morton 1997.

[63] For a more complete description see RFC 2460 at para. 3 accessed at <http://www.ietf.org/rfc/rfc2460.txt?number=2460> on 1 October 2004.

[64] Solum and Minn Chung (2004) refer briefly to this in footnote 208.

regulate content. Regulators of content need a practical means to be able to block the distribution of the unwanted or illegal content. The offending site or content is identified through the IP address of the host machine.[65] Data coming from that IP address can be blocked.

Identification can also have an effect on the users' right to privacy. For example, in one type of IPv6 addresses[66] the standard provided that a part of the IP address would be linked to the unique Medium Access Control (MAC) address embed in the computer's Ethernet network card. MAC addresses are a part of a computer's hardware and are not easily interchangeable.[67] The effect of these addresses can mean that the activities of the particular machine can be traced at all times through the unique MAC address part of the IPv6 address. This is an important difference from other IP addressing schemes (including the IPv4) where the numeric address is not necessarily tied to a specific machine or user. The privacy implications prompted both the European Union[68] and a number of privacy organisations to draw the attention of the IETF IPv6 work group. The issue was partially resolved by the publication of an optional addressing scheme – RFC3041 Privacy Extensions for Stateless Address Autoconfiguration.[69] This part of the standard is dependent on the take-up by host operating systems.

The process followed by IETF in creating and developing a technical standard involves two stages: a technical specification is suggested, developed and reviewed several times by the Internet community. It is then adopted and published as a standard in the 'Requests for Comment' (RFC) series. Agreement on a technical standard is based on a concept of 'rough consensus,' that is, 'a very large majority of those who care must agree'.[70]

The technical requirements of the new IP were arrived at by a call for white papers with suggested specifications to meet the new needs.[71] There were twenty-one responses from different Internet communities (industry, academic, military, and so forth). By 1992, a number of proposals were being discussed. By end 1994, the IETF community agreed on the base requirements of the new IP protocol and an agreement was reached on the specifications to be developed.

---

[65] Solum and Minn Chung 2004.

[66] Addresses generated by stateless address auto configuration.

[67] See Davidson, Morris and Courtney 2002: 3.

[68] See Art. 29 (EU Data Protection Working Party) (2002) Opinion 2/2002 on the use of unique identifiers in telecommunication terminal equipments: the example of IPv6 adopted on 30 May 2002. Doc. Ref 10750/02/EN/Final; and Ecija Abogados 2003.

[69] See RFC 3041 accessed at <ftp://ftp.rfc-editor.org/in-notes/rfc3041.txt> on 7 October 2004.

[70] In practice, this may mean that achieving this consensus takes a considerable amount of time. This length of time is generally balanced against the idea that the standards once accepted by a wide consensus are more widely acceptable. See description of the IETF given by the Center for Democracy & Technology accessed at <http://www.cdt.org/standards/ietf.shtml> on 9 May 2003. The process is defined in Requests for Comment 2026 accessed at <http://www.ietf.org/rfc/rfc2026.txt?number=2026> on 23 August 2004.

[71] See RFC1752 at para. 6 accessed at <http://www.ietf.org/rfc/rfc1752.txt?number=1752> on 23 August 2004.

In December 1995, two Proposed Standards (i) RFC1883 – Internet Protocol Version 6 (IPv6) Specification;[72] and (ii) RFC 1884 – IP version 6 Addressing Architecture[73] were agreed upon and published. From 1995 to 1998, the proposed standard was publicly discussed, modified and changed to correct the problems and difficulties posed by the proposed standard. In 1998, the modified set of IPv6 protocol specification were agreed and published as a 'Draft Standard' (RFC2460 – Internet Protocol Version 6 (IPv6) Specification).[74] A 'Draft Standard', according to IETF practices,[75] 'is normally considered to be a final specification, and changes are likely to be made only to solve specific problems encountered.' This rendered obsolete the earlier RFC1883. The IPv6 Addressing Architecture specifications were modified and re-published as 'Proposed Standards' in 1998 (RFC2373)[76] and later in 2003 (RFC3513).[77]

IPv6 implementations are being developed for many different host operating systems and routers. A number of states (for example, in the United States,[78] in the European Union[79] and in different countries in Asia) have set-up IPv6 implementation task forces to help with the widespread deployment of the IPv6. Once adopted the IPv6 standard is 'auto-enforcing' in that unless all the requirements of the standard are followed the machine cannot be accessed by or access other machines on the network.[80]

Authentication and integrity of Internet transactions

Some transactions on-line, either because of their nature or because of the content that is being sent in the transaction, need to be carried out in a 'secure' way. Technical measures to ensure security of transactions have been developed since the early years of the Internet. Cryptographic technologies have long been developed and used to provide secure transactions in open networks.

Encryption of content, while important to ensure the confidential nature of the content, does not address issues of 'authentication' (verification of the origin of

[72] RFC 1883 accessed at <http://www.ietf.org/rfc/rfc1883.txt?number=1883> on 1 October 2004.
[73] RFC 1884 accessed at <http://www.ietf.org/rfc/rfc1884.txt?number=1884> on 1 October 2004.
[74] RFC 2460 accessed at <http://www.ietf.org/rfc/rfc2460.txt?number=2460> on 1 October 2004.
[75] RFC 2026 – The Internet Standards Process – Revision 3 (Version October 1996) at para. 4, accessed at <http://www.ietf.org/rfc/rfc2026.txt> on 23 August 2004.
[76] RFC 2373 accessed at <http://www.ietf.org/rfc/rfc2373.txt?number=2373> on 1 October 2004.
[77] RFC 3513 accessed at <http://www.ietf.org/rfc/rfc3513.txt?number=3513> on 1 October 2004.
[78] <http://www.nav6tf.org>.
[79] <http://www.euro6ix.org>.
[80] Furthermore, there is a certain inevitability tied to the adoption of the IPv6 standard: sooner rather than later, as the numbers problem becomes more acute the adoption and transition to the IPv6 standard is inevitable. This can already be seen in Asia: Asia had initially been allocated less than 20% of the global address space under IPv4, for most of the Asia population to gain access to the Internet (and hence the economic growth linked to such expansion) most Asian countries (predominantly, Japan, China and India) have adopted the IPv6 standard. See Hagen 2004.

data) and 'integrity' (verification of whether data has been altered in the transmission) of the data. Electronic 'signatures' were developed (by technical developers) to address and regulate 'authentication'[81] and 'integrity' of data issues in transactions.

Electronic signatures are technical systems of authentication or verification. Several methods exist to sign documents electronically varying from simple methods (e.g., inserting a scanned image of a hand-written signature in a word processing document) to very advanced methods (e.g., using cryptography).[82] Most of the simple methods do not satisfactorily address the issues of authentication and integrity of the transaction.[83] 'Digital signatures are a special class of electronic signatures that use public key cryptography[84] to give electronic signatories a unique digital identification.'[85] In its simplest form, a digital signature consists of two parts: (a) a method of encoding information that can identify the user, content or transaction; and (b) a method of verifying the authenticity of the encoded information.

Verification of the authenticity and the integrity of the data do not necessarily, however, prove the identity of the originator of the signature.[86] In response to the need to prove the identity of the originator of the signature, 'certification authorities' were developed. 'Certification authorities' are usually private third parties using technical measures to check and certify the origin of a message. A 'certification

---

[81] 'Electronic authentication can be understood to encompass any method of verifying some piece of information in an electronic environment, whether it the identity of the author of a text or sender of a message, the authority of a person to enter into a particular kind of transaction, the security attributes of a hardware or software device, or any one of countless other pieces of information that someone may want to be able to confirm in the electronic world.' OECD Doc.DSTI/ICCP/REG/CP(2000)1 – updated 7 December 2000.

[82] Communication from the Commission 'Ensuring security and trust in electronic communication: Towards a European Framework for Digital Signatures and Encryption' (COM(1997)503 final 8 October 1997) at p. 3.

[83] Digital Signatures are not the only available form of secure electronic signature but arguable it is the most popular and the most successful as a technical method.

[84] Public key encryption (PKE) is based on asymmetric cryptography. Basically, 'PKE technology manipulates data into numerical digests and vice-versa, with algorithms as the key mechanisms used to manipulate the data. "Schemes" are particular algorithms, or series of algorithms, used to manipulate data in digital signature technology. One of the most common schemes currently used in PKE is the RSA scheme. The basic operation behind this scheme is the use of a "key" as an exponent that is applied mathematically to the number representing the message. The message in its initial or numerical, state is called "plaintext". The number resulting from the enciphering process is called the "ciphertext". In the RSA scheme, the ciphertext is a number that is mathematically manipulated with some other random number by an algorithm; this "other" number is also needed as part of the key. Together, the two numbers form the private key. The other number formed as a result of the applied algorithm is a part of the public key and is used to decipher the ciphertext and to recreate the original plaintext message.' Lupton 1999: 10.

[85] Barofsky 2000: 150.

[86] Communication from the Commission 'Ensuring security and trust in electronic communication: Towards a European Framework for Digital Signatures and Encryption' (COM(1997)503 final 8 October 1997) at p. 3.

authority' authenticates the relationship between a particular public key and the creator of the key.[87]

Creating technical standards for digital signatures ensures that machines can recognise the signatures being sent and enables a recipient to be able to validate or authenticate the information in the transaction. With the increase of commercial transactions, the use of technical measures to verify authenticity has increased considerably. While on a technical (and practical) level these technical measures are considered to be 'signatures' – that is, systems that served as a method of authentication – from a legal perspective, unless specific legislation is introduced confirming their legal validity, traditionally only written signatures are considered legal signatures for contracts.

Two groups, the European Telecommunications Standards Institute (ETSI ESI) and the European Committee for Standardisation (CEN), are responsible to develop the technical standards at a European level. The ETSI ESI looks at interoperability issues at the communication and transaction levels of electronic signatures. CEN focuses on the development of quality and functional standards for signature creation and verification products, as well as quality and functional standards for Certification Providers. Both groups are accredited with the European Commission.[88] While developing the digital signatures standards compliant with the EU Directive (1999/93/EC), ETSI ESI created an electronic open discussion area, providing public access to the draft documents, background material, and supporting the exchange of ideas, comments and contributions for the development of the standards. Once the standards where agreed upon by ETSI ESI, a Commission Decision (2003/511/EC) officially recognised the standards.[89] EESSI stopped functioning in October 2004.[90]

Intellectual property rights on the Internet

In many cases, the favoured solution for the problem of intellectual property infringements on the Internet is called 'digital rights management' (DRM) – what a DRM approach implies is a system to manage/regulate intellectual property rights in a digital context. Often this involves: (a) technical measures to protect and enforce existing rights; and (b) some form of written licensing agreement.[91] Some technical protection measures (TPM) developed by industry to regulate intellectual property are described here.[92] Kerr, et al., define technical protection measures as

---

[87] Lupton 1999: 15.

[88] See EESSI home page at <http://www.ictsb.org/EESSI_introduction.htm> accessed on 2 November 2004.

[89] Cf., *OJ* L175 15 July 2003.

[90] See <http://www.ict.etsi.org/EESSI_home.htm> accessed 5 October 2005.

[91] Hugenholtz 2000 has defined DRM as a contract, typically a licensing agreement, coupled with technology, typically a TPM such as encryption.

[92] In theory, one can also have a DRM solution without a TPM. However the effectiveness of such a solution is rather limited as it would be difficult to implement the DRM solution in a technical space without using technical measures to do so and relying solely on the written agreement.

'a technological method intended to promote the authorized use of digital works. This is accomplished by controlling access to such works or various uses of such works, including: i) copying; ii) distribution, iii) performance, and iv) display. TPMs can operate as safeguards or "virtual fences" around digitized content, whether or not the content enjoys copyright protection.'[93]

Essentially, a TPM gives a content owner a tool to control (at least in part) access and subsequent uses of the content. TPMs can be classified by their function:[94]

(a) to control access to the content – TPMs can be used to prevent users from viewing, reading or hearing the content without authorisation. They can also be used to limit the number of times a user can access the content.

(b) to control the use of the content – TPMs can be used to limit the extent the content can be copied, printed, viewed, heard, shared or distributed.

(c) to protect the integrity and authenticity of information – TPMs can be used to establish the authenticity and integrity of the content.

(d) to track the use of the content – TPMs can be used to track the use made of the content by the user. Based on this information, enforcement action may be taken against unauthorised uses of the content.

In practice, TPMs often do a combination of the above activities, for example, they control both access to and subsequent use of the content. The two most common methods to control access to content are: (i) passwords and (ii) cryptography. Encryption involves two steps: the coding of plain text is converted into an unreadable form and then, using a key to the encryption, the unreadable form is converted (back) to a readable format. Access to the 'key' that allows the decryption of the encrypted text is of course essential for access to the protected content. There are different technical ways to allow access to the key – symmetric and asymmetric encryption.

Various schemes that have been developed to link encrypted files to software and hardware devices so that an encrypted message can only be decrypted using that particular software and hardware arrangement. Rischer[95] lists and describes some of these methods, for example: sealed content; device binding; trusted player; trust-enable player, trusted device (closed environment), trusted device (detection), on-line access controls, multiple-key high security. Some of these methods not only control access to the content but also the subsequent use of the content – for example in 'device binding' content can be accessed on a specific device and will be inaccessible using a different device.

Watermarking or digital marking is the most commonly used technological device to track the use of the content. A watermark is, basically, a set of digital identi-

---

[93] Kerr, et al. 2002: 2.

[94] As was done in the US Digital Millennium Copyright Act see Besek 2004: 449.

[95] Rischer 2000.

fiers built into a digital content and designed in such a way as to remain with the content. By tracking the watermark the contents owner can trace the use of the content and can trace any unauthorised uses. Watermarking does not prevent the unauthorised use of the content but can be used in the enforcement and administration of rights in the watermarked content.[96]

Examples of TPM systems

• Secure Digital Music Initiative (SDMI)
In view of the increase and ease of creating unauthorised digital copies of right-protected music, the main aim of SDMI was to develop a secure system to deliver music in a digital form. The system proposed consisted of a watermark specification to mark content and the development of (hardware) systems able to play music having the authorised watermark. SDMI at a consortium level formulated the policy while the software developers and engineers converted the policy decisions into code – into a working technical system.

The SDMI model suffered two major set-backs: i) the code used for the watermark specification was 'cracked' after an open call to test the specification; ii) only few devices were developed to read the watermark and hence little SDMI compliant music was sold. SDMI has since been dormant.[97]

• Content Scramble System (CSS)
Similarly to the music industry, the motion picture industry "was reluctant to release movies in digital form on digital versatile discs (DVDs) without a technological mechanism to protect against unauthorized copying and distribution."[98] Under the aegis of the Copy Protection Technical Working Group (CPTWG),[99] Matsushita Electric Industrial Co. Ltd. and Toshiba Corp. developed the 'content scramble system' (CSS). CSS is a system of encryption that can only be read by DVD players and DVD-ROM drives licensed to decrypt the CSS.[100] The encryption code for CSS too was 'cracked' and the previously encrypted content can be accessed, viewed and copied by using DeCSS technology. Several lawsuits have been brought in the US under the Digital Millennium Copyright Act of 1998 (DMCA) questioning the legality of offering circumvention tools to circumvent copyrighted content protected by anti-circumvention technology.

---

[96] Besek 2004: 451.

[97] Id. 2004: 453-454.

[98] Id. 2004: 457.

[99] The Copy Protection Technical Working Group (CPTWG) is an informal association of motion picture studios, consumer electronics manufacturers and the computer industry. The CPTWG does not develop technological specifications itself. Its aim is to study and evaluate content protection technologies and to encourage the development of a number of protection technologies (see Besek 2004: 457 and 461).

[100] Kerr, Maurushat and Tacit 2002: 9-10.

Although the (US) Court upheld those provisions and granted eight film studios a permanent injunction prohibiting two defendants from posting DeCSS on their web site and linking to other sites containing DeCSS, this circumvention device continues to be widely available on the internet.[101] Notwithstanding the availability of a means to circumvent the CSS code, CSS is still used by the motion picture industry.

- Adobe Acrobat eBook Reader

Similar to the preoccupations of the music and movie industry, book publishers too have also sought to develop technical measures to protect the content of books in a digital form. One of these technical measures is the Adobe Acrobat eBook Reader ('Adobe Reader'). The Adobe Reader is a software program that users can use (on any hardware) to read content published on-line. Through the Adobe Reader the publisher can place a variety of restrictions on the use that can be made of the content being read, for example copying and printing restrictions.[102] Currently, the Adobe Reader is used by a number of publishers and content distributors who publish content in a format that: (i) can be read by means of the Adobe Reader; and (ii) the Adobe Reader can 'execute' the intellectual property protection rules of the publisher that apply to the specific content.

6.2.4   What do these technical standards achieve?

Technical standards can serve three main functions in the regulation of Internet activities. Primarily, they are an important source of (technical and legal) rules. The rules developed through a process of self-regulation address particular needs for regulation that are otherwise unaccounted for. In the P3P case, the standards provide an important way for users to choose how their personal data is used, hence choosing how much of their personal preferences to disclose to web site owners – a right which is, in practice, not offered through other rule systems. In the IPv6 case, the standards provide important rules that simultaneously co-ordinate communication between machines and determine rights of access and identification for users. In the digital signatures case, the standards provide a means of authentication for digital contents having the same legal effect as handwritten signatures on text documents.

Secondly, technical standards provide a way to implement rules of private groups and states. The electronic signatures example and the creation of technical protection measures in the protection of intellectual property rights both show how self-regulation implements rules coming from state regulation (be it the EU Directive on Digital Signatures or copyright protection legislation). To an important extent,

---

[101] Id. 2002: 10.
[102] Besek 2004: 459.

the P3P example is also an example of self-regulation using technical means to implement rules – in this case, legislation on data protection practices.

Thirdly, technical standards provide rules that apply across territorial borders to regulate activities that states are unable or reluctant to reach. This is an important function especially since Internet activities may take place across national/territorial boundaries. In the IPv6 example, machines irrespective of their geographical location need to communicate with each other; in the P3P example, the standards offer a means to determine the level of data protection irrespective of geographical location or state boundaries. Similarly, in the electronic signatures example, the rules provide a solution that can be used by persons in different states. In addition, technical protection measures limit the use of legally protected content irrespective of any territorial connection with state legislation protecting the content. Technical standards offer customised regulatory solutions that can then be applied in a 'global' context. None of the standards – P3P, IPv6, standards for digital signatures and technical protection measures – have solely a territorial or regional application. They can, and in fact are, applied globally.

6.2.5 Technical standards as rules

Legitimacy of the groups and technical standards

Are technical standards legitimate tools of self-regulation? The groups and the Internet user community follow and adopt these technical standards to varying degrees. The technical expertise and knowledge of the members of the groups developing the technical standards give credibility to the usefulness and reliability of the technical standard. The fact that the technical expertise and knowledge of the IETF members is unrivalled by any other group adds credibility to the IPv6 standard. Similarly, the technical expertise and knowledge of the W3C members reassure the user that the P3P standard is technically (and legally) sound.

The participation and recognition of states and governmental authorities in the standard-making process confirms the legitimacy of the group formulating the technical standard and the technical standard itself. In some instances, the participation of states is limited to an advisory role, such as in the P3P example, where data protection authorities of different states submitted advice on the draft standards. Similarly, in the development of the IPv6 standard, public authorities (as well as private groups) drew attention to the potential privacy risks for users using the IPv6 standard. The advice and participation of states legitimises the rule-making power of the groups.

In the case of the setting of technical standards for digital signatures and in the setting of technical protection measures, the legitimising process by states of the private groups is even more evident. In the case of technical standards for digital signatures, state regulation, such as the EU legislation, provides for a formal accreditation system for the group and the standards developed by the group. The

EU's recognition supplements the claim of EESSI's legitimacy to formulate technical (and legal) standards for digital signatures.

By allowing, supporting and protecting the creation of technical protection measures (TPMs) in intellectual property legislation, states legitimise the participation of private groups (such as SDMI) in the regulation of intellectual property rights through the creation and use of TPMs. This is strengthened further by state legislation specifically protecting technical protection measures.

The fact that most groups can implement the technical standard irrespective of whether members and users agree with the standard can cast doubt of the legitimacy of the group and the technical standard. Yet, as the P3P case illustrates, having technical ability to implement does not necessarily bind users to take up the standard. While W3C members can implement the P3P standards, the actual rate of adoption of the standard is still low.[103]

The direct interest of the members of the groups achieved by following the standard created adds to the acceptability of the technical standards developed.

Accountability of the group

Some of the groups, predominantly IETF and W3C,[104] have internal mechanisms to hold the group to account. They both have a hierarchical decision-making structure within the group. The different parts of the group keep each other in check. For example, the work of the different IETF working groups is reviewed and approved by the Internet Engineering Steering Group (IESG). The IESG determines whether a specification submitted to it satisfies the applicable criteria and maturity to be approved as a technical standard.[105] The IETF working groups are held in check through member voting on the workings of the group. Sometimes the acceptance of a standard is delayed until a rough consensus is reached. This often involves the introduction of modifications to the technical standards to satisfy the demands of the larger consensus.

---

[103] However, one may argue that in fact the problems of take-up and adoption of a rule is common to the adoption of any rule issued by any rule enacting body (including the state) and is not a problem particular to the adoption of P3P qua technical standard or its legitimacy. Adoption of 'laws' is often dependent on 'external' circumstances to have an indirect bearing on the take-up of the 'law' – for example, the possibility of loss of commercial reputation if organisation is seen not to adopt the 'law'.

[104] The W3C has a clearly defined hierarchical decision-making structure that can provide some internal accountability. The W3C Advisory Committee, which is made up of one representative from each W3C member, takes the final decisions on the adoption of the technical standard. The representation of each member on the Advisory Group secures that different values and interests are represented in the final decision taken. The multiple working groups within W3C provide the actual formulation and implementation of the technical standard. The work of the working groups is submitted to the scrutiny of the W3C Advisory Committee and the W3C Director. The scrutiny of the Advisory Committee and Director acts as check on the action of the multiple working groups and ensures that the technical standards address the needs of W3C as a group.

[105] See Art. 6 of IETF RFC 2026 The Internet Standards Process – Revision 3 accessed at <http://www.ietf.org/rfc/rfc2026.txt> on 23 August 2004.

There is also another internal measure of accountability – accountability exercised through financial support or withdrawal of support. As Wapner points out 'members also vote with their pocket-books'.[106] A member's financial support to W3C, for example, is a form of accountability – unless the group follows the agreed direction in the creation and development of the standard, the members can withdraw financial support.

Furthermore, members are often actively engaged in the standard forming process. This is indicative that the members perceive that the group is/can be successful in achieving its aims and satisfy the needs of the members. The direct participation of the members keeps the whole group in check.

To some extent, even commercial groupings, such as the SDMI, are subject to internal scrutiny. The development team, for example, is often answerable to a Board of Directors or specific Directors of the commercial enterprises involved in the grouping. Whether through voting rights or through the payment of membership fees, the groups are accountable to their members and to their hierarchical structures of authority.

In part, the private groups are and can be held in check and accountable by the state and by civil society. The state can use, for example, antitrust legislation and other relevant legislation, such as copyright legislation in the case of technical protection measures and fundamental rights legislation such as data protection in the P3P example, to influence self-regulatory measures. In particular, data protection authorities have examined the compatibility of the standards being set with state legislation and have given advice on changes to be made to ensure compatibility. In many instances, W3C has followed and implemented the advice suggested by the public authorities. Public authorities hence act as external 'overseers' of the action of the private groups.

In the digital signatures example, the EU holds the private groups to account in two different ways – by requiring the accreditation of the group[107] and by requiring that the standards be submitted to the EU Commission for acknowledgment of their legal status.

Both IETF and W3C have revised technical standards when public interest groups or public authorities[108] pointed to the potential damaging effects of the technical standards on the rights of other users. Public interest groups, for example, drew attention to the potential privacy violations produced by the IPv6 specifications. IETF reacted by producing an additional specification that could limit the potential privacy violations.

Another potential tool of accountability comes from technical experts who are in a position to limit the use and efficiency of TPMs.

---

[106] Wapner 2002: 201.

[107] The EU could have held EESSI in check by threatening to withdraw accreditation.

[108] For example: data protection authorities in the development of the P3P standard and public interest groups on privacy in the development of the IPv6 standard.

Legal effect of the rule-making process

Apart from their obvious technical effects, technical standards have important legal implications. For example, the IPv6 standards can be used to determine who is allowed Internet access and allows the person to be identified when on the Internet.

While the setting of technical standards consists largely of discussions about technical details, this does not detract from the legal nature of the process of setting standards. Whenever the technical standards have a regulatory effect the standard-setting process is also a rule-making process. This process is stable and clearly defined. A standard-setting organisation, like a state, identifies the need to regulate an Internet activity (or aspects of it), assesses the relative importance of the need, establishes a policy to address the need and formulates the policy into a workable rule (in this case a technical standard) through the use of (technical) experts. The formulation by the experts is reviewed by the group and implemented into a (technical) rule. The adoption of the (technical) rule is then dependent on the different 'subjects' of the rule and may (like some state legislation) remain 'not-adopted' (or inoperative).

Five steps in the rule-making process can be identified:

(i) *Recognition of need*: In the examples examined, the self-regulation process is prompted by actual needs for regulation of specific Internet activities. For example, the need for the protection of personal privacy in on-line transactions prompted the development of the P3P standards. The (then) limited possibilities of technical access to the Internet motivated the development of the IPv6 standard. The need for means to ensure authenticity and verification in 'sensitive' transactions on-line is the basis for the development of technical standards for digital signatures. The need to extend protection to 'protected' content on-line explains the creation of technical protection measures.

(ii) *Valuation of need*: Rule-making is costly, so the private groups only take action to address particular needs that they regard as particularly important. The expertise and knowledge of the private groups in the area enabled them to acknowledge and determine the importance of the need. The value given to the need may be influenced by the specific circumstances of the group. For example, in the P3P case the importance to take action was influenced by the perceived 'threat' of state legislation, which might have had more onerous consequences for the private groups. In the IPv6 situation, the value of the need was primarily at a technical Internet architecture level. The value in the technical protection measures example is motivated by the alleged financial losses of the content-holders. The groups recognise further that it would be better to address the need themselves and in a collective manner.

(iii) *Formulation of the rule*: In this stage, the groups agree on the regulative direction to be followed to address the need. They agree further that technical standards would be used to achieve the regulative direction agreed upon. For example, in the P3P case, the 'privacy' vocabulary list later to work as the 'backbone' for the technical standard, was developed at this stage. In the technical protection measures scenario, on the other hand, the groups agreed to use current national and international copyright legislation as the rule upon which to base the technical measures.

(iv) *Technical implementation of the rule*: In a process of technical and expert discussions and negotiations, the requirements are formalised into a 'technical standard'. This stage in the process is similar to the state-led process in as much as the process of formalisation is often a process marked with negotiated, consensus building, drafting and re-drafting.[109]

(v) *Adoption and enforcement of the rule*: Similar to state-led processes the implemented technical standards need to come into effect. For example, in the P3P case, the Advisory Committee and the W3C Director approved the technical standards before final publication. There are two differences from state-led processes however:

(a) Unless the technical standards are used by the group and by the addressees of the standard, they are not considered to be binding. For example, the solution offered by the P3P standard only takes effect when it is actually used by websites and 'user agents' developers. It is also depends on users consciously changing the default 'user agent' settings.

(b) Once adopted technical standards often have a 'self-enforcing' character that does not require further enforcement or supervision by the groups. Some criticism has been levelled at the auto-enforcing characteristic of some technical standards, such as TPMs. The main criticism is that the rules 'auto-enforced' by some TPMs go beyond the rights given to content owners by intellectual property legislation. For example, TPMs preventing the user from making copies of content can go against the long established rules of 'fair use' found in most (if not all) copyright legislation.

The auto-enforcement characteristic of TPMs is in practice constantly being undermined by the development of circumvention mechanisms.[110] The development of

---

[109] For procedure followed in the IETF see <http://www.ietf.org/rfc/rfc3160.txt> – this document explains the process followed through RFCs (Requests for Comment) from recommended specifications to standard setting.

[110] Circumvention in this context refers to the breaking of the TPM code to avoid the effect of the TPM. Kerr, Maurushat and Tacit (2002: 4) define 'circumvention' as '"Circumvention" of a TPM refers to the breaking or avoidance of the use of a protection measure to prevent unauthorized access to a system or mechanism such as a database, satellite system, or security mechanism attached to DVD movies.' This definition is derived from *Universal Studio* v. *Reimerdes*, 111 Federal Supplement 2d 294 (S.D.N.Y. 2000).

circumvention mechanisms weakening the potential of TPMs has triggered the introduction in copyright legislation of protection against circumvention mechanisms: circumvention mechanisms being considered an infringement of TPM copyright. For example, the World Intellectual Property Organisation (WIPO) Copyright Treaty requires that

'Contracting Parties shall provide adequate legal protection and effective legal remedies against the circumvention of effective technological measures that are used by authors in connection with the exercise of their rights under this Treaty or the Berne Convention and that restrict acts, in respect of their works, which are not authorized by the authors concerned or permitted by law.'[111]

This requirement has been implemented in both the US Digital Millennium Copyright Act and the EU Copyright Directive (2001/29/EC).

Mostly the time line and stages in the rule-making process are clear, written and available to the public. Often, especially in the work of IETF, W3C and EESSI, the different documents used and discussed in the drafting stages are also available to the public. The groups differ in the degree of regulative formality.[112] While the IETF and the W3C follow fixed steps in the procedure to create and formulate technical standards, other private groups, for example groups creating technical protection measures, have a less formalised technical standards setting procedure. The degree of regulative formality can be used as an indicator of 'legality': once the process followed by the private groups is a transparent, open and stable one, the results can be considered 'legal'.[113]

One can argue that the process followed in the development of TPMs, does not exhibit the same regulative formality as the creation of other technical standards. The process, in fact, is often neither transparent nor open. What is public is the effect of the TPM once it is implemented. TPMs, in short, are less 'legal' than the other technical standards discussed in this chapter.

Legal nature of the technical standards

Laws in a community can be identified both by the manner in which they were created and adopted and by the formal nature of their content.[114] Some authors[115] have argued, against the position put forth by Reidenberg[116] and Lessig,[117] that technical code cannot be considered 'law' as it fails to satisfy the criteria estab-

---

[111] WIPO Copyright Treaty Art. 11 – Obligations concerning Technological Measures accessed at <http://www.wipo.int/clea/docs/en/wo/wo033en.htm#P88_11974> on 12 October 2004.

[112] Benoliel 2003: 1280.

[113] Ibid.

[114] Hart 1994; Dworkin 1997 and Thirlway 2001.

[115] See especially work of the 'Code as Law' IViR research group (in preparation).

[116] Reidenberg 1998.

[117] Lessig 1999.

lished by, for example, the work of Fuller[118] on legal systems. On examination, however, most technical standards fulfil the criteria identified by Fuller and undoubtedly have legal effects on the Internet activities.

Using Fuller's criteria, we can argue that technical standards, like laws, are generally applicable to all similar situations and are not decided upon on an *ad hoc* basis as a specific situation arises. Indeed, technical standards are considered standards specifically because they are agreed upon 'for common and repeated use'[119] in a given context. In the case of the P3P, IPv6, digital signatures standards and also to some extent in the case of technical protection measures, if a standard were to change haphazardly it would be very difficult, if not impossible, to use it as a means of regulating actions. In the case of the IPv6 standard, unless the standard is stable and used for general application there would be no certainty that machines can communicate between each other and have access to cyberspace. Similarly, in the case of digital signatures, for example, if the technical standards were not stable, there would be no standard way of checking the authenticity and integrity of the digital signature used. Technical specifications are only adopted as technical standards once the specifications are stable and consensus has been reached on their stability. For example, in the IETF process only technical specifications that are considered stable are adopted as technical standards.

A law must, according to Fuller, be publicly known and available to the subjects of the law. Technical standards, once implemented, are available to the public and not only to users or members of the community that created and developed the technical standard. The specifications for technical standards, such as the P3P, IPv6 or those for digital signatures, are publicly available. Just as some laws are 'better' understood by persons who are legally trained, some technical standards are better understood by persons who have the technical expertise and familiarity to follow the demands of the technical specifications.

A law should have a prospective character, that is, it applies to future situations or behaviour and not to past behaviour. One cannot be expected to follow a rule unless the 'expected' behaviour to be exhibited is knowable in advance. Technical standards can, from their very nature, only be applied to future behaviour.

Laws should be consistent with existing laws and legal doctrine. A state legal system should also have some mechanism to ensure consistency between laws, such as a review process by the courts to review the consistency of the laws and their conformity with fundamental law and principles found, for example, in the Constitution of the state. Similarly, technical standards need to be consistent to avoid technical 'conflicts'. New technical standards are examined by the private groups for consistency with other technical standards formulated both by the same group of private groups and by other organisations. For example, in the creation

---

[118] Fuller 1964.

[119] ISO/IEC Guide 2 quoted at <http://www.wssn.net/WSSN/gen_inf.html#Whatisstd> (quoted at footnote 4 in Bellagio Conference 2003).

and development of technical standards for digital signatures the EESSI reviewed its standards for consistency with technical standards formulated earlier by the IETF and W3C.

At times, state or supra-state law establishes the legal character of a technical standard. For example, the legal character of the electronic signature is established through approval by the European Union of the technical standards as conforming to the requirements of a 'legal' electronic signature for the purposes of the EU Directive. The legal character of the technical standards is then unmistakable. Furthermore, EU approval indirectly ensures that the technical standard is stable and does not change haphazardly.

Once adopted the technical standards are binding. Some technical standards, such as P3P,[120] do not provide a complete solution for the situation requiring regulation. In regulating the collection and use of personal data two sides of the activity need to be regulated: (i) the actual collection and use of the personal data by the web site; and (ii) the choice of the user to determine what personal information to disclose and under which circumstances. The P3P technical standard addresses this second aspect of the regulation of personal data. It offers a partial, but important, solution to the problem of on-line privacy practices. As pointed out in the Working Document for the modification of the P3P technical standard,

'Although P3P provides a technical mechanism for ensuring that users can be informed about privacy policies before they release personal information, it does not provide a technical mechanism for making sure sites act according to their policies.'[121]

Furthermore, there is no way to check compliance with the P3P standard. A 2003 study of the P3P standard found that a third of the web sites evaluated had syntax errors in their privacy policies, some critical enough to prevent user agents from evaluating the web site's privacy policy.[122] The lack of a compliance enforcement mechanism can undermine the value of the P3P technical standard. As Reidenberg argues,

---

[120] As a W3C document describes 'Although P3P provides a technical mechanism for ensuring that users can be informed about privacy policies before they release personal information, it does not provide a technical mechanism for making sure sites act according to their policies. Products implementing this specification MAY provide some assistance in that regard, but that is up to specific implementations and outside the scope of this specification. However, P3P is complementary to laws and self-regulatory programs that can provide enforcement mechanisms. In addition, P3P does not include mechanisms for transferring data or for securing personal data in transit or storage. P3P may be built into tools designed to facilitate data transfer. These tools should include appropriate security safeguards.' See P3P 1.1 Specification W3C Working draft dated 1 July 2005 at point 1 accessed at <http://www.w3.org/TR/P3P11/> on 5 October 2005.

[121] P3P 1.1 Specification W3C Working draft dated 20 July 2004 at point 1 accessed at <http://www.w3.org/TR/2004/WD-P3P11-20040720/> on 30 September 2004.

[122] See Cranor, Byers and Kormann 2003: 2, 8-9, 11-13.

'the manner in which P3P is incorporated in browsers, including the default setting and the fashion by which websites actually describe their practices, are critical for fair treatment of personal information.'[123]

Often, the regulatory effect of a technical standard is dependent on the level of 'sophistication' of the implementers of the technical standards. For example, in the P3P standard, the current 'user agents' that have been developed are: (i) mostly limited to regulating the practice of 'cookies'; (ii) not very user-friendly. In addition, P3P does not offer any means by which a user can check that the web site is actually complying with its own privacy policy.[124] P3P only provides the user with a means to check the web site's privacy policy at face value. The current standard does not provide a technical means to monitor whether a particular web site 'adheres to a stated privacy policy or automatically withdraws information if a site's stated policies changes.'[125]

6.3   STATES AND THE SETTING OF TECHNICAL STANDARDS

In many instances, such as in the case of standards for electronic signatures, states and state regulation provide a legal framework that influences the development of technical standards. Even though the development of technical standards for authenticity and verification of transactions began earlier than any legislative enactment, once legislation was passed[126] the technical standard setting process was influenced by the legislation. Indeed, future developments of the technical standards for electronic signatures have sought to satisfy legislative requirements (and have been limited by the choice in legislation in favour of a particular technology – public key encryption).

   In the P3P case, the developers of the standard were aware and 'guided' by the definitions and legal expectations found in data protection legislation in a number of European jurisdictions. Arguably, the P3P developers, while not being strictly bound by the legislation of any one country, could not afford not to follow the broad framework found in the legislation. Had the P3P developers completely ignored the existing legislation and created an inconsistent standard, the adoption and use of the technical standard would have been severely limited.

   States also encourage the adoption of technical standards and provide conditions to encourage the development of technical standards. States encourage the development of technical standards in different ways:

---

[123] Reidenberg 1999: 789.
[124] Electronic Privacy Information Center & Junkbusters 2002; McClurg 2003: 94.
[125] Delaney, et al. 2003.
[126] Predominantly the EU Electronic Signatures Directive (1999/93/EC).

- by co-funding the development of technical standards – as in the case of the European Electronic Signature Standardization Initiative (EESSI) standard setting process;
- by providing advice on the formulation and legal effect of technical standards – such as the participation of data protection authorities in the formulation of the P3P specifications. Their contribution 'encouraged' the making of a standard 'useable' in the European context.
- by providing legislation that protects the technical standards against circumvention – for example, by providing anti-circumvention clauses to protect the technical protection measures for copyright protected content.
- by encouraging the adoption of the technical standards – for example, the European Union and Asian countries have encouraged the adoption of IPv6.

Furthermore, states provide an important accountability mechanism for the standard setting process. The ways states can hold the groups in check varies in formality. One way is by offering a system of accreditation to the groups – as when the EU accredits groups providing standards for digital signatures. In the same example, the European Union goes one step further. It requires that the rules developed by the private groups be submitted for scrutiny of the European Union before formal approval. In theory, state law and state courts can hold the standard setting process in check. A broad class of legal measures can be used. These include, *inter alia*, antitrust legislation (or fair competition rules), legislation protecting individual fundamental rights such as the right to privacy and legislation protecting fair use and economic rights.

6.4 CONCLUSION

Technical standards are an important foundation of the technical structure of the Internet. They are created in response to a need perceived by participants in Internet activities. Apart from satisfying a technical need, technical standards are often also instruments of regulation. They are a representation (by technical means) of an acceptable behaviour[127] and technically 'set' the parameters of the acceptable behaviour.

The descriptions show that technical standards are, often, the more appropriate tool to regulate activities or to implement regulation on the Internet. This is consistent with the insight that 'secondary mobilizers' – as Griffiths[128] calls situations where 'local-level structures ... accomplish behavior in conformity with the external rule without any [explicit/active] rule-following by the ultimate addressees' – 'can often implement a rule better by ingenious environmental design'.[129] In the

---

[127] Cargill 1989: 13.
[128] Cf., Griffiths 2003: 64-65.
[129] Id. 2003: 64.

regulation of privacy in on-line transactions, for example, one way of addressing the need for regulation is by setting technical measures addressing the privacy concerns of users. The P3P standards provide this possibility. One can argue that the use of technical standards is inevitable in the regulation of such matters. Statutory or other non-technical regulation alone does not have the means required to control the activity.

There is no question on the regulatory effect of technical standards. Like self-regulation using codes of conduct and contracts, using technical standards is legally binding and effective. Furthermore, once a technical standard is implemented, it has an absolute and 'automatic' enforcement characteristic.

Intertwining and complementary relationship

Technical standards do not exist in a legal vacuum. In regulating the different Internet activities, the technical standards co-exist together with other legal sources, mainly state regulation. The current relationship between self-regulation and state regulation can be described as one of intertwining and of complementarity. The creation of technical standards complements the implementation of rules coming from state legislation and self-regulation. In turn, state regulation provides legal rules to protect the technical standards. This intertwining between self-regulation and state regulation can be seen in particular in the provision of technical protection measures for copyright protected content. Self-regulation implements state copyright legislation and in turn state legislation protects the technical standards against circumvention measures designed to weaken the enforcement capabilities of technical protection. The intertwining in this case continues further. Since a court decision imposing a criminal sanction for the 'cracking' of a technical measure protecting content does not 'heal' the crack in the technical code, self-regulation develops new protection measures and hence the cycle of intertwining and complementarity starts again.

Apart from being complemented by states and state regulation, self-regulation is complemented by other sources too. One source is public interest advocacy groups. For example, in both the P3P and the IPv6 examples the role and participation of public interest groups in the self-regulation process creating and developing the technical standards have helped in keeping W3P and IETF in check. Had public interest groups not alerted the IETF, for instance, the IPv6 protocol could have dangerously threatened the privacy of users using the protocol to access Internet.[130] Another source is private groups who fund the development of the technical standards[131] and eventually adopt the standards developed through self-regulation. In the P3P example, the adoption and support of 'dominant' commercial enterprises,

---

[130] See description in IPv6 example above and Davidson, Morris and Courtney 2002: 3.

[131] For example, technical protection measures are primarily funded by the commercial sector (or 'protected' content holders such as the music or movie industry). The (profit and not-for profit organisations) members of W3C fund the P3P standards.

such as Microsoft of the technical standard, complement in the sustainability of the P3P as a technical standard.

A number of reasons explain the current relationship between technical standards and state regulation. The relationship comes from a strong interdependence between state regulation and self-regulation in the regulation of Internet activities specifically because of the technical nature of the Internet and Internet activities and the a-territorial quality of technical standards. Notwithstanding the regulatory challenge that states and state regulation face due to the technical nature of Internet activities, states are still keen to provide (directly or indirectly) rules and remedies for citizens/users of the Internet. Given that they are unable or cannot offer global regulation and global remedies, states encourage the development of technical standards by private groups, thus assuaging part of their obligation. In many instances, states have effectively delegated the creation and development of the technical standard to the self-regulating groups, especially where technical standards are deemed the appropriate regulatory measure. This is clearly seen in the case of the development of electronic signatures.

Private groups are considered likely to have (and in practice they do have) a 'superior knowledge of the subject compared to a government agency'.[132] States are dependent on the expertise and technical access of private groups to reach activities that states are unable or unwilling to reach. In turn, self-regulation is dependent on the general legal frameworks and structures provided by states (or by other sources) to support the legitimacy and legal effect of the legal and technical standards set through a process of self-regulation. In the P3P example, for instance, states are dependent on experts to provide technical systems to provide means for the protection of personal information of users, while the private groups are dependent on state principles on data protection and privacy. Indeed this deferral to the private sector based on the expertise of the private sector in the activity requiring regulation and in the technical know-how required to formulate an appropriate technical standard, confirms the legitimacy of groups to participate in the regulation of Internet activities.

In some cases, acknowledgement of the expertise and know-how of the groups by states comes after the process of self-regulation has taken place. The groups create the rules and technical standards, which state regulation later takes up or acknowledges. A case in point is the way the EU acknowledged the technical standard for digital signatures developed by the EESSI.[133]

The a-territorial nature of the technical structure of Internet is a *sine qua non* of Internet. If the technical structures are limited by territory, the global exchange of

---

[132] Weiser 2001: 824 quoting Douglas C. Michael (1995), 'Federal Agency Use of Audited Self-Regulation as a Regulatory Technique', *Administrative Law Review*, Vol. 47, pp. 171, 181-182.

[133] A Commission Decision (2003/511/EC) officially recognised the standards in July 2003 (*OJ* L175 15 July 2003) EESSI stopped functioning in October 2004. See <http://www.ict.etsi.org/EESSI_home.htm> accessed 5 October 2005.

information currently supported by Internet could no longer be offered. Limiting the development of technical standards geographically influences the 'global' nature of Internet. The necessity to maintain an a-territorial ('global') Internet implies that the rules of one state alone cannot regulate the technical activity or space. State regulation is dependent on inter-state co-operation and self-regulation. Self-regulation fills in the need for transnational regulation and transnational technical application and implementation of the technical standards.[134] Once adopted the technical standards take effect irrespective of territorial or geographical limitations. For example, digital signatures standards implemented in digital signature systems regulate authentication and verification irrespective of where the 'user' is actually using the digital signatures system. The same can be said of each of the three other examples of technical standards.

Moreover, once adopted technical standards can offer an element of automatic enforcement of the regulation irrespective of the national jurisdictional limitations encountered by statutory regulation. For example, once adopted, technological protection measures added to protected content will protect that content irrespective of the physical geographical location of the user. In self-regulation by technical standards there is much less dependence on *post factum* sanction of punishment than in other instances of self-regulation. Conformity is ensured through automatic means once a technical measure or standard is implemented and not through the threat of a sanction.

While the 'automatic' enforcement characteristic of technical standards can also be seen as limiting the freedom of users to choose whether to follow a particular rule or not, this limitation is present in any situation where a technical solution is used to implement a rule (including the cloverleaf highway interchange praised by Llewellyn).[135] Ultimately however, the user always has the option not to use the particular system using the technical standard at all. Even in the most extreme circumstance, a user can always abstain from following the standard (and endure the consequences of such choices).

Self-regulation is dependent on states to support the regulatory initiatives of self-regulating groups. While states can offer global regulation of standards, as seen, for example, in the case of telecommunications standards by the International Telecommunications Union (ITU), two situations hamper the same development in Internet. First, there is no one body that co-ordinates all the standard-setting on the Internet (and to a certain extent, there cannot be).[136] Secondly, reaching consensus between states (if at all) is a laborious process – a delay that Internet can ill afford. Indeed the urgent need for timely solutions on the Internet also explains the in-

---

[134] Reidenberg (1998) argues that *Lex Informatica* regulates across national jurisdictions. It is only limited by the 'jurisdiction' of the network but not necessarily territorially or geographically. The same can be said specifically of technical standards.

[135] Cf., Karl Llewellyn as quoted in Griffiths 2003: 64-65.

[136] Especially taking into consideration the wide variety of areas that need technical standards.

volvement of private groups in providing solutions (whether by creating rules or by using technical means to implement state regulation).

Similar to the situation of the technical nature of the Internet and Internet activities, states do not relinquish the possibility of participating in the regulation, even if the regulation needs to apply transnationally. States have an obligation to protect their citizens' interests irrespective of the territorial limitations implied in state regulation. This explains the encouragement given by states to self-regulation in the process of creating and developing standards that have an 'automatic' a-territorial effect.

As with Reidenberg's argument that '*lex informatica* allows customized rules to suit particular network situations and preserve choices for individual participants',[137] technical standards are also customised measures created and developed to address the specific needs. No one technical solution fits all the needs. Each regulatory need is addressed by the development of specific technical standards customised to suit the particular regulatory requirements. In this way, technical standards are capable of filling in for the absence of state regulation and of intertwining and complementing the work of state legislation and other forms of self-regulation.

---

[137] Reidenberg 1999: 574.

Chapter 7
SELF-REGULATION IN THE RESOLUTION OF ON-LINE DISPUTES

7.1 INTRODUCTION

Like activities in the off-line world, Internet activities can be a source of disputes. The large number of people using the Internet for commercial and non-commercial purposes has increased the possibility and variety of disputes. Examples of disputes include the non-delivery of goods in e-commerce transactions; copyright infringements in the distribution of content on-line; breaches of privacy; and so forth. An efficient system to resolve disputes helps to maintain trust in use of the Internet. Both states and private groups have an interest in facilitating dispute resolution.

On the Internet, the majority of dispute resolution is not carried out in 'formal' settings (whether offered by states or private groups). Most on-line conflicts are resolved via informal means, such as direct negotiation between the parties involved in the dispute or through the intervention of third parties, for example, moderators in on-line chat spaces.[1] Disputants have recourse to formal settings (where they exist) only when informal dispute resolution does not succeed or does not take place.

This chapter looks at the participation of self-regulating groups in the resolution of three different categories of disputes:

(i) disputes arising from e-commerce transactions. Like disputes about commercial transactions off-line, these may include disputes about the non-delivery of or non-payment for the object of a commercial transaction or disputes about the quality of the object of the transaction. Two self-regulation arrangements are described – SquareTrade and Electronic Consumer Dispute Resolution (ECODIR).

(ii) disputes between trademark or service mark holders and domain name registrants. These may include conflicts about who is entitled to use a same particular string of characters as a domain name. They can also include disputes about whether a domain name is too similar to a particular trademark.[2] Two self-regulation arrangements are described – eResolution and the Asian Domain Name Dispute Resolution Centre (ADNDRC).

(iii) Internet content-related disputes. These include disputes whether the content is defamatory and whether particular content allegedly infringes the rights of

---

[1] Gaitenby 2004.
[2] Smith 2002: 78.

J.P. Mifsud Bonnici, Self-Regulation in Cyberspace
© 2008, T·M·C·ASSER PRESS, The Hague, and the author

copyright holders. Other disputes can include conflicts on the legality of self-regulation in the regulation of Internet content. For example, if an ISP blocks certain content for all its clients the exercise of self-regulation can be a source of conflict between customers who want to access the particular content and the ISP. One self-regulation arrangement is described: IRIS-Médiation.

What makes Internet (or on-line) disputes particularly problematic to resolve is that the disputes take place across traditional territorial boundaries and are regulated (when regulation exists at all) by a heterogeneous collection of state and private regulation.[3] Furthermore, the parties taking part in the activities may not be easily identifiable and have 'fluid identities'.[4]

Private groups have long been involved in the regulation of disputes arising on-line. They have developed legal and technical measures to prevent disputes. The development of trust mark schemes[5] is one example. They have also been involved in the resolution of disputes. This chapter describes and explains the involvement of groups in the resolution of on-line disputes primarily through the development and use of (on-line) resolution systems (ODRS). It discusses the relationship between dispute resolution offered by private groups and by state institutions.

For a number of reasons, states and international governmental organisations support the involvement of private groups in the resolution of disputes, especially in the resolution of e-commerce disputes. Support is based on the expectation that self-regulation can offer a solution to users/citizens where states fail. The discussion in the literature and policy documents is largely based on the assumed advantages of self-regulation in dispute resolution, for example the claim that on-line dispute resolution is effective since it does not face the legal obstacles posed by national legal systems.[6]

Groups are involved in the creation and implementation of substantive and procedural rules for the resolution of on-line disputes. Groups implement some of these rules through the creation of on-line dispute resolution systems (ODRS). At times, the creators of the rules also provide the ODRS – such as in the example of SquareTrade described later in this chapter. In these arrangements of self-regulation, it is difficult to distinguish between the rules and their implementation. At other times the creators of the rules and the ODRS providers are different groups – for example, in the resolution of trademark-domain name disputes the rules are created by one group, such as ICANN, while other groups, such as WIPO, provide the actual ODRS.

---

[3] Tilman 1999.

[4] Choi 2003: 1.

[5] By registering to a trust mark scheme, traders and content providers bind themselves to follow the rules on reliability, trustworthiness and dispute resolution created by the agency issuing the trust marks. Consumer than choose to trade with the trust mark holders because of the guarantees that the trust mark carries with it.

[6] Schultz 2002: 2.

In spite of the long involvement of private groups, dispute resolution systems for on-line disputes are not yet widespread. However, though few in number, they are representative of the potential of self-regulation in the resolution of on-line disputes. In two areas in particular, in the resolution of disputes coming from e-commerce transactions and in trademark-domain name disputes, current cases of self-regulation provide indispensable dispute resolution services. In e-commerce transactions, self-regulation offers dispute resolution for cases that would have for a number of reasons, such as their small financial value, otherwise remain unresolved. The more than 1.5 million disputes submitted to SquareTrade – an on-line dispute resolution provider for e-commerce transactions – show the extent of the need for self-regulation. In trademark-domain name disputes, self-regulation fills in for the absence of state rules concerning such disputes by providing both substantive and procedural rules. The ICANN Uniform Domain Name Dispute Resolution Policy, for example, offers both substantive and procedural rules to resolve trademark-domain name disputes.

Self-regulation serves three main functions. First, it offers a forum and, at times, provides an actual remedy for on-line disputes where access to states courts for dispute resolution is theoretical at best. This can be seen especially in the provision of dispute resolution of e-commerce related disputes. Secondly, self-regulation provides a forum and an actual remedy to resolve on-line disputes in contemporaneous with (yet quicker than) remedies offered by state courts. This can be seen in particular in the case of trademark-domain name related disputes and to a much more limited extent in content-related disputes. Thirdly, it provides substantive rules for the resolution of particular on-line disputes (especially in the absence of specific state legislation regulating the particular disputes). This can be seen in particular in rules on trademark-domain disputes.

These functions intertwine and complement state initiatives. Self-regulation handles cases that state courts are unable to offer an actual remedy to and in situations where state substantive rules to resolve the dispute are missing or incomplete. In turn, states and state regulation provide a general legal background to which self-regulation plugs in, offer an ultimate fall-back opportunity for cases resolved through private dispute resolution and encourage the development of private dispute resolution arrangements.

The next section covers four themes: it first defines the use of the term 'on-line dispute resolution; secondly it gives a brief description of the difficulties involved in the resolution of disputes arising from on-line conflicts; thirdly it introduces the main groups involved in on-line dispute resolution (eBay, SquareTrade, ECODIR, ICANN, eResolution, ADNDRC and Iris-Médiation) and lastly gives a brief description of the rules (and on-line dispute resolution systems) developed by these groups.

7.2 ON-LINE DISPUTE RESOLUTION

An ODRS can be used in the resolution of on-line and off-line disputes. This chapter describes (only) ODRS used for the resolution of disputes arising on-line. The term 'on-line', in this chapter, hence, refers to both (a) the nature of the dispute – a dispute arising from an on-line activity; and (b) the means offered to resolve the dispute.

In the literature, the use[7] of ODRS for the resolution of disputes is referred to as 'on-line dispute resolution' (ODR). As a term, it is used interchangeably to refer to the use of ODRS for the resolution of on-line and off-line disputes.[8] Three types of ODRS are identified in the literature:

(a) systems using 'traditional' Alternative Dispute Resolution (ADR) techniques (such as mediation and arbitration) in an on-line environment.[9] Some examples include on-line arbitration, using a website to resolve disputes with the aid of qualified arbitrators; on-line resolution of consumer complaints, using e-mail to handle certain types of consumer complaints; and on-line mediation, using a website to resolve disputes with the aid of qualified mediators.[10]
(b) automated ADR, that is, where the resolution of the process is done through either an expert system or blind bidding systems (without the direct 'intervention' of a person). On-line settlement, using an expert system to settle financial claims by automated means, is one example.[11]
(c) a combination of automated ADR and traditional ADR in an on-line environment.

The ODRS used for the resolution of on-line disputes (and described in this chapter) fall largely in the third category.

7.2.1 Challenges for state dispute resolution institutions

Resolving disputes arising in an on-line context in state courts or in state-based alternative dispute resolution mechanisms may be problematic. Since many of the activities on the Internet take place across national boundaries, the related disputes often involve parties in different jurisdictions. In such circumstances, it is not always simple to identify which court has jurisdiction to hear and try the dispute.

---

[7] Not the creation of ODRS.

[8] Van den Heuvel (2000: 8), for example, defines ODR as 'the deployment of applications and computer networks for resolving disputes with ADR methods. Both e-disputes and brick and mortar disputes can be resolved using ODR.'

[9] Sometimes also called 'technology assisted ADR' (von Lewinski 2003: 168) and 'e-ADR' (Schiavetta 2004).

[10] Van den Heuvel 2000: 8.

[11] Ibid.

Moreover, laws across states are not homogeneous.[12] Not only are laws on our three categories of disputes in different states not harmonised, they are sometimes in conflict with each other as, for example, in the case of laws on defamation in one state and the laws on freedom of expression in another.[13] Many times, a relevant law only exists in some of the states concerned. At other times, each state may have more than one law to regulate the dispute. Trying to resolve a dispute in such context is, of course, difficult if not impossible.

Furthermore, the court that has jurisdiction to hear the case may at times be in a state different from the state where the decision needs to be enforced. There may be, for example, difficulties in enforcing a decision in the jurisdiction where the opposing party has assets. One well-known case points to the difficulty in enforcement of foreign decisions. In the *Yahoo!* case in France,[14] the plaintiffs could not enforce a decision where a French Court found in their favour since the defendant company had no assets in France. Neither could they enforce the judgment in the United States, where the defendant company had assets, since the US court did not recognise the judgment of the French Court. While traditional principles of private international law can often be used to resolve these conflicts, in certain disputes, for example, e-commerce disputes where the amount or object in dispute does not have a 'high' value, the effort and expense involved in determining the right court and enforcing the decision often exceeds the value of the object of litigation.

In disputes that require particular (technical) expertise, such as in some content-related disputes and trademarks-domain names disputes, state courts may lack the necessary expertise and specialisation to resolve the disputes in an effective manner. Most of the conflicts that arise on the Internet require an understanding of the nature of Internet activities. State courts (at least in the early years of the Internet and to some extent also today) do not offer expert or specialised solutions to the disputes.

Lastly, court procedures are often expensive, especially for a party to pursue legal action in another jurisdiction. For example, the cost of the procedure and time involved in accessing a foreign court to settle a dispute arising from an e-commerce transaction is often far greater than the cost of the object in dispute, making access to court an impractical option. Court proceedings are (almost invariably) long and time consuming, especially compared with the speed with which transactions are concluded on the Internet.

---

[12] Tilman 1999.

[13] The decision in the *Yahoo!* case of the US court not to enforce the French judgment because the French judgment limited freedom of speech shows some of the difficulties involved in obtaining a resolution of an internet content-related dispute. *La Ligue contre le racisme et l'antisémitisme* v. *Yahoo! Inc.* High Court of Paris, 22 May 2000, Interim Court Order No. 00/05308, 00/05309 and also Tilman 1999.

[14] *La Ligue contre le racisme et l'antisémitisme* v. *Yahoo! Inc.* High Court of Paris, 22 May 2000, Interim Court Order No. 00/05308, 00/05309.

Notwithstanding the difficulties, some disputes that arise on the Internet are brought to state courts. The benefit of choosing in favour of state courts is that, to some extent, state courts have wide experience in resolving conflicts of laws and conflicts in jurisdiction. Courts are usually familiar with the traditional principles for solving disputes taking place across territories according to private international law principles. For many disputes (and disputants), however, the option of bringing the dispute to a state court often exists only in theory. In practice, the difficulties pointed out earlier make access to state courts well nigh impracticable and hence disputes irresolvable.

7.2.2 Reasons to self-regulate

Against this setting, two important needs – the need for a forum and actual remedies for on-line disputes – prompt private groups to participate in the creation and provision of private (alternative) means to resolve disputes. One need is the need for an actual (rather than theoretical) dispute resolution forum available preferably where conflicts arise on-line. Satisfying this need can give the necessary security to users to continue using the Internet as their 'market place'.[15] In addition, users need to have the possibility to avoid going to court (especially where the applicable court would be a foreign court)[16] without having to abandon the hope of resolving the dispute. Another need is the need for remedies. A party bringing an action against another party in the dispute expects that the forum not only provides a place to air the dispute and reach a settlement but that the settlement can be applied.

7.2.3 ODR and e-commerce related disputes

I describe here the two most important self-regulation arrangements in the resolution of e-commerce related dispute. One involves the resolution of disputes that arise in the eBay auction space – SquareTrade. SquareTrade is an important example because of the number of people that have made use of the SquareTrade ODRS. The second involves the resolution of e-commerce disputes irrespective of the transaction space where the dispute arises – ECODIR. This arrangement is an important example of an arrangement supported by state (here the European Union) funding and policy.

The development and use of ODRS for e-commerce disputes goes back to the early commercial days of the Internet. The introduction and growth of commerce on-line and consequently related conflicts immediately pointed towards the need for dispute resolution mechanisms other than state courts.

In response, the first ODR systems were created, mostly by academics, for example the On-line Ombuds Office[17] (created by academics at the University of

---

[15] Schultz 2002.

[16] Fenoulhet 2001: 2.

[17] The On-line Ombuds Office offered on-line mediation services for any on-line dispute. Katsh and Rifkin 2001: 56.

Massachusetts) or lawyers funded by research grants, for example The Virtual Magistrate.[18] Though not specifically intended for e-commerce disputes (indeed the Virtual Magistrate project was intended for content-related disputes), the role of these systems was primarily to test the suitability and reception by the on-line communities of on-line dispute resolution systems. The next wave of development was spurred by the successes of these experimental systems. In 1999, the University of Massachusetts developed a pilot on-line dispute resolution service for the e-Bay community.[19] The findings of the pilot study were used as a basis in the current dispute resolution system offered by SquareTrade for eBay related disputes.

States and intergovernmental organisations have sought to support the development and use of on-line dispute resolution systems. Three intergovernmental organisations – the European Union (EU), the Organisation for Economic Co-operation and Development (OECD) and the United Nations Centre for Trade Facilitation and Electronic Business (UN/CEFACT)/United Nations Economic Commission for Europe (UNECE) have been particularly involved.

The involvement of the European Union is based on an 'economic growth' argument – if consumers are not confident, cannot trust the Internet for their purchases, there will be less trading and there will consequently be less economic growth in the EU area. One issue in consumer confidence is that consumers need to have a system that can efficiently resolve disputes if any were to arise in the course of their dealings on-line. Against this background, the European Union has favoured the development of on-line dispute resolution systems. EU support can be seen in three ways:

(a) by co-funding the development of two ODR systems: ECODIR (under Decision 283/1999) (described later in this subsection) and OC Dispute Resolution System (under the TEN-Telecom funding).
(b) by promising to produce a Commission Communication on ODR – a promise still to be fulfilled.[20]

---

[18] The Virtual Magistrate project offered arbitration for resolution of disputes involving: (1) users of on-line systems, (2) those who claim to be harmed by wrongful messages, postings, or files and (3) system operators (to the extent that complaints or demands for remedies are directed at system operators). See The Virtual Magistrate Project Concept Paper (July 1996) accessed at <http://www.vmag.org/docs/concept.html> on 3 August 2004.

[19] A description of the pilot project and findings are found in Katsh, Rifkin and Gaitenby 2000.

[20] This Commission Communication on ODR has long been promised: At the Lisbon Special European Council of March 2000, the European Council called on 'the Commission and the Council to consider how to promote consumer confidence in electronic commerce, in particular through alternative dispute resolution systems.' The Feira European Council in June 2000, which endorsed the Commission's eEurope Action Plan, endorsed a key action 'promoting alternative dispute resolution'. At the Stockholm European Council of 23 and 24 March 2001 the Commission announced its 'intention to present a Communication promoting on-line dispute resolution systems'. (see Fenoulhet 2001: 1) The same intention was reiterated in the Commission Green Paper on alternative dispute resolution in civil and commercial law published in April 2002 (see para. 40 p. 18 of document (COM(2002)196 final 19 April 2002)). In November 2003, a Commission Staff Working Document (see SEC(2003)1387

(c) by including a reference to the possibility of ODR in the e-Commerce Directive (2000/31/EC)[21] – hence accepting 'out-of-court dispute settlement' by 'electronic means' as a legally acceptable means of dispute resolution.

Similar to the European Union, the OECD's main concern with ODR systems is economic growth and consumer protection. The OECD's support for on-line dispute resolution services is mainly through providing the conditions for a debate among OECD Member States on ODR for e-commerce disputes. The OECD support for ODR can be traced to the 1999 OECD Guidelines for Consumer Protection in the Context of Electronic Commerce. In the Guidelines,[22] the OECD recommends, 'Consumers should be provided meaningful access to fair and timely alternative dispute resolution and redress without undue cost or burden.' These ADR methods 'should employ information technologies innovatively'.

In December 2000, the OECD together with the International Chamber of Commerce and the Hague Conference on Private International Law organised a joint conference on on-line ADR in relation to privacy and consumer protection.[23] The conference explored the use of on-line ADR systems for disputes involving small values and/or low levels of harm that arise between businesses and consumers on-line. The primary focus was on informal, flexible systems that allow for the necessary balancing between the type of dispute and the formality of the process for resolution.[24]

This was followed by two reports: one in 2002 and one in 2004. In 2002, the OECD Working Party on Information Security and Privacy issued a report on Legal Provisions related to Business-To-Consumer Alternative Dispute Resolution in Relation to Privacy and Consumer Protection.[25] The 2004 report addressed the

---

27 November 2003 point 64 at p. 29) forecasted that the Commission Communication on ODR would be published before end of 2003. No Communication has been published yet.

[21] E-Commerce Directive 2000/31/EC at Art. 17 – Out-of-court dispute settlement

'1. Member States shall ensure that, in the event of disagreement between an information society service provider and the recipient of the service, their legislation does not hamper the use of out-of-court schemes, available under national law, for dispute settlement, including appropriate electronic means.

2. Member States shall encourage bodies responsible for the out-of-court settlement of, in particular, consumer disputes to operate in a way which provides adequate procedural guarantees for the parties concerned.

3. Member States shall encourage bodies responsible for out-of-court dispute settlement to inform the Commission of the significant decisions they take regarding information society services and to transmit any other information on the practices, usages or customs relating to electronic commerce.'

[22] Part One Art. VI accessed at <http://www.oecd.org/dataoecd/5/34/1824782.pdf> on 22 July 2004.

[23] Conference report at <http://www.olis.oecd.org/olis/2001doc.nsf/LinkTo/DSTI-ICCP-REG-CP(2001)2> accessed 22 July 2004.

[24] OECD Working Party on Information Security and Privacy (2002) Legal Provisions related to business-to-consumer alternative dispute resolution in relation to privacy and consumer protection. Doc. Dated 17 July 2002 Doc. Ref. DSTI/ICCP/REG/CP(2002)1/FINAL at p. 5.

[25] OECD Working Party on Information Security and Privacy (2002) Legal Provisions related to business-to-consumer alternative dispute resolution in relation to privacy and consumer protection.

need for Alternative Dispute Resolution (ADR) on-line mechanisms for small and medium enterprises (SME) having cross-border disputes.[26] The report suggests a number of best practices to be followed in the offering of ADR systems.

Similarly to the OECD, the role of the United Nations has been mostly that of providing a forum for discussion on the use of on-line alternative dispute resolution to facilitate trade relations between Member States. In 2001-2003, the United Nations Centre for Trade Facilitation and Electronic Business (UN/CEFACT) drafted a recommendation on on-line alternative dispute resolution.[27] The draft recommendation recommends that governments promote the development of ODR systems. It also recommends that ODR systems be implemented by the private sector 'in combination with self-regulatory instruments for electronic business such as codes of conduct and trust-mark schemes.'[28] In addition, for two consecutive years (2003-2004), the United Nations Economic Commission for Europe organised an annual conference on ODR. The conferences brought together scholars and practitioners involved in ODR to discuss the developing technical, financial and legal directions of ODR.

The support and interest of international governmental organisations together with the keenness of the private sector to find suitable *fora* to resolve e-commerce disputes has lead to the development of a number of private dispute resolution systems. The more prominent example of private on-line dispute resolution for e-commerce disputes are SquareTrade and ECODIR. A number of other systems, like Econfidence and Risolvionline,[29] offer an on-line dispute resolution system that can be used for both e-commerce and off-line commercial disputes.[30] When used, these systems have been used predominantly for off-line commercial disputes.[31]

7.2.3.1 *The regulation of disputes between buyers and sellers on eBay*

- eBay and SquareTrade

Currently the most important on-line dispute resolution rules and procedures for e-commerce related disputes are the ones created by eBay and SquareTrade specifi-

---

Doc. Dated 17 July 2002 Doc. Ref. DSTI/ICCP/REG/CP(2002)1/FINAL. This report included the results of a questionnaire submitted to OECD Member States on legal issues associated with on-line ADR.

[26] Issued June 2004 at the 2nd OECD Conference of Ministers responsible for Small and Medium-sized enterprises (SMEs): Promoting Entrepreneurship and innovative SMEs in a global economy: Towards a more responsible and inclusive globalisation (held in Turkey 3-5 June 2004) accessed at <http://www.oecd.org/dataoecd/6/8/31919270.pdf> on 21 July 2004.

[27] Various revisions of the text can be found at <http://www.unece.org>.

[28] Draft version 17th December 2002 document reference RESTRICTED CEFACT/2001/LG14/Rev.10 p. 10.

[29] Developed by the Milan Chamber of Commerce. See Sali 2005.

[30] Both these systems have been predominantly used for commercial disputes taking place entirely in the 'off-line' space.

[31] Sali 2005.

cally to address disputes arising in the eBay auction space. eBay is one of the largest auction spaces on the Internet. It houses more than hundred million registered buyers and sellers, trading on the Internet any imaginable legal item.[32] Usually these are 'small' merchants, who use the Internet as their main medium for business. While the relationship between eBay and individual sellers and buyers can be a cause of dispute, this chapter discusses (only) the applicable rules for disputes between buyers and sellers on eBay. These disputes are either 'typical buyer-seller' disputes or eBay specific disputes.[33] The disputes are mainly:

(a) merchandise related disputes involving mostly non-delivery of goods or services and misrepresentation;
(b) payment related disputes involving credit and billing problems;
(c) other issues – mainly disputes involving improper selling practices, un-honoured guarantees or warranties, and unsatisfactory services.
(d) feedback related disputes – eBay gives sellers and buyers the option to evaluate the service and reliability of the seller and buyer in every transaction by filling in 'feedback' forms. The feedback is published on the eBay site. Any person can check the feedback rating given by other buyers and sellers on the performance of the particular buyer or seller one is about to transact with. The feedback represents a seller's or buyer's reputation on-line. Once a feedback rating is given, neither party can retract or change it. At times, the parties do not agree on the feedback received.

There are three sets of groups involved in the regulation of disputes between buyers and sellers on eBay: eBay, SquareTrade Inc and mediators. eBay is a (private) commercial company that created originally founded in San Jose' in 1995 and owns the eBay auction space. eBay Inc. is organised under United States Law. eBay Inc. owns a number of subsidiary companies registered under the laws of the different states. eBay in the United Kingdom for example is registered under United Kingdom law.[34] SquareTrade Inc. is also a private company,[35] founded in 2000 and registered under United States Law. SquareTrade specifically offers an ODRS. Mediators involved in the SquareTrade ODRS are usually trained mediators and have expertise in e-commerce and intellectual property issues. SquareTrade mediators come from over ten countries and are fluent in eight languages. A mediator is assigned to a case based on the type of dispute or specific expertise of the mediator.[36]

---

[32] See <http://pages.ebay.com/aboutebay/thecompany/companyoverview.html> accessed 19 August 2005.

[33] See SquareTrade complaint form at <https://www.squaretrade.com/odr> accessed on 3 August 2004.

[34] See <http://pages.ebay.com/aboutebay/thecompany/companyoverview.html> accessed on 19 August 2005

[35] Accessed at <http://www.squaretrade.com/cnt/jsp/prs/faq.jsp;jsessionid=twlgsav6c1?vhostid=chipotle&stmp=squaretrade&cntid=twlgsav6c1> 3 August 2004.

[36] Abernethy 2003: 14.

In brief, eBay regulates what happens when disputes arise – mainly it 'sends' the parties to SquareTrade. SquareTrade provides procedural rules to be followed in the on-line dispute resolution process offered through the SquareTrade on-line dispute resolution system. The SquareTrade ODRS implements these procedural rules. eBay and SquareTrade have, since August 2000, an exclusive contract[37] – that is eBay has agreed to 'send' disputes arising in the eBay space exclusively to the SquareTrade ODRS. Since its inception, the SquareTrade ODRS has handled more than 1.5 million cases.[38] Mediators participate in the on-line dispute resolution process offered by SquareTrade. They follow the procedural rules developed by SquareTrade.

- The rules

eBay rules regulate the 'beginning' and 'end' of the dispute resolution process. Through the contract with SquareTrade, eBay directs disputes between sellers and buyers to the SquareTrade ODRS. This rule is only binding on eBay users in cases of 'feedback rating' disputes. Only settlements (changing a feedback rating) decided through the SquareTrade mediation process are effective for eBay. In effect, eBay rules 'enforce' settlements reached using the SquareTrade ODRS.

The SquareTrade rules regulate:

(a) what disputes can be submitted to the SquareTrade ODRS: only claims between buyer and seller whose transaction took place on eBay.
(b) the relationship between the parties submitting to the SquareTrade ODRS: the relationship between both the complainant and the respondent and SquareTrade is governed by contract.
(c) the procedure to be followed in the dispute resolution: the SquareTrade ODRS implements these rules of procedure.
(d) the involvement and appointment of mediators in the SquareTrade ODRS mediation stage. The 'SquareTrade Standards of Practice for On-line Dispute Resolution'[39] and the SquareTrade set of 'Ethical Standards'[40] bind the mediators. These standards include that the mediators should be neutral of the parties and act impartially; that any conflicts of interest should be disclosed to all parties; that mediators are bound by confidentiality and a privacy policy; that the mediator is a competent and qualified person to handle the claim in dispute; that the process followed is fair and transparent; and that the process is handled in an expedite manner.

---

[37] See Benyekhlef and Gélinas 2005.

[38] Statistic given by Conley Tyler 2004.

[39] Accessed at <http://www.squaretrade.com/cnt/jsp/lgl/standards_med.jsp;jsession> on 19 July 2004.

[40] Accessed at <http://www.squaretrade.com/cnt/jsp/abt/ethics.jsp;jsession> on 19 July 2004.

There are two phases in the dispute resolution process offered by the SquareTrade ODRS: direct negotiation and mediated resolution. The direct negotiation process is an automated process. The process is set in motion by the filing of a claim by one of the parties in the dispute. The filing of the claim is made through a customised complaint filing process, that is, the complainant fills in a form with pre-set options for both the type of complaint and the claim being made. The pre-set options reflect underlying substantive rules that regulate the dispute resolution process, such as principles of fairness. SquareTrade claims that the pre-set options (especially with the list of potential solutions) is a way to help complainants articulate their demands while focusing on fairness and compromise.[41] Once the complaint is filed, the respondent is informed of the claim by SquareTrade and has 14 days within which to reply. If the respondent replies, he files in a similarly 'guided' response form.

The filing of a complaint and response is free of charge. In the direct negotiation phase, the parties communicate directly with each other through an (asynchronous) communication tool provided in the SquareTrade secure space.[42] The direct negotiation phase can be described as a process of 'self-settlement', that is, the parties try to reach a settlement on the dispute without the intervention of a third party.

If the direct negotiation phase reaches no settlement, either party can initiate mediation, that is, ask for a mediator to be appointed to help resolve the dispute. Asking for a mediator involves a fee of 20 US Dollars. The mediator does not act as a judge or arbiter. The mediator assists the parties to reach a settlement. At the parties' request, a mediator can recommend a settlement.[43] All information relating to a case is stored in a password-protected case page hosted by SquareTrade.[44] When the parties reach a settlement, the mediator draws up a resolution agreement, which both parties click to accept to show that settlement has been reached.[45]

An examination of the SquareTrade example shows that there are a number of reasons why both complainants and respondents use SquareTrade to settle a dispute coming from a transaction on eBay. Firstly, the SquareTrade ODRS is often the only formal dispute resolution option actually available to resolve the dispute. For many of the parties, particularly when the parties are in different territorial jurisdictions and the value of the object is small, the option of taking the dispute to a state court is not in practice viable. Furthermore, the SquareTrade resolution space can easily be accessed, literally by one click away, from the eBay space.[46]

---

[41] Abernethy 2003: 12.

[42] The parties discuss their issues through a password-protected Case Page on the SquareTrade website <http://www.squaretrade.com/cnt/jsp/hlp/odr.jsp;jsessionid=raqks6x9s7?vhostid=chipotle&stmp=squaretrade&cntid=raqks6x9s7&cate=3&ques=1> accessed on 3 August 2004.

[43] <http://www.squaretrade.com/cnt/jsp/odr/learn_odr.jsp;jsessionid=oqgbosxzu1?vhostid=chipotle&stmp=squaretrade&cntid=oqgbosxzu1> accessed 3 August 2004.

[44] Abernethy 2003: 12.

[45] Id. 2003: 14.

[46] Mifsud Bonnic and De Vey Mestdagh 2005b.

Secondly, parties on eBay, in particular those who trade regularly on eBay, are keen to be seen as traders or buyers who, when things have not worked well, are willingly to resolve the dispute. A 'good' reputation is an invaluable asset on eBay. As has been mentioned earlier, eBay provides a software-supported reputation system[47] – parties register feedback rating on this software system, on each other at the end of a transaction. If the trader is unco-operative in the resolution of a dispute, this could imply a negative rating by the other trader and consequently a loss in the key trading asset of reputation.

Thirdly, SquareTrade is the only option for the resolution of 'feedback-related' disputes. When parties do not agree on the rating given by the other party, the only option for the rating to be withdrawn or removed, would be to have the case assigned to SquareTrade mediation. In contrast to other disputes, which require the respondent to reply to the complaint before the dispute resolution can proceed, if a respondent does not reply to a feedback-related complaint SquareTrade will review the complaint and give an assessment on the complaint. If the SquareTrade reviewer finds in favour of the complainant, SquareTrade sends the request to eBay and the disputed feedback is removed from the site.[48]

Fourthly, all eBay traders that have registered with SquareTrade's seal of trust are bound by contract to submit to or respond to a dispute via the SquareTrade ODRS. The SquareTrade seal of trust is a voluntary, against payment, scheme aimed at increasing customer confidence in trading with the registered trader. Seal members commit themselves to abide by a set of selling standards and practices and in return SquareTrade issues a seal of trust after a stringent registration and evaluation process. While SquareTrade does not guarantee a transaction or seller's performance, its service can lower the risks of buying on-line.[49]

7.2.3.2   *The regulation of disputes between buyers and sellers through ECODIR*

Even if less known, other private groups are also involved in the resolution of e-commerce disputes irrespective of the transaction space where the dispute arises. One such group is the **E**lectronic **CO**nsumer **DI**spute **R**esolution (ECODIR). The group offer an on-line dispute resolution process for disputes between consumers and sellers on the Internet. Parties in any cyberspace transaction space can choose to take their dispute to the ECODIR dispute resolution space.[50] ECODIR is a con-

---

[47] See Katsh, Rifkin and Gaitenby 2000.

[48] See 'Improve your score – the SquareTrade process works' accessed at <http://www.square trade.com/spl/jsp/eby/eb_nf.jsp?vhostid=daffy&stmp=squaretrade&disid=p9d3und0w2&cntid= pi2xmrdfb1#eBay> 16 February 2005.

[49] <http://www.squaretrade.com/cnt/jsp/prs/faq.jsp;jsessionid=twlgsav6c1?vhostid=chipotle&stmp= squaretrade&cntid=twlgsav6c1> accessed 3 August 2004.

[50] The aim is to have a system where all types of small disputes between consumers and sellers can be settled in the same environment where they arose. Benyekhlef and Gélinas 2005.

sortium of European and North American Universities,[51] and some private part-ners.[52] A number of consumer associations and professional associations advised on the project.[53] The current secretariat is organised by the University of Dublin. The European Union's Directorate for Health and Consumer Affairs co-funded the creation and development of the ECODIR ODRS.[54] The ECODIR ODRS was launched in Brussels in October 2001[55] and ran as a pilot project until June 2003.[56] During this time, ECODIR handled 62 cases from over 14 countries.[57] The techni-cal environment of the ECODIR ODRS is modelled on the environment used in the eResolution ODRS (also described in this chapter).

As with the SquareTrade rules, the rules developed by ECODIR are primarily procedural rules. These rules outline the way a case submitted to ECODIR is handled. The rules:

(a) determine which cases are allowed and which not: Only cases involving at least one consumer and dealing exclusively with disputes arising from Internet trans-actions are allowed. Disputes relating to illicit content, corporal damages, family, taxation or intellectual property are excluded.[58]

(b) outline the procedural steps that need to be followed from the filing of a claim to termination or resolution: A dispute needs to be filed (on-line) by one of the parties. The respondent is notified automatically by ECODIR. If the respondent replies to the claim, the resolution process starts.

---

[51] The Centre for Computer and Law Research at the University of Notre-Dame de la Paix in Namur, Belgium, The faculty of law at University College Dublin, The Centre d'Études sur la Coopération Jurique Internationale from the CNRS in France, The Public Law Research Centre at the University of Montreal in Canada, the Centre of Law and Computer Studies of the Balearic Islands at the Balearic Islands University in Spain, the Interfaculty Technology Assessment Unit at the University of Notre-Dame de la Paix in Namur, Belgium and the Institute of Information-Telecommunication, Media Law at the University of Muenster, Germany. Accessed at <http://www.ecodir.org/about_us/team.htm> on 14 July 2004.

[52] The Centre de Médiation et d'Arbitrage de Paris, Globalsign (a Belgian private company) and On-lineResolution (a private American company) Accessed at <http://www.ecodir.org/about_us/team.htm> on 14 July 2004.

[53] Presentation given by Vincent Tilman on ECODIR at the Building Trust in the On-line Environ-ment: Business to Consumer Dispute Resolution Joint Conference of the OECD, HCOPIL, ICC held 11-12 December 2000 accessed at <http://www.oecd.org/> on 13 July 2004.

[54] The development of ECODIR benefited from co-funding by the European Commission, Health and Consumer Protection Directorate-General. The legal basis for the funding was Art. 2(c) of Deci-sion 283/1999EC of the European Parliament and Council of 25 January 1999 establishing a general framework for Community activities in favour of consumers. See <http://www.ecodir.org> accessed on 7 June 2004.

[55] Cruquenaire and de Patoul 2002.

[56] ECODIR has been held in abeyance since the end of the project.

[57] Accessed at <http://www.ucd.ie/alumni/html/connections9/2004ucdp38.pdf> on 13 July 2004.

[58] Art. 1: Application of the Rules-ECODIR Resolution Rules accessed at <http://www.ecodir.org/odrp/rules.htm> on 14 July 2004.

The ODR process is a voluntary process, that is, the parties to the dispute submit and respondent to the case voluntarily. There is no binding rule compelling a respondent to respond to a claim submitted to ODR.

There are three stages in the ECODIR process: negotiation, mediation and recommendation. Each stage in the process is free of charge. The rules provide that the negotiation phase cannot take longer than 18 days. If the dispute is not resolved in the negotiation phase, any of the parties can ask for a mediator to be appointed. The mediation phase should not take longer than 15 days. If the parties have not resolved the dispute at the end of 15 days, the mediator can make a recommendation within 4 days. If the parties agree (at any point in the dispute resolution process) on a solution, they can sign an Agreement form to formalise the settlement.

The ECODIR rules include a system of follow-up after a settlement has been reached between the parties. Thirty days after settlement is reached, the Secretariat writes to the parties to enquire whether the settlement had been implemented. If the settlement is not implemented the parties are asked to provide reasons for the non-implementation.[59] Follow-up by the Secretariat has no enforcement power but has, presumably, some 'authoritative' value.

All information relating to a claim and the communication between the parties and the mediator takes place in a secure private web space on ECODIR's server.[60]

(c) provide for the way the ECODIR secretariat and mediators behave. The rules list the number of actions to be performed by the Secretariat, for example, to notify a respondent that a customer has filed a claim; to keep track of time in the different phases of the process; to appoint a mediator; to change a mediator; and to check on the implementation of a settlement.[61]

Mediators are bound by secrecy and confidentiality.[62] They are to assist "the Parties in an independent and impartial manner in their attempt to reach an amicable settlement to their problem."[63] Furthermore, the mediators are to be guided by principles of fairness and justice and undertake not to act as counsel or representative of the parties.[64] Mediators are chosen on the basis of their expertise in the dispute area in question.[65]

---

[59] Art. 3: The Process and Article 4: Implementation of the Settlement-ECODIR Resolution rules accessed at <http://www.ecodir.org/odrp/rules.htm> on 14 July 2004.

[60] Frequently asked questions (answer to question: What is the On-line Dispute Resolution service offered by ECODIR?) accessed at <http://www.ecodir.org/odrp/faq.htm> on 14 July 2004.

[61] ECODIR Resolution Rules accessed at <http://www.ecodir.org/odrp/rules.htm> on 14 July 2004.

[62] Art. 10: Confidentiality-ECODIR Resolution Rules accessed at <http://www.ecodir.org/odrp/rules.htm> on 14 July 2004.

[63] Art. 6: Role of the Mediator-ECODIR Resolution Rules accessed at <http://www.ecodir.org/odrp/rules.htm> on 14 July 2004.

[64] Ibid.

[65] Art. 5: Appointment of a Mediator-ECODIR Resolution Rules accessed at <http://www.ecodir.org/odrp/rules.htm> on 14 July 2004 states 'The Mediators field of expertise, geographic location and language proficiency are taken into consideration in their appointment.'

(d) provide for the way the parties are expected to behave: Parties are bound by rules of confidentiality. They are expected to act in good faith with the mediator and with the other party. They are to submit proposed solutions for the settlement of the dispute and exercise their best efforts to reach an agreement.[66]

The rules for the different stages in the process are based on underlying values found in state law and obligations found in traditional alternative dispute resolution mechanisms.[67] When commenting on the designing of ECODIR, Cruquenaire and De Patoul[68] emphasize that the rules also reflect principles found in two EU recommendations: Commission Recommendation 98/257/EC[69] on the principles applicable to the bodies responsible for out-of-court settlement of consumer disputes and Commission Recommendation 2001/310/EC[70] on the principles out-of-court bodies involved in the consensual resolution of consumer disputes. These include specifically the rules on independence and impartiality of the mediators, the transparency of the process, solution in a reasonable time, and the possibility of being represented or assisted during proceedings.

Despite the similarity in rules between ECODIR and SquareTrade, ECODIR's popularity has been very limited.[71] The reasons for non-use follow from 'legal', social and market rules that have been built into the eBay/SquareTrade space but not in the ECODIR arrangement. Primarily, there is no direct link between the space where the disputes arises and the ODRS. In the SquareTrade example, there is a clear connection between the 'space' where transactions are taking place and the ODRS, that is, eBay and SquareTrade. In contrast, in the ECODIR example, there is no obvious link between the space where ECODIR's potential users transact and ECODIR.

Furthermore, the remedies offered by ECODIR have no real direct effect on the assets of the participants. In the SquareTrade example, participation in the ODRS and the remedies offered have a direct effect on the reputation of the participant in the eBay community. Participating in ECODIR has no clear direct effect on the assets of participants. It depends completely on the 'goodwill' of participants to want to participate and to keep to the agreement reached.[72]

7.2.4   ODR and trademark-domain name disputes

The most important private rule-making process for trademark-domain name disputes is the Uniform Domain Name Dispute Resolution Policy (UDRP) developed

---

[66] Art. 9: Role of the Parties-ECODIR Resolution Rules accessed at <http://www.ecodir.org/odrp/rules.htm> on 14 July 2004.

[67] They are also based on principles of fairness and justice found in the European Convention of Human Rights.

[68] Cruquenaire and De Patoul 2002

[69] *OJ* L115 17 April 1998 p. 31.

[70] *OJ* L109 19 April 2001 p. 56.

[71] 16 cases.

[72] Cf., Mifsud Bonnici and De Vey Mestdagh 2005b.

by the Internet Corporation for Assigned Names and Numbers (ICANN). The increased use and commercial value of domain names in the late 1990s gave rise to a number of disputes between trademark holders and service marks and domain name registrants. Ordinarily the same trademark or service mark can be used in a single (jurisdictional) territory so long as the marks are used in different economic sectors were confusion is unlikely. The use of a domain name is neither restricted to one jurisdiction and nor does it allow multiple registrations of the same name under the same top-level domain. Conflicts between trademark holders and domain name registrants are of, at least, three types: (i) conflicts on the use of the same string of characters; (ii) conflicts where a domain name is similar to a trade-mark and is meant to pass for the other; and (iii) cyber squatting, that is, the registering of a domain name before the trade mark owner has done so with a view to exacting a price for transferring the domain name to the trade mark owner.[73]

These conflicts and disputes need to be resolved. Normally, a state court where the trademark is registered resolves trademark disputes. While the same option is available to trademark-domain name resolution, since the disputes may involve different jurisdictions (and originally many courts were unfamiliar with the notion of domain name) alternative dispute resolution solutions are needed. The need for a prompt and (relatively) easy manner of resolving disputes prompted ICANN to formulate a Uniform Domain Name Dispute Resolution Policy (UDRP) for the resolution of disputes between trademark holders and domain name holders on (originally) the '.com', '.org' and '.net' top-level domains. ICANN-accredited registrars in all gTLDs now adopt it.[74]

Earlier, in July 1998, WIPO Member States had asked WIPO to report on a procedural method that should be adopted in the resolution of conflicts between trademark holders and domain name registrants. The WIPO report was published in April 1999.[75] Later that year (August 1999), ICANN issued the UDRP rules. The UDRP rules included the recommendations proposed by WIPO. As of May 2004, 9377 proceedings involving 15,710 domain names had been brought under the UDRP. Two-thirds of the proceedings resulted in either a transfer or cancellation of the domain name in dispute. Around one-fifth of the proceedings found in favour of the respondent and around one-ninth were terminated without decision. The 15,710 represent about 0.03 per cent of the 46 million domain names subject to UDRP registered during the same years (1999-2004).[76] The majority of cases were submitted in the early years of the UDRP. For a number of reasons,[77] there has been a decline in the number of trademark-domain name disputes.[78]

---

[73] Smith 2002: 78.

[74] That is, the '.aero', '.biz', '.com', '.coop', '.info', '.museum', '.name', '.net', '.org' and '.pro'.

[75] Further details see WIPO Report 1999 and Gibson 2001: 34.

[76] US National Research Council of the National Academies 2005: 3-45.

[77] For example, the 'success' of disputes resolved under the UDRP process; and the introduction of rules for the registration of domain names under new top level domain names to reduce instances of cyber squatting.

[78] Since August 2000, proceedings filed have been steadily declining. See US National Research Council of the National Academies 2005: 3-45.

Contemporaneously, a number of disputes have been submitted to state courts in different countries. Since 997, courts in, amongst others, the United Kingdom, France, India and the United States have decided trademark-domain name disputes.[79]

7.2.4.1   *UDRP rules created by ICANN*

The ICANN[80] UDRP rules consist of three sets of rules. The first set establishes the circumstances where trademark-domain name disputes may be resolved using an administrative (private) dispute resolution process. The UDRP rules provide for administrative dispute resolution proceedings in the event that a complainant (often a trademark holder) asserts that:

(i)   the domain name is identical or confusingly similar to a trademark or service mark in which the complainant has rights; and
(ii)   the registrant has no rights or legitimate interests in respect of the domain name; and
(iii) the domain name has been registered and is being used in bad faith.[81]

The UDRP rules identify how 'bad faith' and 'legitimate interests' in respect of a domain name in dispute can be proved in the proceedings. They also identify the main procedural steps to be followed in the trademark-domain name resolution process. The dispute resolution proceedings are mandatory on domain name registrants of top-level domains. They determine what the results of the dispute resolution process can be. If the Administrative panel finds against a defendant (a domain name registrant) the domain name can be cancelled, transferred or changed.[82] The decision is automatically enforced by the domain name Registry (after ten business days from the decision), which cancels or transfers the domain name according to the decision.

The second set of rules are to be followed by dispute resolution providers approved by ICANN. The approved dispute resolution providers are bound by the Rules for Uniform Domain Name Dispute Resolution Policy.[83] These are procedural rules to be followed when a trademark-domain name complaint is filed with the provider. The rules include:

(a) the rules a complainant must follow in the filing of a complaint;
(b) the method of communication and time limits binding the provider to communicate the complaint to the respondent;

---

[79] US National Research Council of the National Academies 2005: 3-48.
[80] A description of ICANN as a private actor involved in self-regulation is given in Chapter 5 – Self-regulation of the Domain Name System.
[81] Art. 4a of the UDRP accessed at <http://www.icann.org/dndr/udrp/policy.htm> 4 August 2004.
[82] Id. Art. 3.
[83] Accessed at <http://www.icann.org/dndr/udrp/uniform-rules.htm> 4 August 2003.

(c) the rules a respondent must comply with in filing a response;
(d) the appointment of a panel, (the panel can be made up of one panellist or the parties may ask for the appointment of a three-panellists panel);
(e) rules panellists must follow in the dispute resolution procedure, (these include rules on impartiality and independence as well as time limits within which the panel should formulate its decision);
(f) rules on the proceedings, (there are no in-person hearings unless the Panel determines in its discretion and by way of exception that a hearing is necessary).[84]
(g) rules on the delivery of the panel decisions;
(h) rules on fees and
(i) rules on the effect of court proceedings on the panel's proceedings, (if Court proceedings are initiated the panel may suspend or terminate the proceeding before it).[85]

The third set of rules regulates the approval of dispute resolution providers by ICANN. Under UDRP, all mandatory administrative dispute proceedings are to be submitted to ICANN-approved dispute resolution providers. There are five approved dispute-resolution providers: Asian Domain Name Dispute Resolution Centre (ADNRC);[86] the Centre for Public Resources Institute for Dispute Resolution (CPR);[87] eResolution;[88] The National Arbitration Forum;[89] and the World Intellectual Property Organisation (WIPO).[90]

Approximately 60 per cent of the disputes submitted under UDRP have been filed with WIPO, approximately 33 per cent have been filed with the National Arbitration Forum, approximately 6 per cent were filed with eResolution, and approximately 0.7 percent has been filed with the Center for Public Resources Institute for Dispute Resolution.[91]

For a dispute resolution provider to be approved, the provider needs to fulfil a number of criteria identified by ICANN. These include, *inter alia*, that the provider is capable of handling the large number of possible cases to be submitted to it; that the panellists of the proposed provider are well trained with respect to domain name disputes and the UDRP rules; and that the provider develop supplemental rules (including a fee schedule) in line with the UDRP rules and that these rules are public and transparent.

---

[84] Art. 13 of the Rules for UDRP accessed at <http://www.icann.org/dndr/udrp/uniform-rules.htm> 4 August 2003.

[85] Id. Art. 18.

[86] Approved since 28 February 2002.

[87] Approved since 22 May 2000.

[88] Approved 1 January 2000 and not accepting proceedings since 30 November 2001.

[89] Approved since 23 December 1999.

[90] Approved since 1 December 1999.

[91] See US National Research Council of the National Academies 2005: 3-45.

7.2.4.2   The dispute resolution process offered by eResolution

eResolution is one of the ICANN-approved domain name dispute resolution provider. It was the first private dispute resolution to offer providing an entirely on-line dispute resolution process. eResolution stopped receiving disputes for resolution when in November 2001 it filed for bankruptcy. eResolution had less than 8 per cent of the market share of domain name disputes at the time of service.[92] It was involved in the on-line resolution of over 500 cases from around 60 countries in the two years of its operation.[93]

In spite of these circumstances, eResolution is still an important example of self-regulation in the provision of dispute resolution, especially since it was the only provider offering an entirely on-line dispute resolution system. All information regarding the case and all communication took place on-line. eResolution offered a secure platform accessible to the parties in the dispute and the panellist/s assigned to the dispute. The discontinuance of eResolution reflects the still volatile nature of the private provision of dispute resolution.

Though the original eResolution web site is no longer operational, archived copies of a number of different versions of eResolution's web site can be accessed at <http://www.archive.org>.[94]

eResolution was developed and maintained by a consortium made up of Disputes.org – a US-based organisation of qualified arbitrators and eResolution.ca – a Canadian on-line arbitration software and services provider.[95] eResolution was approved by ICANN to act as a domain name dispute resolution provider as from the 1st January 2000. The on-line dispute resolution system went live on 4th January 2000.

The trademark-domain name dispute resolution process offered by eResolution is regulated by two sets of rules.[96] The first set of rules was created by ICANN for the resolution of domain name disputes. The second set is the set of 'Supplemental Rules' created by eResolution. The 'supplemental rules'[97] are primarily procedural rules. These rules conform with and supplement the UDRP rules primarily 'to evaluate Complaints and for conducting administrative proceedings'.[98] These rules regulate, *inter alia*:

---

[92] Selby 2003: 134.

[93] See Benyekhlef and Gélinas 2005.

[94] Accessed at <http://web.archive.org/web/*//http://www.disputes.org> on 26 July 2004.

[95] In practice a consortium of leading academics in the field of on-line dispute resolution (e.g., Prof. Katsh,) and intellectual property. Information from Company Press Release on the launch of eResolultion's website 20 December 1999 accessed at <http://web.archive.org/web/20000612115648/www.eresolution.ca/> on 26 July 2004.

[96] In the resolution of some domain name disputes of specific top-level domains other sets of rules may be applicable. For example, for the resolution of the '.biz' TLD two other sets of rules – STOP and RDRP – also apply (see <http://web.archive.org/web/20011020013126/www.eresolution.ca/> on 26 July 2004).

[97] Accessed at <http://web.archive.org/web/200061032224/www.eresolution.ca/> on 26 July 2004.

[98] Art. 1u Definitions – Supplemental Rules accessed at accessed at <http://web.archive.org/web/200061032224/www.eresolution.ca/> on 26 July 2004.

(a) the filing of the complaint and response. A valid complaint/response has three parts: a coversheet, the complaint proper and annexes to the complaint. The rule is implemented in the technical set-up of the eResolution on-line dispute resolution system. The complaint and response are filed using specific electronic forms. The three parts are to be submitted in electronic format and hard copy. The claim/response forms force the complainant/respondent to follow a given structure in the organisation of the arguments of the complaint or response.

The design of the eResolution forms, it has been argued, have two advantages over the forms of other providers: (i) they are more structured,[99] and (ii) since they are submitted in electronic form, they are clearer and easily accessible to the panellist.[100]

(b) the fees to be paid for submitting the dispute to the eResolution on-line dispute resolution process. Once a complaint is filed for the dispute resolution process to commence, the complainant must pay the prescribed fee. The fee is dependent on the number of panellists (one or three) hearing the case. The choice on the number of panellists lies with the complainant. However, if the complainant opts for a one-panel procedure the respondent can still ask that three panellists hear the procedure.

(c) the method of communication between the parties and the eResolution, between the panellists and the parties, between the panellist and eResolution. All communications are to be done by e-mail unless eResolution prescribes another form for the communication.[101]

(d) the appointment of panellists and the qualifications of panellists. The appointment of the panel is the responsibility of the dispute resolution provider. However, when asking for a three-panellist panel, the complainant and the respondent can nominate three panellists from the list of approved panellists. (Each provider submits the list of panellists to ICANN for approval.)

The panellist must be and remain independent and impartial during the proceedings.[102] The rules provide for challenges to a panellist by a party and the appointment of a replacement.[103]

(e) the termination of the proceedings: proceedings can terminate either on the delivery of a decision by the panel or when the parties reach a settlement.

---

[99] Lametti (2002: 4) argues that the eResolution forms had more leading questions in the form. Using this structure the party could present the arguments in a precise and more complete manner.

[100] Lametti (2002: 2-3).

[101] Rule 4 – Communications in Supplemental Rules accessed at accessed at <http://web.archive.org/web/200061032224/www.eresolution.ca/> on 26 July 2004.

[102] Art. 9 Attributes of Panelist in Supplemental Rules accessed at accessed at <http://web.archive.org/web/200061032224/www.eresolution.ca/> on 26 July 2004.

[103] Arts. 10 and 11 Recusation and Replacement in Supplemental Rules accessed at accessed at <http://web.archive.org/web/200061032224/www.eresolution.ca/> on 26 July 2004.

7.2.4.3   *The dispute resolution process offered by ADNDRC*

ADNDRC is a joint initiative of the China International Economic and Trade Arbitration Commission (CIETAC) and the Hong Kong International Arbitration Centre (HKIAC).[104] Both bodies are private groups. The ADNDRC ODRS is financially supported by the business community and some states.

Three sets of private groups are involved in providing the dispute resolution within ADNDRC. The ADNDRC centre provides the procedural rules to be followed in the dispute resolution process. A Hong Kong based company, Tradelink Electronic Commerce Limited,[105] developed the technical system used for dispute resolution following the dispute resolution rules created by ICANN and ADNDRC. The third group are the panellists who decide the domain name disputes. The panellists are approved by ICANN. They come from a number of jurisdictions, but there is an obvious majority of Asian-based panellists.[106] (The users of the system are predominantly (but not exclusively) Asian trademark holders complaining against Asian based domain name registrants.)

The ADNDRC accepts claims submitted on-line (or physically) to either the Beijing or the Hong Kong office of the ADNDRC. The claimant chooses where to submit the claim. The dispute resolution system offered by both offices is on-line.

Two sets of rules regulate the on-line process: (i) ICANN rules on dispute resolution and (ii) the ADNDRC supplemental rules. The ADNDRC Supplemental rules are predominantly drafted for the running of an off-line dispute resolution system. Like the eResolution Supplemental rules, the Supplemental rules (including the technically inbuilt rules) regulate, *inter alia*:

(a) the filing of the complaint. The ODRS 'walks' the complainant through the filing of a complaint, requiring the complainant to comply with all the rules for submission. Once the complaint form is filed electronically, the complainant must submit a hard copy of the complaint together with any additional documentation and pay the prescribed fee.
(b) the filing of a response. If the respondent chooses to use the on-line system, the respondent is guided through the filing of a response. The on-line form ensures that the respondent complies with all the rules of submission (except that a hard copy of the response must later be sent to ADNDRC).
(c) the method of communication between the parties and the ADNDRC, between the panellists and the parties, between the panellist and ADNDRC. All communication other than the filling in of the forms, can be done by e-mail, postal services, or telephone.[107]

---

[104] See <http://www.adndrc.org/adndrc/index.html> accessed 26 July 2004.

[105] See <http://www.adndrc.org/adndrc/bj_home.html> accessed 26 July 2004.

[106] See <http://www.adndrc.org/adndrc/bj_panelist.html> accessed 26 July 2004.

[107] Art. 3 of ADNDRC Supplemental Rules accessed at <http://www.adndrc.org/adndrc/bj_sup plemental_rules.html> on 5 August 2004.

(d) the appointment of panellists and the qualifications of panellists. The appointment of the panel is the responsibility of the ADNDRC. However, when asking for a three-panellist panel, the complainant and the respondent can nominate three panellists from the list of approved panellists. The panellist must remain independent and impartial during the proceedings.[108]

(e) the publication of the panel decision. All decisions are available on-line at the ADNDRC web site.

(f) the fees to be paid for submitting the dispute to the ADNDRC on-line dispute resolution process. As in the case of eResolution, fees are dependent on the number of panellists (one or three) hearing the case and the number of domain names in dispute.

7.2.5 ODR and Internet-content related disputes

'Informal' private dispute resolution in content-related disputes regularly takes place in Internet communities. Different on-line communities have developed informal ways to resolve conflicts on content within the community. These vary from persons in the group acting as moderators of the content in a news group to persons resorting to flaming[109] to 'resolve' disputes.

Private 'formal' dispute resolution systems to resolve content-related disputes are less common. State courts remain the predominant dispute resolution forum for content-related disputes. One of the earliest examples of a 'formal' dispute resolution system for content-related disputes is The Virtual Magistrate developed in 1996. The Virtual Magistrate was the first to offer on-line arbitration services for resolution of, *inter alia*, disputes claiming harm (damage) by wrongful messages, postings, or files on-line.[110] However, when The Virtual Magistrate issued its first decision a few months after its launch – a default (and unenforceable) decision in favour of a complainant against the non-participating America Online – it drew controversy, and the programme has by and large, become dormant.[111]

The Virtual Magistrate set the trail for the development of other on-line dispute resolution systems for on-line content-related disputes. Among the best known is IRIS-Médiation. It was set-up around the same time as the first Internet content-related disputes were being brought before French courts.

---

[108] Id. Art. 9.

[109] Flaming can be defined as the act of exchanging insults on-line. ['Flaming' is the act of posting messages that are deliberately hostile and insulting, usually in the social context of a discussion board (usually on the Internet) – accessed at <http://en.wikipedia.org/wiki/Flaming> on 9 September 2005].

[110] See The Virtual Magistrate Project Concept Paper (July 1996) accessed at <http://www.vmag.org/docs/concept.html> on 3 August 2004.

[111] This notwithstanding, The Virtual Magistrate is still available and hosted by Chicago-Kent College of Law, at <www.vmag.org>. See also Ambrogi 2005: 13.

7.2.5.1   *The dispute resolution process offered by IRIS-Médiation*

IRIS-Médiation was developed by a French private non-governmental organisation, **I**maginons un **R**éseau **I**nternet **S**olidaire (IRIS). The mediators were volunteers. The list of mediators included lawyers, technicians, academics and others. The users of the system were private parties who agreed voluntarily to submit and respond to a claim.

IRIS-Médiation was launched in March 1998 as an experiment. The intention of the experiment was to show that many small conflicts between private parties concerning on-line content could be resolved without recourse to court.[112] Another reason for the experiment was to establish that ODR could serve as an 'appeal' from decisions on content taken by ISPs.

In the first year of activities of IRIS-Médiation, between March 1998 and March 1999, 125 requests for mediation were submitted. 61 of the claims remained unanswered by the respondent. Of the remaining requests 53 reached a settlement, 2 found no amicable solution and in 6 cases one party failed to participate after agreeing to do so.[113]

The IRIS-Médiation procedural rules are not clearly defined in a list of rules. The rules have been implemented in the on-line system. The rules include rules that determine:

(a) what disputes can be submitted to IRIS-Médiation. Disputes that can be submitted to IRIS-Médiation are Internet content related disputes between parties who have no contractual relationship with each other. Some cases that have been submitted to IRIS-Médiation related to allegations of intellectual property violations on personal web sites and allegations of privacy violations or libel or insult claims.[114]

(b) how the dispute is submitted to IRIS-Médiation. A complainant can fill in a form available on-line or send the complaint via e-mail.

(c) that the respondent can submit a response via e-mail.

(d) how a mediator is appointed.

(e) that the agreement reached between the parties is not binding and based completely on the consent of the parties for its implementation.

(f) that the privacy and confidentiality of the proceedings is to be respected at all times.

(g) that the ODR service is offered free of charge to the parties submitting their claim.

---

[112] Meryem Marzouki 2000: slide 5.
[113] Id. slide 8.
[114] Ibid.

- Other ODRS for content-related disputes

While there is current no ODRS for copyright related disputes, Lemley and Reese[115] argue that ODR can offer a quick and inexpensive system for resolving digital copyright disputes. Seeing that copyright related disputes are an important area of Internet content-related disputes and that state courts (in different jurisdictions), have produced a patchwork of often contradictory decisions, the authors propose a system similar to that described above for resolving trademark-domain name disputes.[116] Private on-line dispute resolution providers would offer the dispute resolution process and the panellists would be experts in intellectual property issues. The authors propose that the system could be limited to 'straightforward conduct that is unlikely to have legitimate justifications, such as high-volume uploading of copyrighted works to p2p networks.'[117] The claims and defences allowed should follow those in the US Digital Millennium Copyright Act. State legislation could provide that all ISP – customer agreements should include a provision that any allegation by a third party of infringement of copyright will be resolved through an administrative procedure.[118] The authors suggest that the panellists could award a financial or other sanction if they find in favour of a complainant.[119] The ISP providing service to the respondent could enforce the decision. The system could be financed through fees paid for the dispute resolution process. Whether this system will be adopted is yet to be seen, it is however indicative of the potential of ODRS in the resolution of on-line disputes.

7.2.6 The function of the self-regulation rules

Although the ODRS used for the resolution of on-line disputes are still in development, self-regulation currently serves three main functions. Primarily it offers a forum to hear disputes and where a remedy can be obtained. This is particularly evident in the resolution of e-commerce related disputes and in trademarks-domain name disputes. In some disputes, such as those that arise in the eBay space, self-regulation offers a forum and remedy where no other practical alternative exits. E-commerce disputes, as noted earlier, can be particularly problematic when the transaction involved takes place transnationally. Access to courts, though theoretically possible, may in practice be too costly and impracticable for the parties in dispute to submit the case to state courts. Indeed, both SquareTrade and ECODIR

---

[115] Lemley and Reese 2004: 4.

[116] With the necessary amendments to the UDRP model keeping in mind the current criticism levelled at the URDP rules especially on the lack of transparency and lack of oversight of panellists' decisions.

[117] Lemley and Reese 2004: 4, 5-6.

[118] This follows the situation prevalent under UDRP. Since in copyright there is no central authority like ICANN to impose that ISP's include mandatory dispute resolution through an administrative process, the state should step in. Lemley and Reese 2004: 5.

[119] Lemley and Reese 2004: 5.

offer a forum for e-commerce related disputes irrespective of the transnational aspects of the on-line dispute. SquareTrade and ECODIR settlements are reached irrespective of the often different nationalities and physical locations of the parties involved in the dispute.

SquareTrade not only offers a forum for on-line disputes but also provides actual remedies. SquareTrade offers a remedy in cases that would otherwise be left unresolved because their 'trivial' value (or the eBay specific nature of the dispute, such as feedback related disputes) makes access to court impractical.

Secondly, the private dispute resolution process has a number of advantages over state courts. This can be seen in particular in the case of trademark-domain name related disputes and to a much more limited extent in content-related disputes. Users submitting a trademark-domain name dispute to (eResolution and) ADNDRC can in practice submit the same dispute to state courts. But an ODRS is often much quicker than court proceedings. On average a dispute submitted to the private dispute resolution process takes only between 40 to 60 days to be resolved.[120] This is much shorter than average times for court proceedings. In addition, and perhaps more importantly, private dispute resolution offers specific expertise and specialised dispute resolution. The panellists have specific expertise in trademark-domain name disputes.

Thirdly, self-regulation provides substantive rules for the resolution of particular on-line disputes (especially where specific state legislation regulating the particular disputes is lacking). This can be seen in particular in the ICANN UDRP rules on trademark-domain disputes. Similarly, this can be seen in the substantive rules created by eBay for the resolution of feedback related disputes.

7.2.7 Self-regulation as a source of dispute resolution rules

Self-regulation arrangements providing dispute resolution share important characteristics of formal legal dispute resolution structures.

Legitimacy and accountability of the dispute resolution providers

The groups involved in the creation and administration of both the substantive rules and the procedural rules of ODRS are experts in the areas of dispute. They understand the needs of the community of users and are familiar with the issues that give rise to disputes. It would be hard to find a more academically and technically qualified private group than ECODIR and (formerly) eResolution, for example. Having technical access, they are able to offer the dispute resolution service on-line making it, literally, 'one click away' for most users to access the dispute resolution space.

Participation of users in the dispute resolution systems confirms that users trust the expertise of the groups and consider the self-regulation arrangements legitimate

---

[120] Benyekhlef and Gélinas 2005.

structures for dispute resolution. The more than 1.5 million cases submitted to SquareTrade, for example, confirm that users consider SquareTrade a legitimate dispute resolution provider. Parties in dispute are free not to follow the SquareTrade rules and ODRS for the resolution of their dispute. They can choose, for example, to submit the dispute to a state court. However, if they choose to submit to the ODRS developed by SquareTrade, they acknowledge SquareTrade's legitimacy. For users, as long as the dispute resolution mechanism offers an actual remedy to the dispute, it makes no difference whether the dispute resolution provider is a state court or a private group. The low level of participation in, for example ECODIR and IRIS-Médiation, can be linked to the remedy (or lack of it) that the private dispute resolution forum provides.

Furthermore, at times the private arrangements are given legitimacy by states, as in the ECODIR example. In other examples, private groups creating substantive dispute resolution rules (such as ICANN in the creation of the UDRP) acknowledge the legitimacy of the private dispute resolution arrangement through either a process of accreditation, such as in the example of eResolution and ADNDRC, or by agreement, as in the case of eBay and SquareTrade.

The legitimacy of the self-regulation is (also) tied to the contractual relationship between the parties who submit to the ODRS and the ODRS. The involvement of eBay in dispute resolution, for example, is based on a contractual relationship between eBay buyers and sellers and eBay. The rules of eBay on dispute resolution – directing the buyers and sellers to use SquareTrade, mandating the use of SquareTrade for 'feedback related' disputes and accepting the settlement reached by SquareTrade ODRS – are part of the contractual relationship between eBay and the buyers and sellers trading in the space provided by eBay.

External sources, such as states, other private groups, and users are also important to keep the groups involved in dispute resolution in check. While the private groups seem to have acted so far in an accountable manner, the internal and external mechanisms of accountability are not always clear. The involvement of states in accountability has been mostly theoretical – there is a theoretical possibility, for example, for the European Union or the Irish government to keep ECODIR in check based on the co-funding arrangement with ECODIR.[121] Under Article 10[122] of the

---

[121] The development of ECODIR benefited from co-funding by the European Commission, Health and Consumer Protection Directorate-General. The legal basis for the funding was Art. 2(c) of Decision 283/1999EC of the European Parliament and Council of 25 January 1999 establishing a general framework for Community activities in favour of consumers. (*OJ* L34 9 February 1999)

[122] Art. 10 of Decision 283/1999EC reads:
'1. The Commission shall ensure the monitoring and supervision of effective implementation of the activities financed by the Community. This shall be done on the basis of reports using procedures agreed between the Commission and the recipient; it shall include checks in situ by means of sampling.
2. Recipients shall submit a report to the Commission for each action within three months of its completion. The Commission shall determine the form and content of this report.
3. Recipients of financial support shall keep at the Commission's disposal all the documentary evidence of expenditure for a period of five years from the last payment concerning an action.'

EU Parliament and Council's Decision under which ECODIR is co-funded, for example, the Commission has the power to monitor and supervise the effective implementation of the project. This secures, at least in theory, some level of accountability of the parties receiving the money from the European Union.

There are in part a number of other mechanisms of accountability. No one mechanism of accountability is enough to secure provider accountability. The different mechanisms are to be taken cumulatively. Private dispute resolution does not exist in a vacuum. It develops and is maintained in a complex relationship with other groups that hold the private dispute resolution systems in account. For example, eResolution and ADNDRC provide dispute resolution services under conditions imposed by ICANN. The approval of ICANN can be withdrawn if the private groups do not follow the ICANN rules. Furthermore, ICANN can be held in check through the oversight mechanisms available to the US government that can review any decision taken by ICANN.

In theory, state courts can also act as an external mechanism of accountability. Courts can, on the request of one or both parties review the substantive and procedural rules of the ODRS and review the decisions/settlements reached.

Users who submit their disputes to private dispute resolution arrangements can keep the groups in check. Unless the regulation created and implemented by the ODRS satisfies the needs of disputants, they can choose not to submit their dispute to the ODRS. In practice, however, the effect of this control mechanism is weak. Buyers and sellers on eBay, for example, have few choices of dispute resolution alternatives. Ensuring that users can select among alternative dispute resolution possibilities increases the effect of this mechanism.

Furthermore, the groups have an inherent (often financial) interest that the system satisfies the needs of the users, as the survival of the private arrangement is dependent on the use of the system by the users. If the system offered does not satisfy users' needs, they will not use the system. While that there may be other reasons (e.g., lack of publicity of the existence of the system) why the members of the community of interest do not use an ODRS, attracting users to the system is one mechanism of accountability of the providing group.

However, satisfying the needs of the users does not necessarily mean that the system provided is intrinsically not an adequate dispute resolution system. The expectations of the users and of other private groups of the dispute resolution may be different from those of the private group involved in the arrangement. In the ECODIR example, the aim of the private group who set it up is essentially an academic research exercise to establish a fair and impartial voluntary dispute resolution system while the users are primarily interested in obtaining an actual remedy to the dispute. Similarly, different expectations seem to have impaired the survival of eResolution. eResolution offered an impartial system where both the claims of the trademark holders and the domain name registrants were equally considered on the merits of the case, with the result that at times eResolution panel decisions were more in favour of a domain name registrant.[123] Their expectations frustrated, trade-mark holders looked elsewhere for a remedy.

Another mechanism of accountability is reputation. Reputation is an intangible asset of any group involved in providing dispute resolution services. First-time users of the system can only trust the provider based on the reputation the group holds. Providers of ODRS are kept in check by the desire not to lose their reputation.

Future private arrangements may need to improve the mechanisms of account-ability. Some authors[124] see a greater role for states in ensuring group accountabil-ity, through for example, accreditation systems or by developing frameworks of procedural guarantees to be followed by the dispute resolution providers. Often, however, criticisms on accountability are not directed at the ODRS provider but more specifically at the panellists, in particular in trademark-domain name dis-putes. The ICANN rules fail to offer a mechanism to review the decisions given by panellists or mechanisms to ensure effectively the impartiality of panellists. Indeed, one could argue that the practice of forum shopping can result in lack of impartial-ity of some of the panellists. The practice of forum shopping encourages panellists and dispute resolution providers to pander to the requests of trademark owners in order to attract a larger market share of disputes. eResolution has not been subject (and could not be subject) to this criticism on panellists bias since the outcome of the disputes showed clearly that eResolution was not indulging the wishes of trade-mark owners but was actually hearing and deciding the disputes on the merits of the cases submitted.

Legal effect of on-line dispute resolution

The substantive rules created by eBay and ICANN are not mere social norms. They are binding, transparent and certain. Similarly, the procedural rules implemented in the dispute resolution systems follow the same principles of fairness and indepen-dence users are accustomed to when using state court systems and other off-line alternative dispute resolution *fora*. It is not surprising that the rules are influenced by existing rules governing other dispute resolution systems. The rules in other systems have been developed over centuries and the willingness of litigants to par-ticipate in the systems is dependent on some of these rules. For example, disputants expect that the mediator or panellist is not biased.

In each example (except in the IRIS-Médiation), the process to be followed is written and easily accessible at the web site of the dispute resolution provider. The sites clearly identify the different steps to be followed in the dispute resolution process. Furthermore, they clearly identify what type of dispute resolution method is offered, for example, SquareTrade offers two dispute resolution methods: direct

---

[123] See Geist 2002a, 2000b.
[124] Like Shultz 2004.

negotiation and mediation. eResolution and ADNDRC offer one system: a panel decision.

The process is open to the parties in each example. The technical set-up of the space offered (except in the IRIS-Médiation case)[125] allows the participants in the process (the parties, the mediators and the administrators) to follow what is going on in the process. The on-line dispute resolution process, like traditional alternative dispute resolution (and unlike state courts), is not accessible to the public. But in the case of the trademark-domain name cases, the final decision reached by the panel is published and is publicly accessible at the web site of the dispute resolution provider.

The rules provide for the impartiality and independence of the mediators/panellists in the dispute resolution process. However, they generally lack mechanisms to check and enforce this. Some authors[126] argue that the lack of mechanisms to enforce the impartiality of panellists disqualifies private ODRS as a dispute resolution forum. Indeed, this has been an important criticism of the current UDRP rules and dispute resolution system. Nor do the ICANN rules provide for any kind of check when a provider condones the bias of the panellists in favour of trademark holders over respondents.

The current private dispute resolution arrangements lack transparency with regard to funding. This lack of transparency can cast doubt on the impartiality of an ODRS. To a certain extent, this is linked with the problem of private groups face in securing long-term funding for the dispute resolution service they offer. In early private dispute resolution experiments, funding was provided mainly through research grants. Currently, private systems (apart from ECODIR and IRIS-Médiation) seek to survive through the fees paid by users for the dispute resolution service. Surviving through fees alone in the long-term is (fairly) ambitious when one considers that private on-line dispute resolution is still unfamiliar to many users. The need to survive financially can entice a dispute resolution provider to favour particular parties in on-line disputes. In the trademark-domain name disputes, for example, one can argue that the dispute resolution provider is directly dependent for its continued existence on trademark owners (rather than domain name registrants)[127] and hence has no interest in providing mechanisms to counter the (perceived) bias in favour of trademark holders over domain name registrants. Where the funding of an ODRS comes from external sources independent of the parties, such as from states, the provider has an incentive to maintain its independence and impartiality transparently intact as in the ECODIR example.

A private on-line dispute resolution system becomes economically viable when it is assured of large quantities of disputes of a similar nature. An agreement or

---

[125] IRIS-Médiation does not offer a technical dispute resolution space (similar to SquareTrade or eResolution for example) – the process is an 'on-line' process so far as it is carried out through e-mail exchanges only.

[126] Benyekhlef and Gélinas 2005.

[127] Davis 2003: 7.

relationship between a dispute resolution provider and a commercial on-line platform where these disputes arise can act as such economic assurance. This is seen in the eBay – SquareTrade arrangement. Assured of a large number of cases, the dispute resolution service can maintain low fees and hence offer a cost-effective solution to the parties in the dispute.

Some authors, like Hörnle[128] and Schultz,[129] see a role for state involvement to ensure impartiality of the on-line dispute resolution processes, for example by creating accreditation agencies for on-line dispute resolution services, requiring third party monitoring/auditing of on-line dispute resolution, or by judicial review of the dispute resolution process. However, these suggestions fail to tackle the issue of long-term financial survival of private dispute resolution arrangements.

Offering actual remedies

Dispute resolution is not only a question of providing a forum to which disputes can be submitted but also of offering actual remedies for on-line disputes. For many users, two central issues are important.[130] The first is that the forum ensures respondent participation and a settlement/decision even in case of the respondent's default. The second is that the systems and the rules ensure that the settlement is binding and can be enforced against a non-compliant party.

The primary incentives for a complainant to participate in dispute resolution are rather obvious. Since a complainant is the aggrieved party in the dispute, a complainant will participate in a dispute resolution process if there is some assurance that the dispute resolution process can offer an actual remedy. Unlike the reasons of a complainant, the reasons why a respondent would submit to dispute resolution are less obvious. Probably, few respondents participate in dispute resolution voluntarily, based on some notion of fairness or equity. More often than not, a respondent participates only because he is compelled to do so. In the case of state courts, there is often a rule of procedure that non-participation of a respondent will not keep the dispute from being decided. Hence, the respondent has an interest in participating and presenting his/her side of the dispute. In the absence of a sovereign authority to compel parties to dispute resolution, the private sector has organised its own rules to secure submission.

Parallels of the same principle (of state courts) can be seen in the case of ICANN's domain name dispute resolution procedure. A domain name registrant is bound by contract to participate in a dispute resolution process provided by ICANN. In case of non-participation of the respondent, the panel can resolve the dispute in favour of the complainant and the respondent's domain name registration cancelled or

---

[128] Hörnle 2003: 25.
[129] Schultz 2003: 1.
[130] These issues are explored in Mifsud Bonnici and De Vey Mestdagh 2005b.

transferred to the complainant. Hence, it benefits the respondent to participate in the panel proceedings to defend the domain name registration.

Some of the rules in the eBay-SquareTrade process have the same compelling effect, such as the SquareTrade rule to review a feedback-rating dispute even when the respondent does not reply to the complaint. The importance of reputation in the market compels a respondent to collaborate in dispute resolution and avoid a negative reputation rating. In short, the incentive for a respondent to participate in an on-line dispute resolution process is inextricably linked with the effects of non-participation: a perceived loss he/she will suffer by non-participation – loss of credibility, loss of trust, financial/economic loss.

As the work of Katsh, Rifkin and Gaitenby[131] documents, specific rules in the transaction space and in the dispute resolution space can influence the participation of users in an on-line dispute resolution system. They argued specifically that eBay 'law' on reputation and the market rules on the value of reputation in the eBay marketplace were an important reason why complainants and respondents alike participated in the SquareTrade dispute resolution process. Indeed, this 'law' is still an important incentive in attracting participants to participate in SquareTrade. Apart from reputation 'law', there are in the current arrangement other 'rules' that influence current participation to SquareTrade dispute resolution process. One example is contract law – all traders committed to SquareTrade's seal of trust are bound by contract rules to submit disputes to the SquareTrade process. The eBay rules on feed-back rating – eBay can make changes to trader feedback only if instructed to do so by SquareTrade on conclusion of a feedback dispute submitted to SqaureTrade's ODRS – is another example. SquareTrade rules on reviewing feedback rating even if respondent does not reply to a complaint is another example. This rule supports the decision of complainants to participate in SquareTrade for feedback rating complaints, as it gives the certainty that the dispute would be addressed and possibly redressed in spite of a respondent's non-collaboration.

To the contrary, the ECODIR and IRIS-Médiation examples lack 'rules' built into the system that effectively compel participation in the dispute settlement mechanism. This lack can explain (in part) the slack use of ECODIR and IRIS-Médiation as an on-line dispute resolution process.[132]

The second important issue is that the system and its rules secure that the settlement/decision reached is binding on the parties and can be enforced against the non-compliant party. A dispute resolution system may have limited value if the process has no effect on the assets of the parties. Similarly, even decisions of state courts may have limited value if the decision of a 'foreign' court will have no practical consequence on the behaviour of the parties. For example, if the respondent

---

[131] Katsh, Rifkin and Gaitenby 2002.

[132] Another reason may be the lack of publicity. Few users are actually aware of the existence of ECODIR and IRIS-Médiation while SquareTrade, thanks to the relationship with eBay, is well-known. Similarly the accreditation of eResolution and ADNDRC by ICANN is a source of publicity.

has no financial assets in the jurisdiction of the court then there is little that the respondent can in fact lose if the court finds in favour of the complainant. Unless an efficient system of recognition of foreign court judgments is in place there is little incentive to participate in the dispute resolution.

In the trademark-domain dispute resolution cases, the decision reached by the panellists is binding on the parties in the dispute. Furthermore, the relevant domain name registry (after a delay of 10 business days)[133] automatically enforces the decision. The rules developed by ICANN and the system provided by eResolution and ADNDRC not only provide a forum where a trademark-domain name dispute can be submitted but also provides an actual enforceable remedy – the transfer or cancellation of the domain name.

The settlements reached through SquareTrade, ECODIR and IRIS-Médiation are dependent on the parties. Abiding by the decision, like participating in the on-line dispute resolution system, is voluntary. In the SquareTrade case, the perceived effects of loss of reputation may be sufficient to compel compliance. Parties in the ECODIR resolution process may opt to agree 'formally' to the settlement by clicking the 'agree' button once the mediator draws up the settlement agreement. In such a case, the common method of enforcement of the settlement (if at all) is through another action (this time before a state court) for breach of contract. State courts and legislation can act as backup systems for further action. They are not enough to entice parties to participate and abide by a settlement but offer some further recourse. In the ECODIR example, the dispute resolution provider communicates with the parties after settlement has been reached to follow-up whether the settlement has in fact been implemented. The provider has no actual power to enforce the settlement on the parties but this follow-up mechanism may in practice have a persuasive effect on the parties. Agreement to and compliance with the mediation settlement in IRIS-Médiation is entirely voluntary.

7.3 STATES AND ODRS

As described earlier, states have actively supported the development of ODRS in particular for the resolution of e-commerce related disputes. Indeed, one can argue that self-regulation is able to carry out the functions discussed earlier in section 7.2 (in 'The function of the self-regulation rules' section) thanks to the assistance it receives from states.

States are involved in encouraging the development of private dispute resolution arrangements. In particular, states (and intergovernmental organisations) have encouraged the development of on-line dispute resolution for the resolution of e-commerce related disputes. The encouragement of states has taken various forms:

---

[133] Art. 4k UDRP accessed at <http://www.icann.org/udrp/udrp-policy-24oct99.htm> on 10 August 2004.

- co-funding of on-line dispute resolution arrangements. The co-funding of ECODIR for the resolution of e-commerce related disputes by the European Union is an important example of co-funding by states.
- the drafting of guidelines that could be followed in the development and provision of on-line dispute resolution – such as the development of guidelines on e-commerce by the OECD which include some guidelines on the use of on-line dispute resolution.[134]
- advice on possible (best) remedies to be offered by private groups in cases of on-line disputes – such as the WIPO advisory report on the resolution of trademark-domain name disputes, parts of which were adopted by ICANN in the UDRP set of rules (see The Management of Internet Names and Addresses: Intellectual Property Issues).[135]

Furthermore, states and state regulation provide a general legal (principles) background to which self-regulation plugs into. In the dispute resolution process, for example, self-regulation rests on and follows general legal procedural principles used in state dispute resolution *fora*. In addition, self-regulation borrows from (or uses) general principles of contract law to regulate, for example, the relationship between a dispute resolution provider and a party submitting a dispute. At other times, self-regulation borrows from general state rules on the provision of alternative dispute resolution (such as rules on arbitration and mediation).

States can have an important oversight function over on-line dispute resolution. The oversight function is carried out in three ways. Firstly, the contractual agreement for co-funding initiatives of states includes clauses to hold the self-regulation arrangements in check. Secondly, state courts can, theoretically at least, through the possibility of judicial review, keep private dispute resolution in check. Thirdly, state legislation on unfair trading and consumer protection can be used to review the activities of private dispute resolution. Indirectly, through keeping private dispute resolution in check, states legitimise the presence of private dispute resolution and the action of private groups involved. Furthermore, state courts and state law provide a backup mechanism when private dispute resolution fails.

7.4   CONCLUSION

The greater the number of participants in cyberspace, the greater the number of disputes over transactions and hence, the greater the need for suitable *fora* to submit disputes to and achieve remedies. As can be seen in the descriptions given in

---

[134] OECD (1999) Guidelines for Consumer Protection in the Context of Electronic Commerce <http://www.oecd.org/dataoecd/5/34/1824782.pdf> 22 July 2004.

[135] Final Report of the WIPO Internet Domain Name Process 30 April 1999 accessed at <http://wipo2.wipo.int/process1/report/pdf/report.pdf> on 4 August 2004.

this chapter, both self-regulating groups and states currently offer *fora* for the resolution of on-line disputes and actually resolve some disputes, even if a large number of on-line disputes remain unresolved.

In limited ways, states offer traditional dispute resolution *fora* and remedies to resolve on-line disputes. Using state courts for on-line disputes is often fraught with legal and financial obstacles. In practice, state courts are not efficient fora for financially inconsequential or on-line environment specific (such as feedback related disputes) disputes. Yet, courts still offer an ultimate (fall-back) dispute resolution forum for on-line disputes.

In the past ten years, groups have introduced and developed a number of on-line *fora* for dispute resolution. In part, these on-line *fora* for dispute resolution developed from the need to address particular types of disputes for which access to state courts is theoretical at best. Groups address the need for dispute resolution knowing that the current set of state court alternatives, where they exist at all, do not, nor are they likely to do so any time soon, address the specific characteristics of on-line disputes. The SquareTrade case, for example, offers remedies specifically in cases where users would in practice not have an alternative forum to which to submit their dispute.

In part, they have been developed as experiments or trials testing the feasibility of private dispute resolution on-line for on-line disputes. There are only a limited number of private initiatives. Some – like SquareTrade and the UDRP – are particularly successful, others – such as ECODIR and Iris Médiation – are less successful.

Intertwining and complementary relationship

Self-regulation and state legislation and dispute resolution institutions do not exist independently of each other. Contrary to the initial expectations, in the early promotion of on-line dispute resolution, self-regulation has not taken over the resolution of on-line disputes. Neither have state institutions offered sufficient (or efficient) remedies in all on-line disputes. They both attempt to offer *fora* and remedies for on-line disputes with only limited success.

Even if the success of self-regulation in formal on-line dispute resolution is still limited, the contribution of the existing ODRS is important. This importance is two-fold. On the one hand, some ODRS, SquareTrade and the UDRP, offer practical remedies to users in disputes. This is especially relevant for e-commerce disputes arising on eBay.

On the other hand, they fill in for the non-existence or limitations of state dispute resolution legislation and institutions. In particular, self-regulation offers a forum and a remedy for on-line disputes where access to states courts is not a practical alternative. It provides substantive rules for the resolution of particular on-line disputes especially where specific state legislation regulating the particular disputes is lacking. ODRS also offer a forum to resolve disputes irrespective of the transnational aspects of the activity and dispute.

SquareTrade settlements are reached in spite of the often-different nationalities and physical location of the parties involved in the dispute. Similarly in trademark-domain name disputes, the panel decisions are implemented and enforced, irrespective of the physical location of the parties. Furthermore, they can offer this forum in a cost effective manner: The fees for dispute resolution, where levied, are much cheaper when compared to fees in state courts for transnational cases. While state courts are accustomed to apply private international law norms for transnational disputes, the effort and costs involved in reaching a settlement would often exceed the value of the object in litigation in on-line disputes. In e-commerce related disputes, for example, where the object in dispute has a 'low' (financial) value, the effort and expense involved in determining the right court and enforcing the decision would usually far exceed the value of the object of litigation. Furthermore, since there is still little international agreement on the recognition and enforcement of judgments issued by foreign courts, there is little assurance that the user submitting a dispute to a state court would actually obtain a remedy to the dispute. Hence, self-regulation fills in for the limitations of state solutions.

Self-regulation offers a forum that has special expertise in the dispute matters submitted. The settlement or panel decision is reached in a relatively short time by specialised assistance and expert panellists. The panellists in the trademark-domain name ODRS and the mediators in e-commerce disputes and Internet content related disputes are experts in the field. In contrast, state courts often lack the expertise needed for some on-line disputes.

The functions that self-regulation performs complement solutions provided by state courts. Self-regulation handles cases that state courts are unable to offer an actual remedy to and in situations where state substantive rules to resolve the dispute are missing or incomplete. In turn, state courts, at least in theory if not in practice, offer an ultimate fall back ('appeal') opportunity for disputes resolved through private dispute resolution. Where, as in trademark-domain name disputes, users in dispute have a choice of submitting the dispute to a state court or to an ODRS, the choice of forum may ultimately depend on the remedy the claimant is seeking. For example, if the remedy is pecuniary, then the choice will be state courts, if the remedy is one of cancellation or transfer of the domain name then using the UDRP process is sufficient (and quicker).

In managing to complement state dispute resolution systems, self-regulation is dependent on the reciprocal action of states and state law. Indeed as Galanter,[136] notes, private dispute resolution acts continuously 'in the shadow of the law' – that is, the dispute resolution process provided by the groups is framed by the rules of other sources, in particular state regulation. Self-regulation plugs into a general legal framework provided by state law. In on-line dispute resolution, the groups

---

[136] Galanter 1981: 2. See also Katsh, Rifkin and Gaitenby 2000: 705-734 and Van den Heuvel 2000. The phrase 'in the shadow of the law' is borrowed from Mnookin and Kornhauser 1979 and Cooter, Marks and Mnookin 1982.

borrow general principles of procedural fairness and impartiality; rules on participant commitment to the dispute resolution process and rules to secure implementation and enforcement of the settlement achieved through the dispute resolution
process. The current state court systems set a benchmark for standards of procedural fairness and impartiality and remedies that users expect as well of private
dispute resolution systems. To some extent, the success (and survival) of the private
dispute resolution systems is dependent on the integration of the state court standards in the private dispute resolution systems. This is seen for example, in the need
for private dispute resolution systems to include rules encouraging the participation
of respondents (besides complainants) in the dispute resolution system and in finding ways to make the settlements reached in the dispute resolution system binding
on the parties.

Self-regulation is also dependent on the encouragement and support, be it advisory or financial, of states. Through encouragement and support, states supplement
the efforts of the groups to provide *fora* and actual remedies for on-line disputes.
Furthermore, through state actions and state courts, states strengthen the legitimacy
and accountability of the groups providing on-line dispute resolution. Some on-line
dispute resolution processes have a number of shortcomings, primarily that they
lack mechanisms to keep the dispute resolution providers and process in check.
Through the action of states and state regulation, some of the effects of these weak-
nesses are reduced.

States are content to see the responsibility of dispute resolution being taken up
by groups, in particular in areas where they are unable to offer remedies, while they
keep an oversight position. Equally, groups providing dispute resolution services
benefit from the oversight position of states. Being seen and acknowledged as legitimate and accountable dispute resolution providers improves the profile of the
groups and can attract more users to submit the on-line dispute to the private resolution system.

Hence, self-regulation and state legislation and dispute resolution institutions do
not merely co-exist. They complement each other and are intertwined. What explains this complementary and intertwined relationship between self-regulation and
state regulation is an underlying interdependence between state and groups in the
resolution of on-line disputes. A particular combination of transnational aspects,
the need for quick resolution, specific knowledge to resolve the dispute and an
expectation that the costs of the dispute resolution are low, stimulate the underlying
interdependence between self-regulation and state legislation.

The current ODRS show that self-regulation is still in the learning curve. Though
the current self-regulation arrangements manifest all the characteristics of an actual
dispute resolution structure, there is room for improvement of each characteristic.
A number of problems afflict the current set of private rules and systems for on-line
dispute resolution. The problems range from specific normative considerations to
the more mundane, yet indispensable, problem of securing long-term funding of
the dispute resolution systems.

Yet, the current set of ODRS is an important set of models (with some improvement) for future systems. The achievements in resolving e-commerce-related disputes (by SquareTrade) and trademark-domain name disputes (following the UDRP rules) are indicative of the potential of on-line dispute resolution systems. Examining the elements that make these on-line dispute resolution examples 'successful' could be used to develop other dispute resolution systems for on-line disputes. As Lemley and Reese[137] suggest, the trademark-domain name dispute resolution system (with some important improvements) can be used as a model for the settlement of other on-line-related disputes, such as specific alleged infringements of copyright.

The examples reviewed in this chapter clearly indicate that given the right circumstances of funding and interrelation with states and state regulation, on-line dispute resolution offers effective, customised, and localised[138] solutions for on-line disputes – solutions that state courts are mostly unable to provide.

Seeing that the need for dispute resolution of on-line disputes remains, future development of more on-line dispute resolution systems is inevitable. Keeping in mind that states have an interest and an obligation towards citizens to see that its citizens have access to a dispute resolution forum and actual remedies when involved in a dispute, states should support the development of ODRS by offering long-term funding of initiatives and by providing legal backup. Building on the current examples, self-regulation can, with the necessary encouragement, continue to improve, develop and satisfy the need of users for effective remedies for on-line disputes.

---

[137] Lemley and Reese 2004.

[138] Also 'near' to where the dispute has taken place (the dispute resolution space is literally 'one click' away from the transaction space where the dispute arose).

Chapter 8
CONCLUSION: SELF-REGULATION IN CYBERSPACE

This study was set against a background of uncertainty: 'What is the function of self-regulation in cyberspace?' in the light of increasing influence and participation of states in the regulation of the Internet. 'Is self-regulation still active or appropriate?' – was the question. In attempting to answer these questions, I have sought to avoid partisanship as to whether self-regulation should be the dominant form of regulation or that it should be replaced by or kept under the strong hold of state regulation. Instead, I record and explain what is going on in four areas of Internet activities – Internet content (see Chapter 4), the administration of the Domain Name System (see Chapter 5), the setting of technical standards on the Internet (see Chapter 6) and the provision of dispute resolution for on-line disputes (see Chapter 7).

In each case I have tried to identify the groups involved in self-regulation, the regulation they create and follow, how this self-regulation came about, and how it relates to regulation by states. On the basis of the insights I derived from the case studies, I am now in a position to answer the questions and to draw some conclusions.

Succinctly put, the descriptions of self-regulation in chapters 4 to 7 show that self-regulation has been, is and is likely to remain a distinctive and indispensable form of regulation on the Internet. Yet, it was and will not be, the sole form of regulation of the Internet. Like other areas of regulation, participants on the Internet are subject to multiple rules and rules systems. The legal pluralism existing outside the Internet also persists on the Internet. Self-regulation intertwines with and is complementary to state regulation forming an intricate mesh of rules that now regulates behaviour on the Internet. While this mesh of rules has developed mostly without a predetermined plan, now that the reasons for the evolution are clearer, one could use these observations to seek to guide the development of future meshing.

8.1 Self-regulation on the Internet is distinctive

The nature of the Internet and the activities taking place there shape self-regulation. The groups involved in self-regulation, the reasons for the formation of the groups, the particular self-regulation rules and ways to apply and implement them are all determined by the nature of the Internet and the activities taking place there.

A wide variety of groups on the Internet are involved in a process of self-regulation. Internet business groups, such as Internet Service Providers (ISPs), are important and easily distinguishable groups. They are, however, not the only groups

J.P. Mifsud Bonnici, Self-Regulation in Cyberspace
© 2008, T·M·C·ASSER PRESS, The Hague, and the author

involved in self-regulation. Groups of technical experts, such as the Internet Engineering Task Force (IETF); Internet user groups; groups sharing common interests, such as the Internet Watch Foundation, are also important groups on the Internet.

The different groups have three characteristics in common. Each group: (i) has specific technical expertise; (ii) is familiar with the activities needing regulation; and (iii) has technical access to the activities on the Internet. ISPs, for example, have the technical knowledge of how Internet content-related activities take place on the Internet. They are familiar with current practices of content providers and users and have technical access to the actual activities. Internet Corporation for Assigned Names and Numbers (ICANN) has technical expertise on the working of the domain name system, is familiar with the activities that need regulation – such as ways of ensuring the uniqueness of domain names, and has access to the technical architecture of the domain name system. Similarly, SquareTrade has the technical expertise necessary to provide an on-line dispute resolution system, is familiar with on-line disputes and has technical access to the Internet to provide the dispute resolution system.

Given the three characteristics, the groups are able to identify the need for regulation and to identify the 'best' way and means to address the need for regulation. Domain name registrars, for example, have technical expertise, are familiar with the domain name system and have technical access to identify the need for specific rules and means to apply and implement rules relating to the registration of domain names under particular top-level domains.

The three characteristics of the relevant groups – technical expertise, familiarity and technical access – can be taken as an explanation of the emergence of self-regulation groups on the Internet.[1] That is, in practice, one may argue that self-regulation will exist on the Internet as long as the group concerned has exclusive technical expertise, familiarity with the activity and technical access to the activity. These characteristics hold such groups together to react to 'threats' the individual members have in common. The group gets together to reach a common solution, based on their technical expertise, familiarity and technical access. One 'threat' is legal uncertainty due to the absence of other sources of regulation or due to unclear regulation or due to the insufficient reach of the regulation where some regulation already exists. ISPs in many countries, for example, formed associations and created rules in response to increasing threats of legal liability on Internet content at a time before state legislation specifically provided for ISP liability in Internet content-related transactions. Another 'threat' is the introduction of state legislation introducing more onerous conditions for the group. For example, the P3P standard was develop in an attempt to pre-empt state legislation on privacy and data protection.

Formal or informal pressure by states or law enforcement authorities to self-regulate or to collaborate in the regulation of activities also motivate the groups.

---

[1] Furger 2001.

The Internet Watch Foundation in the regulation of Internet content, ICANN in the regulation of the DNS, the Electronic Consumer Dispute Resolution (ECODIR) in the provision of on-line dispute resolution for e-commerce related disputes and the European Electronic Signature Standardization Initiative (EESSI) in the formation of digital signatures are all influenced by formal or informal pressure from states to get together and provide regulation.

Some authors[2] have argued that another reason for the emergence of self-regulation arrangements comes from the legal traditions (or pre-disposition) in certain states in favour of self-regulation. While this may explain the emergence of self-regulation arrangement in some states, the United Kingdom, for example, it is less persuasive where groups on the Internet are not strictly linked to particular legal systems or are linked to states traditionally less in favour of self-regulation. In spite of the different legal traditions, for example in the United Kingdom and France, ISPs in both territories have both chosen to create self-regulation rules on the regulation of Internet content-related transactions.

Self-regulation on the Internet is predominantly a 'bottom-up' process, that is, the group carries out the process of regulation on its own initiative to address the needs for regulation as perceived by the group. At times, the 'bottom-up' process is carried out in collaboration with other groups and the advice of states. The development of 'hotlines' is one such example, where ISPs worked together with other private groups (such as the Internet Watch Foundation in the United Kingdom) and the state enforcement agencies.

A completely 'bottom-up' process carried out by the group alone is more frequently found in the regulation of three types of activities. Those that: (a) are private in nature, for example, in the provision of dispute resolution for e-commerce transactions; (b) have attracted little interest from states, such as the regulation of the allocation of generic top-level domain names; or (c) are of a technical nature, such as, in the setting of technical standards.

In the majority of arrangements, states participate in the creation of the self-regulation rules. States do this where the activities and transactions affect the interests of the state. For example, there is a strong presence of states in the regulation of illegal Internet content, where states have an interest in the prohibition of publication of specific categories of illegal content such as the prohibition of content on bomb making in the interests of national security, and the prohibition of child pornography. Another example is the growing participation of states in the regulation of their respective country code top-level domains, now that states perceive the country code top-level domain as a form of representation and/or marketing device for their country.

States also participate in the self-regulation process where the activities and transactions affect the interests of the citizens of the state. Some examples include the participation of states in the self-regulation process to protect users from unsolic-

---

[2] Lex Fori 2000; Rossi 2002.

ited (unwanted) Internet content; in the protection of intellectual property rights (by supporting the development of technical protection measures); in protecting the processing of personal information on the Internet (through participation in the development of technical standards for privacy protection such as P3P, for example).

The involvement of the state may be direct or indirect. It is direct when the self-regulation is actually mandated by state legislation or where the rules created and formulated by the group are subject to state approval. The predominant example here is the regulation of illegal Internet content related activities. It is indirect when though the different steps in the process are carried out by the group(s), states contribute in some way to the self-regulation process. The contribution can be a financial one – as in the support of self-regulation for the regulation of harmful Internet content and the development of on-line dispute resolution systems for e-commerce disputes. It can also consist in giving advice – as is the participation of the GAC in the ICANN set-up and the participation of governmental authorities in the development of technical standards. States can also be involved in assisting in the enforcement of the self-regulation rules – in particular, where courts enforce the contractual agreements developed by the groups.

8.2   SELF-REGULATION PROVIDES 'HARD' REGULATION

In the literature, regulation developed through a process of self-regulation is referred to, at times, as 'soft law'. The implication of using the 'soft law' metaphor is that the legal effect of the self-regulation rules is 'softer', less powerful than regulation coming from states.[3] But in the case of the Internet using the 'soft law' metaphor for self-regulation would not be accurate. The strength of the rules created by self-regulation is confirmed by both: (a) the formal nature of the self-regulation rules and the processes followed to make them; and (b) the legal effect of those rules.

The formal nature of self-regulation rules

Like state rules, the self-regulation rules described in the preceding chapters are created following a formal and systematic process. The process is similar to that followed by states when enacting state legislation. The groups go through a process of identifying a need for regulation and then proceed to draft and formulate the necessary rules. The rules are then approved, applied and implemented, and finally are enforced if breached. The same formal and systematic process is also followed in the creation of technical standards.

Following a predefined process of rule-making is what contrasts self-regulation from both 'market norms' and 'informal group norms'. The latter are created spo-

---

[3] Lex Fori report 2000: 28.

radically and haphazardly to regulate behaviour as the need arises. Norms created by moderators in on-line chat groups, for example, are usually created by the moderator according to the need for moderation in a particular discussion. The moderator decides what norms should be followed mostly without following a formal process.

The legal effect of self-regulation rules

Testing self-regulation rules against the characteristic legal requirements of transparency, legal certainty and binding effect shows the 'hard' legal nature of the self-regulation rules. The rules conform to a minimum measure of transparency, both in the process of making the rules and in the availability of the rules. The groups disclose (mostly accurate and timely) information about the rule-making process and the rules they create. Self-regulation rules are, for example, publicly available on-line. In specific instances, particularly in the use of technical standards to implement rules, the information disclosed relates to the (technical) implementation of the rules and not to the underlying rules as such.

Transparency of the rule-making process and of the rules themselves contributes significantly to the legal certainty the rules provide. Thanks to transparent practices, the members of the group and participants are aware of the rules and the responsibilities that follow from participation in certain activities or transactions. In addition, given that for rules to be changed that group needs to follow a determined (formal) process, the rules do not change frequently or unpredictably. This is another element in support of legal certainty.

The binding effect of the self-regulation rules differs from 'absolutely' binding as in the case of technical rules, to rules that are dependent on participants' willingness to accept their binding effect. The differences in binding effect of the rules is closely related to three situations:

(a) whether the implementation of the rules is done through technical means that automatically bind the behaviour of the participants – as in the case of technical standards. The use of technology in the implementation of the rules increases the binding effect of the rules and limits the room for non-compliance;
(b) whether the rules provide for measures to sanction non-compliance with the rules – as in the case of, for example, ISPA rules which provide for sanctions the association can take against members not conforming to the association rules; and
(c) whether through non-participation, the participant would lose (tangible) assets – as in the case, of trademark-domain name disputes, where the decision of an adjudicating panel is binding on the domain name holder and automatically enforced by the registry even if the respondent fails to participate in the dispute resolution proceedings.

Though all three characteristics are present in the different cases described, the descriptions show that there is a broad variation in the 'legal effect' of the various self-regulation rules created. As in the case of state regulation, the legal effect of self-regulation rules depends on the activity being regulated; on the strength and organisational arrangement of the rule-makers; and on the acceptance of the rules by participants.

The effect of self-regulation rules can be more binding than state legislation. In particular, the effect of technical rules and technical measures implementing rules often has an 'absolute' binding effect once the rule is applied. 'Code' is an absolute law. Once implemented, the technical rules direct the behaviour of users and participants, allowing little or no scope for users to deviate from the rule.

Conversely, on the Internet, while state legislation is theoretically applicable, and state courts could sanction behaviour contrary to the legislation, the practical application and enforcement of state law is often difficult if not impossible. State law, in such circumstances, can be 'softer' than self-regulation.

Legitimacy and accountability

The legal effect of the rules of self-regulation is recognised and honoured in practice by the members of the groups and third parties (users and customers) and by states. Members and third parties acknowledge the legitimacy of the rules and of the groups as rule-makers.

The three characteristics of groups involved in regulation – technical expertise, familiarity and technical access – lend credibility to the groups as law-makers and induce members of the groups and third parties including states to accept the authority of the rule-making groups.

The various arrangements of self-regulation show that the groups involved in the regulation of Internet activities on the Internet, largely, have a legitimate interest in providing rules for the group. For example, ISPs involved in the regulation of Internet content-related activities have a generally legitimate interest in such regulation. Similarly, the members of the IETF had a legitimate interest in creating the technical standards that permit machines to communicate and identify each other on the network. This legitimate interest contributes to both the authority of the group and the legal effect of the rules. Members have an interest in acknowledging the rules and in following them.

The notion of legitimacy is important when comparing self-regulation to other sources of regulation, such as state regulation. It may be argued that from a user/ participant perspective, the issue of authority of the group as rule-makers is not very important. What is important for users is that rules (whether provided by groups or states) provide a means to solve a problem and provide an actual remedy. In this context, whether a rule is enacted by a private or public source is immaterial. The critique for example, of ECODIR as a dispute resolution provider for on-line disputes is mainly that it fails to provide actual remedies, not that ECODIR has no authority to make such rules.

The legal effect of the rules is strengthened by the fact that the groups are accountable to the members of the group and to third parties, including states. The descriptions of the cases show that there are both internal (that is, by the group itself)[4] and external mechanisms (that is, by third parties) for holding the self-regulating groups to account. Four types of internal accountability mechanisms have been described. These are:

(a) a hierarchical decision-making structure within a private grouping – most of the larger groups, like ISPs, W3P and ICANN, have a clear hierarchical decision-making structure. The draft rules go through an internal process of scrutiny before being approved as formal rules binding on the members of the group.
(b) member voting rights – in most of the groups the members of the group have voting rights that are used to show support or challenge the process followed by the group. In IETF, for example, the drafting group is held to account through member voting on the workings of the group. In the IETF process, technical standards are agreed by a 'rough' consensus of the members of IETF. Sometimes the acceptance of a standard is delayed until a rough consensus is reached. This often involves the introduction of modifications to the technical standards to satisfy the demands of the larger consensus.
(c) the payment of membership fees – a member's financial contribution to, for example, the W3C, is a form of accountability. Unless the group follows the generally desired line in the creation and development of the rules, the members can withdraw or stop financial support.
(d) the adoption of the regulation by the members – in all cases the rules become formally binding on the members once they are formally adopted by the group.

External mechanisms of accountability from private and public sources complement the action of the internal mechanisms. The cases show that rules and practices of groups can be challenged by both states mechanisms and by other groups. States can question the activities of private groups. For example, states can use antitrust legislation to 'inspect' the practices of a group. Some authors[5] have suggested that the US government could hold ICANN in check by subjecting it to antitrust scrutiny. While in practice, this mechanism of accountability is hardly used; the mere threat is often sufficient to keep some groups in check.

In cases where self-regulation is co-funded by states, such as in some cases of self-regulation in the regulation of Internet content-related activities and ECODIR, states can use the contractual relationship (on which the funding is based) as a means of holding groups to account. Indeed, the contractual terms of the co-funding often include specific clauses that allow states to scrutinize the self-regulating actions of the group. In some cases, states[6] require that groups register their rules

---

[4] Wapner 2002.
[5] For example while Froomkin and Lemley (2003) suggest that ICANN can be subject to antitrust proceedings, antitrust proceedings were never brought against ICANN.
[6] Australia for example.

with a public authority established by law. Once registered the public authority can inspect the actions of the group and hold the group to account.

One ultimate check on the actions of the group can come from courts. Courts can review (and sporadically have reviewed[7]) the practices and rules of the groups. Courts can and have been invoked with some success. In some countries, such as the United Kingdom, Germany, France and Belgium, private parties and state prosecutors have brought actions against ISPs for hosting content inciting racial or xenophobic hatred, or child pornography, or human trafficking.[8]

Other groups also hold self-regulating groups in check. They follow the actions of groups closely and draw the attention of the members of the groups to situations where the action of the group threatens the rights of others. For example, public interest groups drew attention to the potential privacy violations produced by the IPv6 specifications. IETF reacted by producing an additional specification to limit the potential privacy violations.

The willingness of groups to act on the advice of other groups is tied to reputation. Reputation is one of the most significant intangible resources any commercial enterprise can have.[9] The potential loss of reputation from adverse publicity influences the behaviour of the group. The potential loss of reputation was one of the factors that lead ISPs, for example, to attempt to regulate unwanted content.[10]

The traditional rules of contractual liability also act as a safeguard against capricious behaviour, per definition in cases where the relationship between the group and the participants is based on a contract (as in the case of the relations between ICANN and domain name registries).

Finally, an (informal) mechanism of accountability comes from the ability of users/participants to switch loyalty from one group to another when dissatisfied with the practices of the group.[11] This, for example, keeps certain ISPs in check.

8.3   SELF-REGULATION IS AN INDISPENSABLE SOURCE OF RULES AND REMEDIES

Self-regulation is an indispensable non-state process of rule creation and enforcement activities on the Internet. Groups are able to provide rules and remedies: (a) where state regulation does not exist; and (b) to fill in procedural and substantive gaps in state legislation. Self-regulation fills in a legal vacuum by providing rules and remedies tailored to the particular regulatory needs of the group.

---

[7] For example, by reviewing the validity of panel decisions in trademark-domain name disputes.

[8] Perhaps the most famous are the German AOL case, the French case against Yahoo France.

[9] Zyglidopoulos 2002.

[10] US House of Representatives Commerce Committee meeting 3 November 1999 (as reported in Hillebrand 1999).

[11] De Vey Mestdagh and Rijgersberg 2006.

8.3.1 Self-regulation fills in gap in the absence of state legislation

Self-regulation provides rules for the regulation of particular activities where no specific substantive state regulation exists to regulate the activities. The absence of state regulation can be explained by the fact that states at times cannot or do not want to regulate particular activities on the Internet. The need of specific expertise and access to the technical space where the activity takes place may also preclude states from intervening. State regulation can also simply be subject to delays which the activities concerned cannot live with.

The groups respond to the inability of states to regulate directly. Using their technical expertise and access, the groups fill in for the missing regulation addressing the needs of the group. The self-regulation rules regulating the domain name system, for example, were developed thanks to the technical expertise and access of the group. The current self-regulation rules for the domain name system fill in for the absence of state regulation in the domain name allocation process.

The unwillingness and inability of states to regulate specific activities on the Internet may also be the result of difficult political and (legal) cultural issues that preclude states from either regulating independently or together with other states. In the regulation of Internet content-related activities, for example, states are at times unable to deal with the tension between the need for specific regulation and fundamental (and constitutionally protected) rights such as freedom of expression. Groups are often not willing to maintain a situation of legal uncertainty for the group and so regulate the activities themselves. The self-regulation rules fill in for the absent state regulation by providing the necessary rules. ISPs, for example, have taken a major role in the regulation of content specifically to reduce the situation of legal uncertainty coming the absence of specific state legislation.

In the regulation of the domain name system, it would be politically untenable to have only one state regulating such an essential resource. This political reality induced the US government to push for private regulation of the domain name system and to 'delegate' the authority to administer the DNS to ICANN.

Often, while self-regulation provides the first set of rules to regulate the activity, the rules are later taken up (and reinforced) by state regulation. Important examples include the rules on 'notice and take down' of Internet content developed by ISPs to handle claims concerning allegedly illegal or harmful content and rules, also developed by ISPs, to retain information on the Internet practices of their users. Both sets of rules were later included in state legislation, more specifically in the EU e-Commerce Directive (2000/31/EC) and the EU Data Retention Directive (2006/24/EC).

8.3.2 Self-regulation fills in procedural and substantive gaps in state legislation

Where state legislation regulating particular activities exist, self-regulation intertwines with and complements it by filling in procedural and substantive gaps in the legislation. The technical nature of the activities regulated limit (or challenge) the ability of state legislation to provide a 'complete' regulatory solution. The groups, conversely, have technical expertise about, familiarity with and technical access to the activities. Furthermore, by participating in the state process, the groups can address the needs of their group better than had they remained as bystanders.

In particular, self-regulation applies, implements and enforces state legislation. It does so either through the creation of codes of practice and other rules or by creating technical standards and technical measures. The groups, for example, create rules on collaboration with law enforcement authorities in the enforcement of some laws, such as with the creation of hotlines to report illegal content or rules on data retention for the enforcement of criminal law. Technical standards and technical measures can be a more appropriate tool to apply and implement state regulation in particular technical settings. In the regulation of privacy in on-line transactions, for example, a technical standard applying state law can be more effective than state rules on their own. Another is the creation of technical measures to protect copyright content. The creation and development of e-signature mechanisms implementing state legislation on the use and application of e-signatures is another example. Mostly, self-regulation converts the state rules into technical rules. Once implemented these technical rules become 'self-enforcing'. The technical rules will enforce the state rules automatically.

Self-regulation also provides effective remedies where access to state courts for dispute resolution for on-line disputes is in practice difficult (or expensive). Particularly in e-commerce related disputes, self-regulation is involved in the provision of 'alternative' dispute resolution processes on-line. Self-regulation in this case offers a remedy where state regulation, though available, does not serve the needs of the on-line community. In the resolution of trademark-domain name disputes, while self-regulation offers a faster remedy for the cancellation or transfer of a domain name, only state courts can impose a pecuniary penalty.

8.3.3 Self-regulation is complemented by state regulation

The rules created by the self-regulating groups plug into rules from other sources, specifically state regulation. Self-regulation rules tie up with the general legal framework provided by state regulation. This happens in all the situations of self-regulation. Even where specific state legislation is absent, general principles of state law influence self-regulation. The general state legal framework complements the legal effect of the self-regulation rules. For example, some rules of self-regulation, like most of the rules regulating the DNS, use contracts as the main instrument of regulation, thus making use legal procedures and scholarship on contract law developed by states and lawyers over the centuries. Hence, this use of contracts improves the possibility of having an actual remedy in case a party breaches one or more of the rules of self-regulation.

At times, state legislation provides the framework within which self-regulation can and indeed is expected to develop. This framework can determine how the rules of self-regulation are 'monitored' for compatibility with the state legislation. Furthermore, the legislation may provide ways to ensure compliance with the self-regulation rules.

States often encourage and support the growth of self-regulation by contributing financially to the development of the rules. Many self-regulation rules and technical measures used to regulate Internet content were developed thanks to the financial support of the European Union.[12] Similarly, the co-financing of the European Union enabled the development of the ECODIR ODRS for the resolution of e-commerce disputes.

States provide advice to groups on the way to regulate particular activities. They assist in the training of staff applying the self-regulation rules.[13] The cases show different examples of states providing advice in the drafting and application of self-regulation rules. In the development of the P3P technical standard for the protection of personal data on-line, data protection authorities of different states contributed to the development process. This supplements (and complements) the technical expertise and familiarity of the groups with the Internet activities needing regulation.

8.4   SELF-REGULATION AND STATE RULES FORM A MESH OF RULES

The descriptions of self-regulation in chapters 4 to 7 show that the actual function of self-regulation on the Internet is rather different from what is often supposed in the literature. The function of self-regulation on the Internet is neither that of a subordinate to state regulation, as identified in the co-regulation approach, nor that of a substitute for state regulation as identified in the substitution approach. Neither is the function of self-regulation that of creating, together with state regulation, hybrid arrangements where self-regulation combines with state regulation becoming one. Instead, self-regulation and state regulation intertwine and reciprocally complement each other. Each source of rules retains its identity and regulatory strengths while complementing the rules and processes of the other. The relative importance and authority of each is greater or lesser according to the nature of the activity and the participants being regulated.

Self-regulation and state rules form a mesh of rules. I use here the analogy used in the literature on mesh regulation[14] of a steel mesh in reinforced concrete structures or mesh in fishing nets, where, when put together, different strands provide a

---

[12] The EU, as pointed out earlier in Chapter 4, has financed many self-regulation initiatives under the Safer Internet Action Plan that has been running since 1999.

[13] This was particularly evident in the training of hotline employees in the regulation of illegal Internet content (discussed in Chapter 4).

[14] See Chapter 2 – Ost and Van Kerchove 2002, Schultz 2005, Cannataci and Mifsud Bonnici 2006 and Poullet 2006.

structure much stronger than that of the individual components.[15] Over the years, self-regulation on the Internet has gradually developed specific interconnections with state regulation. It now functions as intricate and indispensable part of the whole mesh of rules that governs the Internet. It fills the substantive or procedural gap where no specific state regulation exists or where existing state regulation is incomplete or ineffective, thus complementing the reach of state regulation. Simultaneously, states supply legal, and at times financial, frameworks that enable or complement self-regulation. The behaviour of users and participants on the Internet, like that of citizens in the off-line world, is regulated by a plurality of rules some coming from states and others coming from a wide variety of self-regulating private groups.

The intertwined mesh of rules provides a stable regulatory framework on the Internet. Simple co-existence between different legal systems is not new. Theories of legal pluralism in legal theory literature point to the co-existence and different forms of relationships between multiple rule systems. Even within the most centralised of state legal systems, parallel rule systems developed by groups exist and interact with the state rule system. But what goes on on the Internet goes beyond co-existence and simple interaction. The intertwining and complementary relationship between state regulation and self-regulation is complex and tightly knotted and pervasive across the various areas of activities on the Internet and in the various procedural steps of regulation. On the Internet, state regulation and self-regulation are interdependent in the creation, adoption, application, implementation and enforcement of regulation.

8.5 SELF-REGULATION IS INTERDEPENDENT WITH STATE-REGULATION

The intertwining and complementary relationship between state law and self-regulation comes from the interdependence[16] of the two forms of regulation in the regulation of Internet activities.[17] One can identify three forms of interdependence between self-regulation and state regulation in the Internet:

---

[15] Cannataci and Mifsud Bonnici 2006.

[16] The concept of 'interdependence' involves an explanation of reciprocal relationships between two separate entities – here self-regulation and state regulation. The reciprocal relationship is not a casual relationship but one of reciprocal dependence. The concept of 'interdependence' is used in the political science literature to explain power relationships in transnational issues (Keohane and Nye 1977; 1998) and in the public policy literature (Lazer 2001) to explain the effect of a regulatory policy of one state on another in the regulation of transnational activities. In both areas of study, otherwise weak independent power (or regulatory) entities survive in transnational spaces because they develop interdependent relations between entities. Core conditions in the transnational space affect the space and consequently dictate interdependence between entities.

[17] Lazer (2001) identifies three forms of interdependence between regulatory policies of states in the regulation of international activities – competitive, co-ordinative and informational interdependence. From the cases of self-regulation described in this study, it is difficult to identify instances of 'competitive interdependence' – that is, interdependence to resolve prisoner-dilemma situations.

(a) *informational interdependence*: Both states and groups suffer from one or more forms of information deficit. At different instances, each lack essential information on which to base rules and remedies for participants/citizens on the Internet. Both self-regulation and state regulation need to cope with the uncertainty as to their best regulatory option.[18] The regulatory choices of the other and their success or failure provide signals indicating good regulatory options.

In the early attempts to regulate Internet content-related activities, both states and groups were at a loss as to how to regulate the different activities. Given the technical expertise and familiarity of the groups with the activities taking place, ISPs in particular, were from an information perspective, in a better position to create rules on content regulation. States subsequently followed the rules adopted by the ISPs. On the other hand, once state regulation had identified particular content that should be considered illegal, the groups followed the choices made by states. Choosing to follow and implement state regulation is a choice in favour of legal certainty over uncertainty.

The same pattern of information interdependence can be seen in the regulation of the domain name system. The groups having technical expertise, familiarity with the activities and technical access develop the rules for the allocation of domain names. States acknowledge the self-regulation rules and support their enforceability. Where states, in particular in country code top-level domains, introduce particular legislation, the groups adopt and implement it.

(b) *organisational interdependence*: Groups on the Internet lack the general reputation of states for being capable, legitimate and accountable sources of regulation. Groups are often still in the process of building their reputation. They depend on the acknowledgment and support of states. By recognising the need for self-regulation, accepting the regulation carried out by the groups and adopting the self-regulation rules, states indirectly give signals on the reputation and reliability of self-regulation.

States depend on the technical authoritativeness and stability provided by technical standards and the technical implementation of rules to counter the turbulent nature of activities on the Internet. States are dependent on the absolute binding effect of technical standards once implemented.

(c) *co-ordinative interdependence*: States and groups realise that having rules that are compatible with those of the other sources of regulation is desirable,[19] providing among other things better legal certainty for the groups and users. By co-ordinated regulation by states and groups, users benefit from a wider protection in the regulation of illegal Internet content, for example.

---

[18] Lazer (2001) uses the same argument to explain interdependence in the regulatory policies between different states in the regulation of international problems.

[19] Lazer 2001.

8.5.1   Conditions underlying the interdependence

The interdependence between the two sources of regulation results from a combination of specific circumstances on the Internet namely, from its technical nature and type of activities, and the creation of multiple communities based on shared interest. Trends in regulation due to globalisation too contribute to the increasing interdependence between state regulation and self-regulation.

8.5.1.1   *The nature of the Internet and the Internet activities*

A number of aspects of the nature of the Internet and the Internet activities – namely the a-territorial nature; issues of technical expertise and access; and the decentralised structure – affect the relations between state regulation and self-regulation and push towards interdependence.

The *a-territorial nature* (and decentralised nature) of most activities on the Internet challenges the traditional notions of state territorial jurisdiction and the tradition to regulate activities in a defined geographical space. The limits on (individual) state jurisdiction and consequently the limits on the sovereignty of state courts implies that state regulation is dependent on other sources of regulation (be they inter-state sources or private sources) to regulate the a-territorial activities.[20] In the regulation of Internet content, for instance, individual states are dependent on inter-state regulation and agreements such as the Council of Europe Cybercrime Convention and on the regulation provided by the self-regulating groups such as ISPs.

Self-regulation at times extends the territorial effect of state legislation to activities that are taking place in other jurisdictions. The application and adoption of technical standards extends the application of individual state laws and principles to a wider, global community. For example, since the principles on data protection applicable in European states were incorporated in the development of the P3P privacy standard, the European legal principles regulate even beyond European states, wherever the standard is applied.

Conversely, while self-regulation is capable of providing rules across national boundaries (such as in the regulation of the DNS, the provision of dispute resolution for on-line relate disputes, and through technical methods that implement rules), it is dependent on state courts for the enforcement of some rules (and the application of sanctions). Ultimately, only states have the power to hold users/citizens to account.

The development of the Internet rests on the *technical expertise* (and familiarity with the Internet) of persons involved on the Internet activities. States, primarily in the early stages of the regulation of the Internet chronology, lacked the necessary expertise to understand the technical intricacies that needed to be regulated in some activities on the Internet while groups have this technical expertise. This marked a

---

[20] See Knill and Lehmkuhl 2002: 41.

dependence of states on private regulation to regulate the intricate technically based activity.

Then again, employing technical expertise to implement regulation requires financial backing to produce and maintain. Groups, especially when the groups are not business groups, are not always in a position to secure long-term financing to produce and maintain the technical implementation systems. They are dependent on the financial support of states. In the regulation of Internet content, for example, the private groups develop technical tools, such as content filtering tools, implementing rules (coming from both the state or other groups) on the receipt and blocking of Internet content. These technical tools are an important means to effectively control Internet content. A number of these tools are financed by states (particularly the European Union).

Occasionally, the groups having technical expertise depend on protection granted by state legislation to be able to use their technical expertise in the implementation of rules. In using technical protection measures in the implementation of copyright legislation, for example, while the actual implementation is left to the group, state legislation provides protection against circumvention of the implementing technical measures.

The *technical access* to the behaviour or the Internet activity rests predominantly with the groups and only in limited ways with states. On the one hand, the issues of technical access affect the efficiency of state-centred regulation and hence states are dependent on non-state regulation to reach the activity. On the other hand, it also implies that gatekeepers and intermediaries (who authorise access to the behaviour) may be liable for either the activity taking place or the lack of action, if they fail to regulate the access. Consequently, groups are keen on state regulation acknowledging their position and limiting their liability. As a result, state and self-regulation are mutually interdependent.

In the regulation of Internet content-related activities, technical access to the activities affects the way they are regulated. Technical access to the content is essential for the actual regulation. On the one hand, the groups, like ISPs, have a dominant position in the access to the content. On the other hand, involvement in the regulation of content may expose ISPs to legal liability. States and groups depend on the collaboration of each other in regulating the activities.

The *turbulent nature of activities* on the Internet demands timely regulation. Activities on the Internet challenge the established legal practices of the off-line world. The ease with which to publish and access content on the Internet, for example, challenges the long established legal principles of copyright that were enacted well before the creation of the Internet. Similarly, current practices on the Internet challenge the established legal protection for the misuse of personal data. Here again, legislation and legal principles on the protection of a right to personal data were established before the commercial opening of the Internet.

States are mostly unable to act in time and provide appropriate regulation when the new activities (and technologies) on the Internet challenge established rights of citizens and participants. The inability of states to act in certain situations is often simply due to the states' lack of motivation to act. There seems to be a pattern that states intervene more readily where economic issues (for example, copyright or country-code top-level domains) or public concerns (for example, illegal content) relating to the state or its citizens are present. Otherwise, in a number of cases where the cost of intervening, whether fiscal, social or political, appears to be disproportionate to the likelihood of results, states lack the motivation to act and are 'happy' enough to leave regulation to self-regulation. The 'delegation' to ICANN is a case in point.

At other times, the activity is simply beyond the confines of states' territorial or substantive jurisdiction. States are dependent on the ability of self-regulation to regulate both irrespective of territory (as with the implementation of technical standards) and irrespective of substantive issues. States are, for example, dependent on self-regulation in the regulation of harmful Internet content, where, considering that the choice of what is considered harmful lies with the user and not the state, state legislation could infringe other users' rights.

Mostly, the inability of states to act in real time is due to the long and laborious process that accompanies the creation and implementation of inter-state law. The process of achieving consensus on an international level is a slow process. Furthermore, the process of achieving consensus has often reduced the eventual regulation to a much watered-down version of the regulation actually needed. Additionally, different cultural values and traditions in regulation can be difficult to surpass at a state or inter-state level. States are dependent on self-regulation for 'preliminary' regulation that can be used as a basis for inter-state law and fill in the regulatory gap till states can negotiate consensus between states.

8.5.1.2 *Multiple communities of shared interest*

The Internet facilitates the getting together and accommodation of growing communities of users coalescing on shared interest in a way not possible in a physical forum.[21] The basis of the communities is often not of shared nationality or citizenship but one of shared interest. At times, the members of the community communicate and get together solely on one dimension – the shared interest – irrespective of other characteristics they may hold in common or differ upon. For example, members in the same community of 'garden lovers' often interact with fellow members only on gardening irrespective of the fact of having, potentially other shared or different interests in common. The option granted by technology to act anonymously, or under a partial or different identity from that used in the physical world, further enhances the coming together of the Internet communities based exclusively on specific interest(s).

---

[21] Burstein, de Vries and Menell 2004.

The situation that cyberspace is not inhabited by a single community of persons of one 'nationality' accounts for the limited regulatory grip of states over these communities. However, this does not mean that the state has no responsibility towards the participants. Participants in these communities of interest have shared allegiances: an allegiance to the rules of each community they participate in and an allegiance to a state they are connected with in the physical world. The multiple loyalties of each citizen/user shape some interdependence between state and non-state regulation to reach and regulate the activities members of communities are involved in.[22]

8.5.1.3 Trends in regulation due to globalisation

The intertwining and complementarity of state and self-regulation in Internet regulation is also influenced by the effect of globalisation of economic activities on regulation. The Internet, on the one hand, plays a central part in the globalisation of economic activities. The majority of transnational transactions (in globalisation), be they commercial or informational, take place on the Internet or are, at least, carried out through communication technologies. Indeed, one can argue that it is only on the Internet that an almost complete globalisation of information services has been achieved.[23] The increase and widespread availability of vital communication technologies (including the Internet) are essential to globalisation. Examining the position of states and groups in the regulation of the Internet is important in understanding some of the regulatory needs brought about by globalisation.

On the other hand, Internet regulation is affected by the trends in regulation, noted in the literature, influenced by globalisation.[24] Globalisation,[25] that is the integration of economic activities via transnational markets and the consequent increase in activities taking place across multiple territories, has an important impact on regulation. It is reconfiguring the regulatory powers of the modern state.[26] There is a shift in the role of states in the regulation of (global) activities – a shift towards more interaction (and interdependence) between states and groups in the provision of regulatory solutions. This can be seen, for example in the regulation of interna-

---

[22] The situation of multiple authorities and multiple loyalties has led some authors (such as Friedrichs 2001) to develop a theory of neo-medievalism – using the situation pertaining in the middle ages as a model for current trends in regulation.

[23] Wolf 2004.

[24] Goldsmith and Wu (2006) counter-argue that globalisation is influenced by regulatory practices.

[25] The term 'globalisation' is used here to refer to two situations: (a) 'integration of economic activities via markets. Here the driving forces of integration are technological and policy changes'. Wolf 2004 (b) what Scholte (2000) calls 'deterriorialization' (or as the spread of supraterritoriality). Here 'globalisation' entails a reconfiguration of geography, so that social space is no longer wholly mapped in terms of territorial places, territorial distances and territorial borders but becomes transcontinental through inter-regional flows and networks of activity.

[26] Jayasuriya 2001: 101.

tional environmental issues where both states and groups are increasingly involved in the regulation of the global issues.

Globalisation has strongly influenced a shift in relations between states and groups in regulation. Like the balance developed in *lex mercatoria* over the centuries, where states have acknowledged the usefulness of regulation developed by private traders, and supported and adopted the same private trading rules,[27] new balances are being worked out in other areas of activities brought to fore through globalisation. In the working of the new balances some trends in regulation due to globalisation – shifting foci of control, privatisation of the costs of regulation, and the emergence of global regulatory networks – are appearing. The relations between states and groups on the Internet are also influenced by these trends.

Shifting foci *of control*: One of the trends in regulation of transnational activities is that states no longer focus on regulating the behaviour of individuals but are more concerned with what Jayasuriya calls 'system enforcement'.[28] States succumb to increased pressure (of globalisation and open markets) to privatise traditionally key state monopolies. Together with the shift of ownership of the resources, states introduce shifts in regulation. The definition of rules and behaviour to be regulated is increasingly left to groups while states have shifted their attention to monitoring and enforcement of the rules created and the monitoring of the rule-making bodies.[29]

Similarly, for example, in the regulation of the DNS, states have adopted an oversight role toward the action of groups, leaving the actual regulation to the groups (ICANN, registry operators and registrars). Even though the current situation, where the United States has the predominant oversight position for the root server, is unacceptable to many states, the alternative proposals[30] still propose an oversight position for states with the involvement of more states (while leaving the actual day-to-day regulation of the DNS to groups).

---

[27] For a discussion on the balance between states and group in *lex mercatoria* see Cutler 2003.

[28] Jayasuriya (2001: 111) illustrates this claim through two examples: a case study (carried out be Aalder and Wilthagen 1997) of the Dutch occupational safety and health regulations. The study shows that 'occupational and health and safety inspectors place less importance on intervention at the shop-floor level and instead seek to "monitor and regulate the operation of self-control systems and subsequently, intervene at the system level".' The other example is about the Australian competition watchdog who increasingly relies on compliance regimes within corporate bodies rather than direct enforcement of competition legislation.

[29] This claim is supported by Wallace, Ironfield and Orr (2000: vi). The authors claim 'From a government perspective, an important objective is to reduce potentially adverse effects that market failure has on the welfare of consumers and the wider community' and not in actual regulation of the area with an intention to improve consumer welfare or industry profitability. The regulation of the area is left in the hands of the firm/s whose objective of self-regulation is ultimately 'to improve the firm's profitability which, in some circumstances, will also improve consumer welfare and bring benefits to the wider community.'

[30] The Working Group on Internet Governance 2005b; see also EU proposal dated 28 September 2005 'Proposal for addition to Chair's paper Sub-Com A internet Governance on Paragraph 5 "Follow-up and Possible Arrangements".' Document Reference: WSIS-II/PC-3/DT/21-E dated 30 September 2005 accessed at <http://www.itu.int/wsis/docs2/pc3/working/dt21.html> on 2 October 2005.

With a shift in responsibility for self-regulation from the regulation of predominantly private relations to the regulation of public (and global) activities, self-regulation is increasingly dependent on the formal legitimisation of self-regulation rules by states. Furthermore, the shift in control to groups means that the actions of the groups are subject to wider scrutiny and accountability. Groups are dependent on oversight carried out by states to validate not only their position as legitimate groups but also the fact that they can be held in account.

Privatisation of regulation costs: Linked with the shift in *foci* of control, states are allocating less financial resources to regulation and depend on groups to shoulder the cost of regulation. The process of legislation and effective enforcement of legislation is a costly process and states are content to support any alternatives that are less costly for the state. States seem increasingly eager to share or transfer part of the financial burden to the private sector. Similarly, on the Internet, states are willing to co-finance and support the self-regulation process rather than attempt to regulate the activity. One can argue that this is a sensible approach by states especially in the situations where states are unable (because of political or technical situations) to actually regulate the activities (alone, without the involvement of self-regulation).

States seem to recognise that supporting regulatory measures created by groups can be a less costly affair than creating and implementing such measures themselves.[31] The reduction of financial costs depends in part on the willingness of groups to shoulder the charge of participating in regulation and the financial costs attached. States seem increasingly to use measures to shift the burden of regulation to the group or to those on the receiving end of such regulation. Similarly, on the Internet, the costs attached for retaining content (data) that can be used in the enforcement of regulation are now the responsibility of groups (predominantly ISPs) and not the state even though the data retained will eventually help in the prosecution by the state of the wrong doers.[32]

Governments are faced with budgeting for the cost of drafting ever-more specialised legislation to cover the behaviour of participants in new technologies and new realities; for the operation of these new laws; for the co-operation with other regulatory authorities in other jurisdictions. The whole function of the state in issuing legislation is being burdened with costs that states no longer want to assume while at the same time they are reluctant to relinquish any position of power that they might have.[33]

---

[31] One could point here (apart from the Internet) at an example from environmental protection regulation. Environmental protection in Europe is one of the areas where States have experimented with self-regulation and where self-regulation systems have proved to be comparatively successful and at a relatively cheaper cost. See for example Verweij 2000 on a comparison of the effect of legislation and self-regulation (and costs) on the pollution levels of the River Rhine in Europe and of the Great Lakes in the North America.

[32] Cf., EU Data Retention Directive (2006/24/EC).

[33] Lex Fori 2000: 46 'La réglementation étatique a souvent été jugée comme étant excessive, coûteuse et inefficace. La fonction judiciaire de l'État a également été soumise à de nombreuses attaques.

Similarly in the regulation of the Internet, states depend on self-regulation to take on regulation that may seem too costly for states, while at the same time retaining some power over the regulation, shifting the focus of control to oversight of the regulatory process and substantive regulation. The support and 'delegation' by the US government of the regulation of the DNS to ICANN is an important example. The US government shifted the focus of control from the costly regulation of the actual day-to-day running of the DNS to oversight of ICANN.

Groups, particularly economic players, are unlikely to tolerate situations of inertia for too long especially since situations of inertia are unpredictable and can create uncertainty in the market. They fill in the regulatory void resulting from political inertia. A regulatory vacuum can have financial implications for the group. Silence, brought by a regulatory vacuum, on the liability of the groups taking part in a particular transaction can have incalculable financial implications for the groups, making participation in the transaction too risky to pursue.

Industry is known to have in situations of unpredictable state legal systems created its own predictable system in parallel to the state system to restore consumer and client confidence.[34] Some self-regulation initiatives have in fact been started to fill in a void not filled in by State regulation.[35] Similarly, on the Internet, in the provision of on-line dispute resolution systems for the resolution of e-commerce related disputes, for example, groups have sought to fill-in for lacking actual dispute resolution. In the regulation of Internet content-related activities, the absence of legal clarity on the responsibility of Internet Service Providers for Internet content, motivated ISPs to participate in self-regulation of content. For the private sector, participating in regulation is an attempt to reduce financial risks.

It can be argued that increasingly, states seem willing to offer regulatory solutions only when the situation is financially rewarding for the state or in response to pressures or perceptions of strong constituencies. Similar trends, as discussed earlier, are seen in the regulation of activities on the Internet. States seem to be interested only to take an active role in regulation when financial or political stakes for the states are high – such as, in the regulation of country-code top-level domains and illegal Internet content.

Emergence of global private regulatory networks: One of the consequences of globalisation, it has been argued, is the growing number of groups who have taken

Le système des tribunaux étatique est considéré comme trop complexe, coûteux et lent. L'encombrement qui caractérise les tribunaux contribue à dégrader l'image que se font les citoyens de la justice.'

[34] For example Ginsburg 2000:834 'The harsh and sometimes unpredictable exercise of law in traditional China led merchants to seek to avoid encounters with the formal legal system. Similarly, societies under colonial rule developed informal orders that paralleled the system of state law.'

[35] As the Conflict Diamonds consortium; or the Australian Code of practice for Computerised Checkout Systems in Supermarkets 1989. Another example comes from the Brazilian derivative markets and their regulation. Lazzarini and Carvalho de Mello (2001) claim that the primary reason of the success and effectiveness of self-regulation of the Brazilian derivative markets stems from the fact that the Brazilian government had failed so dramatically to provide the necessary regulation.

authoritative roles and functions in the regulation of inter-national activities.[36] States are no longer the only groups involved in the regulation of international activities. A wide variety of groups are involved in different types of regulation and varying levels of transparency and legitimacy. These include norms created by global market forces, rules of private institutions such as international standards organisations, rules of human rights and environmental non-governmental organisations, norms of transnational religious movements and, *à la limite*, rules of mafias and mercenary movements. The important function of self-regulation in Internet regulation fits in this trend.

8.6 MESH REGULATION IS A 'WORK IN PROGRESS'

8.6.1 'Open spaces' in the regulation mesh

Current regulation of activities on the Internet is neither static nor exhaustive. The meshing of rule systems provides some direction and some remedies and solutions to transactions on the Internet. In a number of areas of activities, the gaps in the mesh of regulation are too wide and some activities fall through, (temporarily) unregulated, until the private and public pieces of twine darn the gaps through complementary actions. The darning process is in continuous evolution and some issues remain (to date) unresolved.

As with a fish net, the current rule meshes can (often) secure that 'big' participants follow the rules (mostly because they cannot afford to be seen as not following rules) while 'small' players slip through the gaps. Simply put, in e-commerce, for example, transaction participants like amazon.com are more likely to honour contracts of sale with consumers than individual traders who can shut down and 'disappear' from the Internet leaving consumers with few if any remedies. Similarly, in the regulation of Internet content, for example, large groups (such as large ISPs) are more likely to follow rules (whether created by the state or by self-regulation) than small players who can move relatively unnoticed on the Internet.

Swire uses a metaphor of elephants and mice to explain this situation.

'In short, "elephants" are organizations that will be subject to the law, while "mice" can hope to ignore it. Elephants are large companies or other organizations that have major operations in a country. Elephants are powerful and have a thick skin, but are impossible to hide. They are undoubtedly subject to a country's jurisdiction. Once laws are enacted, they likely, will have to comply. By contrast, mice are small and mobile actors, such as pornography sites or copyright violators, who can reopen immediately after being kicked off of a server or can move offshore. Mice breed annoyingly quickly – new sites can open at any time. Where harm over the Internet is caused by mice, hidden in crannies in the network, traditional legal enforcement is more difficult.'[37]

---

[36] See Hall and Biersteker 2002: 4.
[37] Swire 2005: 1978-1979 and 1998.

There are also two other types of gaps in the mesh. The first involves areas where the meshes of regulation have not yet been adapted to new developments – due to technology, changes in circumstances and new needs – on the Internet. The current mesh may provide a frame for the regulation but the details of the regulation are yet to be filled in.

The second type involves areas where, although the meshes of state and self-regulation rules are intertwined and provide some rules and fora, some problems in the meshing of regulation still remain to be solved. 'Conflict of laws' is the primary problem running through all areas of activities.

'Conflict of laws' issues include choice of law and enforcement of foreign judgments problems. On the one hand, it is unacceptable that a particular state court – territorially bound – should have the jurisdiction to try a case that took place in an essentially a-territorial space and apply laws only valid for that state. Using traditional concepts of state sovereignty, where governments have exclusive power over their citizens and territory, to resolve internal disputes is inconsistent with the global nature of the Internet. It would imply, for example, that a provider of content in one jurisdiction is subject to the jurisdiction of any country from which the content can be accessed.

On the other hand, states and state courts have a long experience in resolving disputes that take place across national boundaries or even not in the territorial limits of a state. Private international law rules on jurisdiction, choice of laws and in a more limited way, on the recognition of (foreign) judgments have existed long before the arrival of the Internet and transactions on the Internet. These rules are now also used for Internet disputes. State courts, for example, are involved in resolving trademark-domain name disputes as long as the court can establish a territorial or personal link between the dispute and the jurisdiction of the court.

Important difficulties remain unresolved however. These include the possibility that state courts take a parochial approach to the resolution of on-line conflicts, preferring narrow interpretation of jurisdiction, preferring their own jurisdiction over possibly the jurisdiction of other courts, preferring the application of local state law over international law and self-regulation rules and refusing to enforce judgements given by foreign courts.[38] It is often argued in literature[39] that state courts need to 'fight' off a parochial approach to the resolution of conflicts and move towards a more cosmopolitan and pluralistic approach. Depending on courts to be more cosmopolitan in accepting jurisdiction to hear a dispute and pluralistic in acknowledging not only the rules of different states but also of groups in choosing the applicable law to resolve the dispute may be problematic.

---

[38] The refusal of the US court to enforce the injunction of a French court in the *Yahoo* case is a 'classic' example of the problems involved.

[39] See for example, Berman 2005; Stein 2005.

8.6.2 **Darning the gaps**

Self-regulation plays an important function in darning the gaps. As far as trapping the 'mice' is concerned, self-regulation is involved in the enforcement of state rules such as in the case of the provision of hotlines for the reporting of illegal Internet content, in particular child pornography. There is a growing trend to use groups as intermediaries between state law and the alleged wrongdoer. The development of (initially self-regulation rules then followed by state) rules on data to be retained by Internet Service Providers (amongst others) to assist in the prosecution of alleged wrongdoers is another example.

As far as conflicts of law and the limited jurisdiction of states is concerned technological measures have been used to enforce and implement state regulation and self-regulation rules[40] and hence reduce the need of access to state courts. One example is the creation of the W3P technical measure for the protection of personal data on-line which implements some of the principles found in European legislation on data protection. Another example is the creation and use of technical protection measures for copyright protected content on-line.

Jurisdiction and choice of law clauses in self-regulation instruments in particular in contracts is another way that self-regulation complements state rules on conflict of laws. The rule in the ICANN Uniform Dispute Resolution Policy that a domain name registrant is subject to a mandatory administrative dispute resolution process in case of trademark-domain name disputes is an example of choice of jurisdiction and choice of law rules in self-regulation instruments.[41]

Furthermore, self-regulation is involved in providing measures to resolve disputes on-line by providing on-line dispute resolution systems and at times, by determining which 'laws' apply to the dispute. Hence, for example self-regulation provides a system to resolve trademark-domain name disputes and provides the rules that apply to the dispute. Similarly, the eBay-SquareTrade arrangement offers both a forum to resolve e-commerce related disputes that take place in the eBay space but also provide rules that should apply to the disputes (for example, in feedback-related disputes). By providing a forum and rules that should apply to the dispute, transactions are likely to be conducted without recourse to national courts and thus avoiding judicial pronouncements (and difficulties) about which jurisdiction and which laws apply.[42]

States too are involved in the darning of gaps in the regulatory meshes complementing both existing state and self-regulation rules. One effort is the proposed Hague Convention on Jurisdiction and Foreign Judgments in Civil and Commer-

---

[40] See Reidenberg 2004, 2005.

[41] Only in part as the UDRP policy does not block the right to submit the dispute to any state court (that is, it does not include rules on choice of state forum and choice of applicable law when dispute is submitted to a state court).

[42] See Swire 2005: 1992.

cial Matters designed, *inter alia*, to set-up harmonised rules for determining which jurisdiction's laws should apply to e-commerce transactions on the Internet.[43] The drafting process has been stalled due to lack of agreement between some states (some European countries and consumer protection lobbies) favouring a country-of-destination rule and some states (predominantly the United States and e-commerce companies) favouring the seller's country of origin. Until a compromise is reached it is unlikely that there will be formal harmonisation of conflict of laws issues for e-commerce transactions.

States have been relatively more successful in achieving consensus on co-operation for the enforcement of law on cybercrime (including the prohibition of illegal Internet content, in particular, child pornography) through the Council of Europe Cybercrime Convention.

The darning process, including the intertwining of self-regulation and state rule meshes, though evolving, requires more work. States and groups have a critical interest – that of providing actual remedies to citizens/participants – in providing more closely knit meshes of regulation.

8.7   WHAT FUTURE?

Will the darning process continue in the future? Given that the need for regulation and remedies will not subside and that the capacity of states to regulate everything alone is decreasing, I would argue that the intertwining and complementary relationship will continue to evolve.

So far, the intertwining and complementary relations between self-regulation and state regulation tended to evolve piecemeal, without a predetermined plan. As the discussion in the preceding chapters shows, the processes of regulation and providing remedies for problems on the Internet are still in development. Content regulation has attracted the most attention in the literature, but balancing the right to freedom of expression against other rights and values is still being tentatively addressed. Similarly, while in the discussions at the recent International Summit on the Information Society in Tunis in November 2005 the *status quo* on the regulation of DNS has been maintained, the wish for greater involvement of states in DNS governance will continue to feature in the coming years. The development of new technical standards is no exception. As new standards are developed the problem of maintaining a balance between the effects of standards and the rights of users is bound to recur. Providing effective remedies for disputes on the Internet is also still in development.

Now that the reasons for the evolution of the intertwining and complementary relations are clearer, one could use this insight to seek to guide the development of

---

[43] Id. 2005: 1988-1989 for a discussion of the stalling of the drafting process and <http://www.cptech.org/ecom/jurisdiction/hague.html> for relevant drafts (accessed 2 October 2005).

future meshing. The darning process could become less haphazard and event driven and more systematic. I do not propose a grand scheme that states should follow imposing intertwining and complementary relations with self-regulation. There are enough examples in history to show that grand schemes ultimately fail, as in their grandeur they often miss out what actually needs to be regulated.[44] Instead, I suggest that one should instead look at what groups do best and how they do it, and build on it.

What self-regulation does best is to provide customised solutions moulded to meet the needs and expectations of the group making the regulation, often in a fast and expedient way and does so at the same level where the need for regulation arises. Paradoxically, while the customised approach of self-regulation seems to be very localised and small, aimed only at the needs of the group, the effect of the rules are often far wider, reaching transnationally. Self-regulation reaches where different groups in the particular activity interact irrespective of territorial or national links. The legal effect of the technical standards, for example, reaches the particular activities irrespective of territorial or physical location of the user. The 'customised' self-regulation rules regulate transnationally in spite of their 'localised' nature.

States can then use these rules as a basis for further regulation where more co-ordination and uniformity in regulation is needed. This approach is not new. States have done so in the development of the Cybercrime Convention and in the development of the EU e-Commerce Directive (2000/31/EC). A similar approach seems to be evolving in the regulation of the DNS where self-regulation still fills in the immediate needs of the groups and users while states negotiate an alternative regulatory set-up.

The advantages of the customised regulation of self-regulation cannot be achieved however without the constant support of states and state legislation. As this study shows, there is a continuing relevance of national legal orders. States are especially indispensable in providing a general framework of legislation and legal mechanisms that ground self-regulation. It is also important that states continue acting as 'watchdog' on the regulatory actions of the groups. Oversight by states is indispensable for the fair running of the customised rules. States should continue to assist in the development and maintenance of the self-regulation rules, including by continuing financial assistance.

Ultimately, states need to consider self-regulation as an intertwining and complementary source of regulation. It is neither its competitor nor its subordinate. Thinking in this way, which corresponds to the reality of current self-regulation on the Internet, states can consider moulding state legislation and policies to complement self-regulation. This is not a situation of 'losing' or abandoning power to groups. It is instead a way to honour the states' responsibility to citizens to provide adequate regulation and remedies and to protect the public interest.

---

[44] See Scott 1999 for an eloquent presentation of all the grand schemes that have failed.

BIBLIOGRAPHY

Aalder, Marius and Ton Wilthagen (1997), 'Moving beyond command and control: reflexivity in the regulation of occupational safety and health and the environment', *Law and Policy*, Vol. 19, Issue 4, pp. 415-443

Abernethy, Steve (2003), 'Building large-scale online dispute resolution & trustmark systems'. Proceedings of the UNECE Forum on ODR 2003 <http://www.odr.info/unece2003> [accessed 25 May 2004]

Akdeniz, Yaman (2001), 'Internet Content Regulation: UK government and the control of Internet content', *Computer Law & Security Report*, Vol. 17, No. 5, pp. 303-317

Alesina, Alberto and Edward Glaeser (2005), 'Work and leisure in the US and Europe'. Study prepared for the NBER Macroeconomic Annual, 2005 <http://paper.nber.org/papers/w11278.pdf> [accessed 22 May 2005]

Ambrogi, Robert J. (2005), 'Virtual Justice: Resolving disputes online', *Bench and Bar Minnesota*, Vol. 62, p. 13

Anonymous (1992), 'The Digital Signature Standard proposed by NIST', *Communications of the Association for Computing Machinery*, Vol. 35, Issue 7, pp. 36-40

Article 29 (EU Data Protection Working Party) (2003), Working Document on Online Authentication Services Doc. Dated 29 January 2003 Doc. Ref. 10054/03/EN WP68 <http://www.europa.eu.int/comm/justice_home/fsj/privacy/docs/wpdocs/2003/wp68_en.pdf> [accessed 5 October 2005]

Article 29 (EU Data Protection Working Party) (2002), Opinion 2/2002 on the use of unique identifiers in telecommunication terminal equipments: the example of IPv6 adopted on 30 May 2002. Doc. Ref 10750/02/EN/Final

Article 29 (EU Data Protection Working Party) (1998), Opinion 1/98 Platform for Privacy Preferences (P3P) and the Open profiling standard Adopted by the Working Party 16 June 1998 Doc. Ref. XV D5032/98 WP11

Asscher, Lodewijk and Sjo Anne Hoogcarspel (2006), *Regulating Spam: A European perspective after the adoption of the E-privacy directive*, T.M.C. Asser Press: The Hague, the Netherlands

Azmi, Ida Madieha (2004), 'Content Regulation in Malaysia: Unleashing Missiles on Dangerous Web Sites', *The Journal of Information, Law and Technology*, Issue 3 <http://www2.warwick.ac.uk/fac/soc/law/elj/jilt/2004_3/azmi/> [accessed 20 April 2005]

Baldwin, Robert and Martin Cave (1999), *Understanding Regulation: Theory, Strategy, and Practice*, Oxford University Press: Oxford, United Kingdom

Barlow, John Perry (1996), 'A Declaration of the Independence of Cyberspace'. Electronic Frontier Foundation <http://www.eff.org/barlow> [accessed 20 October 2001]

Barofsky, Andrew (2000), 'The European Commission's Directive on Electronic Signatures: Technological "Favoritism" towards digital signatures', *Boston College International and Comparative Law Review*, Vol. 4, pp. 145-159

Bellagio Conference (2003), Advance materials of the Bellagio Conference on Public Values, system design and the public domain (March 3-7, 2003) <http://homepages.nyu.edu/rag111/Bellagio/agenda.materials.doc> [accessed 20 June 2004]

Benoliel, Daniel (2003), 'Cyberspace Technological Standardization: An institutional theory retrospective', *Berkeley Technology Law Journal*, Vol. 18, Issue 4, pp.1259-1340

Benyekhlef, Karim & Fabien Gélinas (2005), 'Online Dispute Resolution', *Lex Electronica*, Vol. 10, Issue 2 <http://www.lex-electronica.org/articles/v10-2/benyekhlef_gelinas.pdf> [accessed 12 July 2005]

Berleur, Jacques and Tanguy E. de Wespin (2001), 'Gouvernance de l'Internet: reglementation, autoregulation' <http://www.creis.sgdg.org/presentation/...tations/is01_actes_colloque/berleur.htm> [accessed 21 August 2002]

Berman, Paul Schiff (2002), 'The globalization of Jurisdiction', *University of Pennsylvania Law Review*, Vol. 151, pp. 311-545

Berman, Paul Schiff (2005), 'Towards a cosmopolitan vision of conflict of laws: Redefining governmental interests in a global era', *University of Pennsylvania Law Review*, Vol. 153, pp. 1819-1882

Besek, June M. (2004), 'Anti-Circumvention Laws and Copyright: A report from the Kernochan Center for Law, Media and the Arts', *Columbia Journal of Law & the Arts*, Vol. 27, pp. 385-519

Biegel, S. (2001), *Beyond our control? Confronting the limits of our legal system in the Age of Cyberspace*, Cambridge, Massachusetts, United States: The MIT Press

Black, Julia (1996), 'Constitutionalising Self-Regulation', *The Modern Law Review*, Vol. 59, Issue 1, pp. 24-55

Bomse, Amy Lynne (2001), 'The dependence of cyberspace', *Duke Law Journal*, Vol. 50, Issue 6, pp. 1717-1750

Boulding, Mark E. (2000), 'Self-regulation: who needs it? By developing and enforcing a well-designed set of rules, e-health codes of ethics can direct attention to the best-quality sites', *Health Affairs*, Vol. 19, Issue 6, pp. 132-139

Brousseau, Éric (2001), 'Internet Regulation: Does self-regulation require an institutional framework?' <http://www.brousseau.info/pdf/EBISNIERegInt0801.pdf> [accessed 4 September 2002]

Burstein, Aaron, Will Thomas de Vries and Peter S. Menell (2004), 'Foreword: The Rise of Internet Interest Group Politics', *Berkeley Technology Law Journal*, Vol. 19, Issue 1, pp. 1-20

Cannataci, Joseph A. and Jeanne Pia Mifsud Bonnici (2007), 'Weaving the mesh: finding remedies in Cyberspace', *International Review of Law, Computers and Technology* (Special Edition), Vol. 21, Issue 1, pp. 59-78

Cargill, Carl F. (1989), *Information technology standardization: theory, process and organisations*, Digital Press: United States

Carr, Indira (2002), 'Draft cyber-crime convention: Criminalization and the Council of Europe (Draft) Convention on cyber-crime', *Computer Law and Security Report*, Vol. 18, Issue 2, pp. 83-90

Center for Democracy and Technology (1999), 'An analysis of the Bertelsmann Foundation Memorandum on Self-Regulation of Internet Content: Concerns from a User Empowerment Perspective' <http://www.cdt.org/speech/991021bertelsmannmeno.shtml> [accessed 16 September 2003]

CENTR (2003), Preliminary Report: Some Comments on Professor Michael Geist's "Government and country-code top level Domains: A global survey" <http://www.centr.org/docs> [accessed 29 November 2004]

Choi, Daewon (2003), 'Online Dispute Resolution: Issues and Future Directions'. Proceedings of the UNECE Forum on ODR 2003 <http://www.odr.inof/unece2003> [accessed 25 May 2004]

Clerc, Evelyne (2001), 'La Gestion semi-privée de l'Internet', in Morand, Charles-Albert (ed.), *Le droit saisi par la Mondialisation*, Bruylant: Bruxelles

Conley Tyler, Melissa (2004), '115 and Counting: The state of ODR 2004', in Conley Tyler, Melissa, Ethan Katsh and Daewon Choi (eds.), *Proceedings of the Third Annual Forum on Online Dispute Resolution*, Melbourne, 5-6 July 2004, <http://www.odr.info/ unforum2004> [accessed 14 February 2005]

Conley Tyler, Melissa and Di Bretherton (2003), 'Seventy-six and Counting: An Analysis of ODR Sites'. Proceedings of the UNECE Forum on ODR 2003 <http://www.odr.inof/ unece2003> [accessed 25 May 2004]

Cooter, Robert, Stephen Marks and Robert Mnookin (1982), 'Bargaining in the Shadow of the law: a testable model of strategic behavior', *Journal of Legal Studies*, Vol. 11, p. 225

Cranor, Lorrie Faith (2002a), 'The Role of Privacy Advocates and Data Protection Authorities in the Design and Deployment of the Platform for Privacy Preferences'. Remarks for "The promise of privacy enhancing technologies" panel at the Twelfth Conference on Computers, Freedom and Privacy, San Francisco, April 16-19, 2002 <http://lorrie.cranor. org/pubs/p3p-cfp2002.html> [accessed 28 September 2004]

Cranor, Lorrie Faith (2002b), *Web privacy with P3P*, O'Reilly & Associates: Sebastopol

Cranor, Lorrie Faith, Simon Byers and David Kormann (2003), 'An analysis of P3P deployment on Commercial, Government, and Children's Web Sites as of May 2003'. Technical Report prepared for the 14 May 2003 Federal Commission Workshop on Technologies for protection Personal Information <http://www.research.att.com/projects/p3p/p3p-census-may03.pdf> [accessed 30 September 2004]

Cranor, Lorrie Faith, Parveen Guduru & Manjula Arjula (2004), User Interfaces for Privacy Agents Draft paper under review version dated 2nd August 2004 <http://lorrie.cranor.org/ pubs/privacy-bird-20040802.pdf> [accessed 30 September 2004]

Cruquenaire, Alexandre & Fabrice de Patoul (2002), 'Le développement des modes alternatifs de règlement des litiges de consumation: Quelques réflexions inspirées par l'expérience ECODIR', *Lex Electronica*, Vol. 7, No. 2 <http://www.lex-electronica.org/articles/v7-2/ cruquenaire-patoul.htm> [accessed 7 June 2004]

Cukier, Kenneth Neil (2005), 'Who will control the Internet?', *Foreign Affairs* November/ December 2005 issue <http://www.foreignaffairs.org/20051101facomment84602/ kenneth-neil-cukier/who-will-control-the-internet.html> [accessed 6 February 2006]

Cutler, A. Claire (2003), *Private Power and Global Authority: Transnational Merchant Law in the Global Political Economy*. Cambridge Studies in International Relations, Cambridge University Press: United Kingdom

Cutler, A. Claire, Virginia Haufler and Tony Porter (eds.) (1999), *Private Authority and International Affairs*, State University of New York Press: New York

Davidson, Alan, John Morris and Robert Courtney (2002), 'Strangers in a Strange Land: Public Interest Advocacy and Internet Standards' <http://tprc.org/papers/2002/97/ Strangers_CDT_to_TPRC.pdf> [accessed 9 May 2003]

Davis, Benjamin G. (2003), 'Disciplining ODR prototypes: true Trust through true independence'. Proceedings of the UNECE Forum on ODR 2003 <http://www.odr.inof/ unece2003> [accessed 25 May 2004]

Delaney, Edwin M., Claire E. Goldstein, Jennifer Gutterman and Scott N. Wagner (2003), 'Automated Computer Privacy Preferences slowly gain popularity', *Journal of Proprietary Rights*, Vol. 15, Issue 8, p. 17

Dixon, Ruth (2001), 'Co-operative forms of regulating the Internet presentation given at the European Forum on Harmful and Illegal Cyber Content: Self-Regulation, User Protection and Media Competence' organized by the Council of Europe Strasbourg 28 November 2001

Van Driel, Marina (1989), *Zelfregulering: Hoog Opspelen of Thuisblijven*, Kluwer: Deventer, the Netherlands

Dumortier, Jos, Stefan Kelm, Hans Nilsson, Georgia Skouma and Patrick van Eecke (2003), 'The legal and market aspects of Electronic Signatures: Legal and Market Aspects of Directive 1999/93/EC and practical applications of electronic signatures in the Member States, EEA, the Candidate and Accession Countries'. A report presented to the European Commission October 2003. Report prepared by the Interdisciplinary Centre for Law & Information Technology of the Katholieke Universiteit Leuven <http://europa.eu.int/information_society/eeurope/2005/all_about/security/electronic_sig_report. pdf> [accessed 29 September 2004]

Dworkin, R.M. (1977), 'Is there a System of Rules?', in *The Philosophy of Law*, Oxford University Press: Oxford.

Eberwine, Eric T. (2004), 'Sound and Fury signifying nothing?', Jürgen Büssow's battle against hate-speech on the Internet, *New York Law School Law Review*, Vol. 49, Issue 1, pp. 353- 410

Ecija Abogados (2003), 'Privacy and Civil Liberty Concerns in Relation to Ipv6'. Report prepared for the European IPv6 Internet Exchanges Backbone. (published 30th June 2003) <http://www.euro6ix.org/Reports/public/euro6ix_pu_d4_2_v3_6.pdf> [accessed 1 October 2004]

Electronic Privacy Information Center & Junkbusters (2002), 'Pretty Poor Privacy: An Assessment of P3P and Internet Privacy' <http://www.epic.org/reports/prettypoorprivacy. html> [accessed 1 October 2004]

Ellickson, Robert C. (1991), *Order Without law: how neighbors settle disputes*, Harvard University Press: Cambridge, Massachusetts

Farrell, Henry (2002), 'Hybrid Institutions and the law: Outlaw arrangements or interface solutions?', *Zeitschrift für Rechtssoziologie,* Vol. 23, Issue 1, pp. 25-40

Feeley, Matthew J. (1999), 'EU Internet Regulation Policy: The Rise of Self-Regulation', *Boston College International and Comparative Law Review*, Vol. 22, Issue 1, pp. 159- 174

Fenoulhet, Timothy (2002), 'La Co-Régulation: une piste pour la régulation de la société de l'information?', Dossier Droit et Nouvelles technologies <http://www.droit-technologie. org> [accessed 10 January 2003]

Fenoulhet, Timothy (2001), 'An introduction to activities related to Online Dispute Resolution in the Information Society at EU Level'. Paper presented at the International Colloquium Internet law European and international approaches 19-20 November 2001, Paris. <http://droit-internet-2001.univ-paris1.fr/pdf/ve/Fenoulhet_T.pdf> [accessed 7 June 2004]

Ferdinand, Peter (2005), '*Cyberpower*: il solo potere di interferire?', *Concilium: rivista internazionale di teologia*, Vol. XLI, Issue 1, pp. 36-46

Frankel, Tamar (2004), 'Governing by Negotiation: The Internet Naming System', *Cardozo Journal of International and Comparative Law*, Vol. 12, pp. 449-492

Frieden, Rob (2001), 'Does a hierarchical Internet necessitate multilateral intervention?', *North Carolina Journal of International Law and Commercial Regulation*, Vol. 26, pp. 361-405

Friedrichs, Jorg, (2001), 'The Meaning of New Medievalism', *European Journal of International Relations*, Vol. 7, pp. 475-502

Froomkin, A. Michael (2005), 'US Drops ICANN/DNS Bombshell (on WSIS?)' (Blog 30 June 2005) <http:www.discourse.net/archives/2005_06_30.html> [accessed 5 August 2005]

Froomkin, A. Michael (2004), 'When we say US™, we mean it!', *Houstan Law Review*, Vol. 41, pp. 839-884

Froomkin, A. Michael (2003), 'ICANN 2.0: Meet the New Boss', Loyola of *Los Angeles Law Review*, Vol. 36 pp. 1087-1101

Froomkin, A. Michael (2002a), 'Form and Substance in Cyberspace', *Journal of Small & Emerging Business Law*, Vol. 6, pp. 93-124

Froomkin, A. Michael (2002c), 'ICANN's "Uniform Dispute Resolution Process": Causes and (Partial) Cures', *Brooklyn Law Review*, Vol. 67, pp. 605-718

Froomkin, A. Michael. (2000a), 'Wrong Turn in Cyberspace: Using ICANN to route around the APA and the Constitution', *Duke Law Journal*, Vol. 50, pp. 17-186

Froomkin, A. Michael (2000b), 'Semi-Private International Rulemaking: Lessons learned from the WIPO Domain Name Process', in Marsden, Christopher (ed.), *Regulating the Global Information Society,* Routledge: London

Froomkin, A. Michael & Mark A. Lemley (2003), 'ICANN and antitrust', *University of Illinois Law Review*, Issue 1, pp. 1-76

Frost, Mervyn (2002), *Constituting human rights: global civil society and the society of democratic states*, Routledge: London

Fuller, Lon L. (1964), *The Morality of Law*, Yale University Press: New Haven

Furger, Franco (2001), 'Global Markets, new games, new rules: The challenge of international private governance', in Appelbaum, Richard P., William L.F. Felstiner and Volkmar Gessner (eds.), *Rules and Networks: The Legal Culture of Global Business Transactions*, Hart Publishing: London

Gaitenby, Alan (2004), 'Draft of Chapter on Online Dispute Resolution' in Wiley & Sons, Inc, *The Internet Encyclopedia*, 2004 <http://www.odr.info/papers.php> [accessed 13 July 2004]

Galanter, Marc (1981), 'Justice in many rooms: Courts, private ordering, and indigenous law', *Journal of Legal Pluralism*, Vol. 19, pp. 1-47

Gauthronet, Serge & Etienne Drouard (2001), 'Unsolicited commercial communications and data protection'. Study presented to Commission of the European Communities <http://www.europa.eu.int/comm/internal_market/privacy/docs/studies/spamsum_en.pdf> [accessed 22 April 2005]

Geelhoed, L.A.(1993), 'Deregulering, herregulering en zelfregulering', in Eijlander, Ph., P.C. Gilhuis and J.A.F. Peters (ed.), *Overheid en Zelfregulering: Alibi voor vrijblijvendheid of prikkel tot aktie?*, Schoordijk Instituut W.E.J. Tjeenk Willink: Zwolle

Geist, Michael (2004), 'Governments and Country-Code top level domains: A global survey Version 2.0' <http://www.michaelgeist.ca/resc/Governments%20And%20Country-Code%20Top%20level%20Domains%20(V.2).pdf> [accessed 29 November 2004]

Geist, Michael (2002a), 'Fair.com? An Examination of the Allegations of Systematic Unfairness in the ICANN UDRP', *Brooklyn Journal of International Law*, Vol. 27, pp. 903-937

Geist, Michael (2002b), 'Fundamentally FAIR.COM? An update on bias allegations and the ICANN UDRP' <http://aix1.uottawa.ca/~geist/fairupdate.pdf> [accessed 20 September 2004]

Gibson, Christopher (2001), 'Digital Dispute Resolution: Internet Domain Names and WIPO's role', *Computer und Recht international*, Vol. 2, Issue 2, pp. 33-39

Gidari, Albert (1998), 'Observations on the state of self-regulation of the Internet' prepared for the Ministerial Conference of the OECD (7-9 October 1998)

Ginsburg, Tom (2000), 'Does Law Matter for Economic Development?' Evidence from *East Asia Law & Society Review*, Vol. 34, Issue 3, pp. 829-856

Van Gestel, Rob (2005), 'Self-Regulation and Environmental Law'. *Electronic Journal of Comparative Law*, Vol. 9, Issue 1 <http://www.ejcl.org> [accessed 3 June 2005]

Goldberg, Kimberely Rose (2003), 'Platform for Privacy Preferences ("P3P"): Finding consumer assent to electronic privacy policies', *Fordham Intellectual Property, Media and Entertainment Law Journal*, Vol. 14, pp. 255-278

Goldsmith, Jack and Tim Wu (2006), *Who Controls the Internet? Illusions of a Borderless World*, Oxford University Press: Oxford, United Kingdom

Greif, Avner and Paul Milgrom (1994), 'Coordination, Commitment and Enforcement: the case of the Merchant Guild', *Journal of Political Economy*, Vol. 102, Issue 4, pp. 745-779

Grewlich, Klaus W. (1999), *Governance in 'Cyberspace': Access and Public Interest in Global Communications*, Kluwer Law International: The Hague

Griffiths, John (2003), 'The Social Working of Legal Rules'. *Journal of Legal Pluralism and Unofficial Law*, Vol. 48, pp. 1-84

Griffiths, John (2001), 'Legal Pluralism', in *International Encyclopedia Of The Social And Behavioral Sciences*, Pergamon: Oxford at p. 8650 <http://keur.eldoc.ub.rug.nl/wetenschappers/2/158/> [accessed 15 June 2005]

Griffiths, John (1986), 'What is legal pluralism?', *Journal of Legal Pluralism and Unofficial Law*, Vol. 4, pp. 1-55

Gunningham, Neil and Joseph Rees (1997), 'Industry self-regulation: an Institutional Perspective', *Law and Policy*, Vol. 19, Issue 4, pp. 363-414

Hagen Silvia (2004), 'The Case for IPv6 in the World'. Networking Tips <http://search networking.techtarget.com/tip/1,289483,sid7_gci990082,00.html> [accessed 7 October 2004]

Hall, Rodney and Thomas J Biersteker (eds.) (2002), *The Emergence of Private Authority in Global Governance*, Cambridge University Press: United Kingdom

Hart, H.L.A. (1994), *The Concept of Law*, Oxford Clarendon Press: United Kingdom

Haufler, Virginia (2001), *A Public Role for the Private Sector: Industry Self-Regulation in a Global Economy*, Carnegie Endowment for International Peace: Washington, D.C.

Van den Heuvel, Esther (2000), 'Online Dispute Resolution as a solution to cross-border e-disputes: an introduction to ODR'. Scriptie (University of Utrecht) <http://www.e-mediation.nl> [accessed 23 July 2004]

Hillebrand, Mary (1999), 'U.S. House Committee Mull Spam Crackdown', *Ecommerce Times* 4th November 1999 <http://www.ecommercetimes.com/perl/story/1647.html> [accessed 12 March 2002]

Holahan, Catherine (2001), 'Yahoo removes pro-eating-disorder Internet sites', *Boston Globe* 4 August

Hörnle, Julia (2003), 'Online Dispute Resolution – More than the Emperor's New Clothes'. Proceedings of the UNECE Forum on ODR 2003 <http://www.odr.inof/unece2003> [accessed 25 May 2004]

Hugenholtz, P. Brent (2000), 'Copyright, Contract and Code: What will remain of the public domain?', *Brooklyn Journal of International Law*, Vol. 26, pp. 77-90

Hunter, Dan (2003), 'ICANN and the concept of democratic deficit', Loyola of *Los Angeles Law Review*, Vol. 36, pp. 1149-1183

The Internet Governance Project (2005a), 'The Future US role in Internet Governance: 7 points in response to the U.S. Commerce Dept.'s "Statement of Principles"' (published 28 July 2005) <http://www.internetgovernance.org> [accessed 5 August 2005]

The Internet Governance Project (2005b), 'Internet Governance: Quo Vadis?' A response to the WGIG Report (published 16 July 2005) <http://www.internetgovernance.org> [accessed 5 August 2005]

The Internet Governance Project (2005c), 'What to do about ICANN: A proposal for structural reform' (published 5 April 2005) <http://www.internetgovernance.org> [accessed 5 August 2005]

The Internet Governance Project (2004), 'A Framework Convention: An Institutional Option for Internet Governance' <http://www.internetgovernance.org> [accessed 5 August 2005]

Jayasuriya, K, (2001), 'Globalization and the changing architecture of the state: the regulatory state and the politics of negative co-ordination', *Journal of European Public Policy*, Vol. 8, Issue 1, pp. 101-123

Johnson, David R. (1997), 'Let's Let the Net Self-regulate: the Case for Allowing Decentralized, Emergent self-ordering to solve the "public policy" problems created by the Internet' <http://www.cli.org/selford/essay.htm> [accessed 18 April 2002]

Johnson, David R. and David G. Post (1998), 'The New 'Civic Virtue' of the Internet: A complex systems model for the Governance of Cyberspace' <http://www.temple.edu/lawschool/dpost/Newcivicvirtue.html> [accessed 18 April 2002]

Johnson, David R. and David G. Post (1996a), 'Law and Borders – The Rise of Law in Cyberspace', *Stanford Law Review*, Vol. 48, pp. 1367-1402

Johnson, David R. and David G. Post (1996b), 'And how shall the Net be Governed?' A meditation on the relative virtues of decentralized, emergent law. <http://www.cli.org/emdraft.html> [accessed 20 October 2001]

Jones, Richard (1998), 'The Internet, Legal Regulation and Legal Pluralism'. Paper presented at the 13th Annual BILETA Conference: 'The Changing Jurisdiction' 27-28th March 1998 in Dublin <http://www.bileta.ac.uk/98papers/jones/html> [accessed 15 June 2005]

Julià-Barceló, Rosa (1998), 'Liability for on-line intermediaries: A European perspective', *European Intellectual Property Review*, Vol. 20, Issue 12, pp. 453-463

Julià-Barceló, Rosa and Thomas Vinje (1998), 'Towards a European framework for Digital Signatures and Encryption': The European Commission takes a step forward for confidential and secure electronic communications, *Computer Law & Security Report*, Vol. 14, Issue 2, pp. 79-86

Kaspersen, Rik, Kees Stuurman, Natascha van Duuren and Evert Neppelenbroek (1999), 'Contracten van Internet-Providers: een adequate basis voor zelfregulering?', *Iter series*, No 21 Kluwer: the Netherlands

Katsh, Ethan & Janet Rifkin (2001), *Online Dispute Resolution: Resolving Conflicts in Cyberspace*, Jossey-Bass: California

Katsh, Ethan, Janet Rifkin and Alan Gaitenby (2000), 'E-Commerce, E-Disputes, and E-Dispute Resolution: In the Shadow of "eBay law"', *Ohio State Journal on Dispute Resolution*, Vol. 15, Issue 3, pp. 705-734

Keohane, Robert O. and Joseph S. Nye (1998), 'Power and Interdependence in the Information Age', *Foreign Affairs*, Vol. 77, Issue 5, pp. 81-94

Keohane, Robert O. and Joseph S. Nye (1977), *Power and Interdependence. World politics in transition*, Boston: Little Brown

Kerr, I, Alana Maurushat and Christian S. Tacit (2002), 'Technical Protection Measures Part 1': Trends in Technical Protection Measures and Circumvention Technologies report prepared for Canadian Heritage <http://www.canadianheritage.gc.ca/progs/ac-ca/progs/pda-cpb/pubs/protection/protection_e.pdf> [accessed 19 August 2004]

Kleinwächter, Wolfgang, (2003), 'From Self-governance to public-private partnership: The Changing role of governments in the Management of the Internet's Core Resources', Loyola of *Los Angeles Law Review*, Vol. 36, pp. 1103-1126

Klensin, John C. (2002), 'A Policy look at IPv6: A tutorial paper'. ITU-Telecommunication Standardization Sector Information Document 15-E <http://www.itu.int/itudic/itu-t/com2/infordocs/015.pdf> [accessed 1 October 2004]

Knill, Christoph and Dirk Lehmkuhl (2002), 'Private Actors and the State: Internationalization and Changing Patterns of Governance'. Governance: An *International Journal of Policy, Administration, and Institutions*, Vol. 15, Issue 1, pp. 41-64

Koops, B.J. and Lips, A.M.B. (2003), 'Wie reguleert het internet? Horizontalisering en rechtsmacht bij de technische regulering van het internet', in Franken, Hans (ed.), *Zeven essays over informatietechnologie en recht*, Iter 46, Sdu Uitgevers, Den Haag

Krim, Jonathan (2005), 'Spammers' New Strategy: Unsolicited e-mail sent using ISP Computers', *The Washington Post*, Friday 4th February 2005 <http://www.washingtonpost.com/wp-dyn/articles/A61901-2005Feb3.html> [accessed 19th April 2005]

Lammetti, David (2002), 'The Form and Substance of Domain Name Arbitration', *Lex Electronica*, Vol. 7, No. 2 <http://www.lex-electronica.org/articles/v7-2/lametti.htm> [accessed 16 October 2002]

Lazer, David (2001), 'Regulatory interdependence and international governance', *Journal of European Public Policy*, Vol. 8, Issue 3, pp. 474-492

Lazzarini, Sergio G., Gary J. Miller & Todd R. Zenger (2001), 'Order with Some Law: Complementarity vs. substitution of formal and informal arrangements', *Journal of Law, Economics and Organization*, Vol. 20, Issue 2, pp. 261-298

Lazzarini, Sergio G. and Pedro Carvalho de Mello (2001), 'Governmental versus self-regulation of derivative markets: examining the U.S. and Brazilian experience', *Journal of Economics and Business*, Vol. 53, Issue 2-3, pp. 185-208

Lehmkuhl, Dirk (2002), 'The Resolution of Domain Names vs. Trademark Conflicts: A Case Study on Regulation Beyond the Nation State, and Related Problems', *Zeitschrift für Rechtssoziologie*, Vol. 23, Issue 1, pp. 61-78

Lemley, Mark A. and Anthony R. Reese (2004), 'A Quick and Inexpensive System for Resolving Digital Copyright Disputes', *UC Berkeley Public Law Research* No. 525682 <http://ssrn.com/abstract=525682> [accessed 22 July 2004]

Leonardi, Danilo A. (2004), 'Self-regulation and the Broadcast media: availability of mechanisms for self-regulation in the broadcasting sector in countries of the EU'. Document dated 30th April 2004 <http://www.selfregulation.info/iapcoda/0405-broadcast-report-dl.htm> [accessed 22 April 2005]

Lerouge, Jean-François (2002), 'Internet Effective Rules: The Role of Self-Regulation', *EDI Law Review*, Vol. 8, Issue 4, pp. 197-207

Lessig, Lawrence (1999a), *Code and Other Laws of Cyberspace*, New York Basic Books

Lessig, Lawrence (1999b), 'The limits in Open Code: Regulatory Standards and the Future of the Net', *Berkeley Technology Law Journal*, Vol. 14, pp. 759-769

Lessig, Lawrence (1996), 'The Zones of Cyberspace', *Stanford Law Review*, Vol. 48, Issue 6, pp. 1403-1412

Von Lewinski, Kai (2003), 'Alternative Dispute Resolution and Internet: A practical survey of the conditions for a successful blend', *CRi*, Issue 6, pp. 167-173

Lex Fori (2000), 'La meilleure pratique dans le recours à des norms juridiques "douces" et son application aux consommateurs au sein de l'Union Européen' - report for Health & Consumer Protection DG. <http://europa.eu.int/comm/consumers/cons_int/safe_shop/fair_bus_pract/green_pap_comm/studies/enfo02_fr.pdf> [accessed 20 October 2001]

Lombardi, Julian (2004), 'Meta Rules of Cyber Space' <http://jlombardi.blogspot.com/2004/10/meta-rules-in-cyberspace.html> [accessed 6 September 2005]

Lombardi, Marilyn May (2005), 'Standing on the Plateau' <http://jlombardi.blogspot.com/2005/04/standing-on-plateau.html> [accessed 6 September 2005]

Lupton, Everett W. (1999), 'The Digital Signature: Your identity by the numbers', *Richmond Journal of Law and Technology*, Vol. 6, pp. 10-52

Macaulay, Stewart (1963), 'Non-contractual relations in business: a preliminary study', *American Sociological Review*, Vol. 28, pp. 55-70

Macey, Jonathan R. (1997), 'Public and Private Ordering and the production of legitimate and illegitimate legal rules', *Cornell Law Review*, Vol. 82, pp. 1123-1149

Manheim, Karl M. and Lawrence B. Solum, (2003), 'An Economic Analysis of Domain Name Policy', *Hastings Communications and Entertainment Law Journal*, Vol. 25, pp. 359-497

Marsden, Christopher (ed.) (2000), *Regulating the Global Information Society*, Routledge: London

Marsden, Christopher T. (2004), 'Co- and self-regulation in European media and Internet sectors: The results of Oxford University's study', www.selfregulation.info, *Communications Law*, Vol. 9, Issue 5, pp. 187-195

Maxwell, John W., Thomas P. Lyon and Steven C. Hackett, (2000), 'Self-regulation and social welfare: the political economy of corporate environmentalism', *Journal of Law and Economics*, Vol. 43, Issue 2, pp. 583-618

McClurg, Andrew J. (2003), 'A Thousand words are worth a picture: a privacy tort response to consumer data protection', *Northwestern University Law Review*, Vol. 98, Issue 1, pp. 63-144

McGeveran, William (2001), 'Programmed Privacy Promises: P3P and Web Privacy Law', *New York University Law Review*, Vol. 76, Issue 6, pp. 1812-1855

Melissaris, Emmanuel (2004), 'The More the Merrier? A new take on legal pluralism', *Social & Legal Studies*, Vol. 13, Issue 1, pp. 57-79

Meryem Marzouki (2000), 'Iris Mediation Experiment': a presentation made during Alternative Dispute Resolution Workshop at DG INFSO (Brussels, 21 March 2000) <http://www.iris.sgdg.org/documents/adr-wshop/index.htm> [accessed 23 July 2004]

Michael, Douglas C. (1995), 'Federal Agency Use of Audited Self-Regulation as a Regulatory Technique', *Administrative Law Review*, Vol. 47, Issue 2, pp. 171-254

Micossi, Stefano (1999), 'The European approach to self-regulation in electronic commerce', in (Document) – Self-regulation and Electronic Commerce in the Netherlands, *EDI Law Review*: legal aspects of paperless communication, Vol. 6, Issue 2-3

Mifsud Bonnici, J.P. and C.N.J. de Vey Mestdagh (2005a), 'Right Vision Wrong Expectations: the EU and self-regulation of harmful Internet content', *Information and Communications Technology Law*, Vol. 14, Issue 2, pp. 133-149

Mifsud Bonnici J.P. & C.N.J. de Vey Mestdagh (2005b), 'On the Use of Legal Measures to Entice Participation in Online Dispute Resolution Systems for the settlement of online-related disputes', in: Zeleznikow, John & Arno R. Lodder (eds.), *IAAIL Workshop Series*, Second International ODR workshop, Wolf Legal Publishers: Tilburg, the Netherlands

Mifsud Bonnici J.P. and C.N.J. de Vey Mestdagh (2004a), 'Balancing norms in cyberspace: non-state economic actors and international norms in cyberspace', in Dekker, I and W. Werner (eds.), *Governance and International Legal Theory*, Martinus Nijhoff: Dordrecht

Mifsud Bonnici, J.P. and C.N.J. de Vey Mestdagh (2004b), 'Tracing the sources of non-state actor regulation: the setting of global technical standards in cyberspace as and example', in Wybe P. Heere (ed.), *From Government to Governance: The Growing Impact of Non-State Actors on the International and European Legal System*, T.M.C. Asser Institute: The Hague

Mifsud Bonnici, Jeanne Pia (2003), 'Internet Service Providers and Self-Regulation: A Process to Limit Internet Service Providers Liability in Cyberspace', in Weyers, H.A.M. and J.N. Stamhuis (eds.), *Zelfregulering*, Elsevier: Den Haag

Mnookin, Robert N. & Lewis Kornhauser, (1979), 'Bargaining in the Shadow of the Law: The Case of Divorce', *Yale Law Journal*, Vol. 88, p. 950

Moore, Sally Falk (1973), 'Law and Social Change: The Semi-Autonomous Social Field as an Appropriate Subject of Study', *Law and Society Review*, Vol. 7, pp. 719-746

Morton, David (1997), 'Understanding IPv6', *PC Network Advisor*, Issue 83 <http://www.pcsupportadvisor.com/nasample/c0655.pdf> [accessed 4 October 2004]

Muller, Milton (1999), 'ICANN and Internet Governance sorting through the debris of 'self-regulation'', *Info*, Vol. 1, Issue 6, pp. 497-520

Newman, Abraham L. and David Bach (2004), 'Self-Regulatory Trajectories in the Shadow of Public Power: Resolving Digital Dilemmas in Europe and the United States', *Governance*, Vol. 17, Issue 3, pp. 387-414

OECD Directorate for Science, Technology and Industry (2004), Background paper for the OECD Workshop on Spam dated 22 January 2004 Doc. Ref. DSTI/ICCP(2003)10/FINAL

OECD Working Party on Telecommunication and Information Services Policies (2003), Comparing Domain Name Administration in OECD Countries Report dated 8 April 2003 Doc. Ref. DSTI/ICCP/TISP(2002)11/FINAL

OECD Working Party on Information Security and Privacy (2002), Legal Provisions related to business-to-consumer alternative dispute resolution in relation to privacy and consumer protection. Doc. Dated 17 July 2002 Doc. Ref. DSTI/ICCP/REG/CP(2002)1/FINAL

OECD (1999), Guidelines for Consumer Protection in the Context of Electronic Commerce <http://www.oecd.org/dataoecd/5/34/1824782.pdf> [accessed 22 July 2004]

OECD Directorate for Science, Technology and Industry Committee for Information, Computer and Communications Policy (1998), Proceedings of the OECD/BIAC Forum on Internet Content Self-Regulation held in Paris, 25 March 1998. Document dated 14 December 1998 Doc. Ref. DSTI/ICCP(98)18/FINAL

Ogus, Anthony (1995), 'Rethinking Self-Regulation', *Oxford Journal of Legal Studies*, Vol. 15, Issue 1, pp. 97-108

OpenNet Initiative (2005), Internet Filtering in Iran 2004-2005 <http://www.opennetinitiative.net/studies/iran/ONI_Country_Study_Iran.pdf> [accessed 11 July 2005]

OpenNet Initiative (2004), A starting point: Legal Implications of Internet Filtering <http://www.opennetinitiative.org> [accessed 22 April 2005]

Ost, François and Michel van de Kerchove (2002), 'De la pyramide au réseau? Pour une théorie dialectique du droit'. Publications des Facultés universitaires Saint-Louis: Bruxelles

Paltridge, Sam and Masayuki, Matsui (2004), 'Generic Top Level Domain Names: Market Development and Allocation Issues' report produced for the OEDC Working Party on Telecommunications and Information Services Policy Document Reference DSTI/ICCP/TISP(2004)2/FINAL (dated 13 July 2004) <http://www.oecd.org/dataoecd/56/34/32996948.pdf> [accessed 9 January 2005]

Perritt, Henry H. (1997), 'Cyberspace and State Sovereignty', *Journal of International Legal Studies*, Vol. 3, pp. 155-204

Poppo, Laura and Todd R. Zenger (2000), 'Substitutes of Complements?' Exploring the relationship between formal contracts and relational governance. <http://papers.ssrn.com/paper.taf?abstract_id=223518> [accessed 15 May 2005]

Post, David G. and David R. Johnson (1997), 'Chaos prevailing on every continent: Towards a new theory of decentralized decision-making in complex systems' <http://www.temple.edu/lawschool/dpost/writings.html> [accessed 18 April 2002]

Postel, Jon (1994), 'Domain Name System Structure and Delegation' (Networking Working Group, Request for Comments No.1591) <http://www.isi.edu/in-notes/rfc1591.txt> [accessed 6 December 2004]

Poullet, Yves (2006), 'Les aspects juridiques des systèmes d'information', *Lex Electronica*, Vol. 10, Issue 3 <http://www.lex-electronica.org/articles/v10-3/poullet.htm> [accessed 2 May 2006]

Poullet, Yves (2004), 'Technologies de l'information et de la communication et «co-régulation»: une nouvelle approche?' <http://www.droit-technologie.org> [accessed 28 May 2004]

Poullet, Yves (2001a), 'How to regulate Internet: new paradigms for Internet governance Self-regulation: value and limits', in Monville, Claire (ed.), *Variations sur le droit de la société de l'information Cahiers du Centre de Recherches Informatique et Droit*, Bruylant: Bruxelles

Poullet, Yves (2001b), 'Towards Confidence: Views from Brussels: a European Internet Law?' Some thoughts on the specific nature of the European regulatory approach to cyberspace. Paper presented at the International Colloquium on Internet Law: European and international approaches (Paris, 19-20 November 2001). <http://droit-internet-2001.univ-paris1.fr/pdf/ve/Poullet-ve.pdf> [accessed 28 May 2004]

Poullet, Ives (2000), 'Some considerations on Cyberspace Law', in Fuentes-Camacho, Teresa (ed.), *International dimensions of cyberspace law*, Ashgate/Darthmouth: London

Price, Monroe E. and Stefaan G. Verhulst (2005), *Self-Regulation and the Internet*, Kluwer Law International: The Hague, the Netherlands

Price, Monroe E. and Stefaan G. Verhulst (2000a), 'The concept of self-regulation and the Internet', in Waltermann, Jan and Marcel Machill (eds.), *Protecting our children on the Internet. Towards a New Culture of Responsibility*, Bertelsmann Foundation Publishers: Gütersloh

Price, Monroe E. and Stefaan G. Verhulst. (2000b), 'In search of the self: charting the course of self-regulation on the Internet in a global environment', in Marsden, Christopher (ed.), *Regulating the Global Information Society*, Routledge: London

Programme in Comparative Media Law and Policy at Oxford University (2003), 'Internet self-regulation: An Overview' <http://www.self-regulation.info/iapcoda/030329-selfreg-global-report.htm> [accessed 28 May 2004]

Programme in Comparative Media Law and Policy at Oxford University (2002), 'ISPA Code Review: Self-regulation of Internet Service Providers Version 1.0' (dated 10th June 2002) <http://www.selfregulation.info> [accessed 29 March 2003]

Radin, Margaret Jane and R. Polk Wagner (1998), 'The Myth of Private Ordering: Redis-
    covering Legal Realism in Cyberspace', *Chicago-Kent Law Review*, Vol. 73, Issue 4, pp.
    1295-1317

Reidenberg, Joel (2005), 'Technology and Internet Jurisdiction', *University of Pennsylva-
    nia Law Review*, Vol. 153, pp. 1951-1974

Reidenberg, Joel (2004a), 'States and Internet Enforcement', Fordham School of Law, *Pub-
    Law Research Paper*, No. 41 <http://papers.ssrn.com/sol3/papers.cfm?abstract_id=
    487965> [accessed 10 December 2004]

Reidenberg, Joel R. (2004b), 'Challenges to International Law Making: Law and Networks',
    International Law FORUM du droit international, Vol. 6, Issue 1, pp. 5-8

Reidenberg, Joel R. (1999), 'Restoring Americans' privacy in electronic commerce', *Berke-
    ley Technology Law Journal*, Vol. 14, pp. 771-792

Reidenberg, Joel R. (1998), '*Lex Informatica*: The formulation of information policy rules
    through technology', *Texas Law Review*, Vol. 76, Issue 3, pp. 553- 593

Risher, C (2000), 'Technological protection measures (anti-circumvention devices) and their
    relation to exceptions to copyright in the Electronic environment', IPA Copyright Forum
    Frankfurt Book Fair 20 October 2000

Rodota', Stefano (2001), 'The EU Data Protection Directive: Implications for the U.S. Pri-
    vacy Debate'. Prepared witness statement for the US House of Representatives Subcom-
    mittee on Commerce, Trade and Consumer Protection submitted 8 March 2001 <http://
    energycommerce.house.gov/107/hearings/03082001Hearing49/Rodota100.htm> [ac-
    cessed 5 March 2004]

Rossi, Giuseppe (2002), 'Il Cyberlaw tra metafore e regole', *Rivista di Diritto Civile*, Vol.
    48, Issue 6, pp. 751-799

Rotert, Michael (2005), 'Combating SPAM: What the Industry can do?' Presentation 10th
    March 2005 at OECD Forum session on emerging SPAM issues <http://www.euroispa.org/
    docs/050310_Spam_mr-oecd.pdf> [accessed 19 April 2005]

Sali, Rinaldo (2005), 'Crossing Dispute and Information Technology: The Experience of
    Risolvionline' www.risolvionline.com, Paper presented at the Second International ODR
    Workshop held in Bologna, Italy June 2005 <http://odrworkshop.info/papers2005/
    sali2005notincl.pdf> [accessed 19 August 2005]

Sand, Inger-Johanne (1998), 'Understanding the New Forms of Governance: Mutually in-
    terdependent, Reflective, Destabilised and Competing Institutions', *European Law Jour-
    nal*, Vol. 4, Issue 3, pp. 271-293

Schenker, Jennifer L. (2004), 'EU readies new tools in fight against Spam', *International
    Herald Tribune* 26 January 2004

Schiavetta, Susan (2004), 'The Relationship Between e-ADR and Article 6 of the European
    Convention of Human Rights pursuant to the Case Law of the European Court of Human
    Rights', *The Journal of Information, Law and Technology (JILT)*, Issue 1 <http://
    elj.warwick.ac.uk/jilt/04-1/schiavetta.html> [accessed 22 July 2004]

Scholte, J. A. (2000), *Globalization. A critical introduction*, Palgrave: London

Schultz, Thomas (2005), 'La Régulation en réseau du cyberspace', *Revue Interdisciplinaire
    d'Études Juridique*, Vol. 35 p. 31 <http://ssrn.com/abstract=899078> [accessed 5 April
    2006]

Shultz, Thomas (2004), 'Does Online Dispute Resolution need governmental intervention?
    The case for architectures of control and trust', *North Carolina Journal of Law & Tech-
    nology*, Vol. 6, Issue 1, pp. 71-106

Schultz, Thomas (2003), 'An essay on the Role of Government for ODR: Theoretical considerations about the Future of ODR'. Proceedings of the UNECE Forum on ODR 2003 <http://www.odr.inof/unece2003> [accessed 25 May 2004]

Schultz, Thomas (2002), 'Online Arbitration: Binding or Non-Binding?' ADR online Monthly (November 2002) <http://www.ombuds.org/center/adr2002-11-schultz.html> [accessed 19 July 2004]

Schultz, Wolfgang and Thorsten Held (2001), 'Regulated Self-regulation as a Form of Modern Government'. Study commissioned by the German Federal Commissioner for Cultural and Media Affairs Interim Report (October 2001), Hans Bredow Institute for Media Research at the University of Hamburg <http://www.humanrights.coe.int/media/documents/interim-report-self-regulation.pdf> [accessed 4 June 2005]

Scott, James C. (1999), Seeing like a State: How certain schemes to improve the human condition have failed, Yale University Press: New Haven, Connecticut

Selby, John (2003), 'Provider Selection Under the ICANN UDRP: An Analysis whether ICANN's original goals are being achieved', Computer und Recht International, Issue 5, pp. 133-138

Sieber, Ulrich (2001), 'Responsibility of Internet Providers: Comparative Analysis of a Basic Question of Information Law', in Lederman, E and R. Shapira (eds.), Law, Information and Information Technology, Kluwer Law International: the Netherlands

Simitis, Spiros (1998), 'Autodisciplina: approccio europeo e statunitense a confronto'. Speech delivered at Internet & Privacy – Quali regole? 9 May 1998 <http://www.privacy.it/garante relsim.html> [accessed 5 March 2004]

Sinclair, Darren (1997), 'Self-regulation versus Command and Control: Beyond False Dichotomies?', Law and Policy, Vol. 19, Issue 4, pp. 529-560

Sitompoel, Nirmala, Flip Tonkens, Nico van Eijk and Egbert Dommering (2001), (Zelf)regulering van nummers en domeinnamen, Iter 46, Sdu Uitgevers, Den Haag

Smith, Graham J.H. (2002), Internet Law and Regulation, Sweet & Maxwell: London

Snyder, Francis G. (1999), 'Governing Economic Globalisation: Global Legal Pluralism and European Law', European Law Journal, Vol. 5, Issue 4, pp. 334-374

Solum, Lawrence B. and Minn Chung (2004), 'The Layers Principle: Internet Architecture and the Law', Notre Dame Law Review, Vol. 79, Issue 3, pp. 815-948

De Sousa Santos, Boaventura (1995), Towards a New Common Sense – Law, Science and Politics in the Pardigmatic Transition, Routledge: London, United Kingdom

Spinello, Richard A. (2001), 'Code and moral values in cyberspace', Ethics and Information Technology, Vol. 3, Issue 2, pp. 137-150

Starr, Sandy (2003), 'The diminishing importance of constitutional rights on the Internet age: From Quill to Cursor: Freedom of the Media in the Digital Era' (Vienna: OSCE) (Papers from the Workshop on Freedom of the Media and the Internet, Vienna 20th November 2002) <http://www.osce.org/documents/rfm/2003/04/41_en.pdf> [accessed 5 March 2004]

Stein, Allan R. (2005), 'Parochialism and pluralism in cyberspace regulation', University of Pennsylvania Law Review, Vol. 153, pp. 2003-2016

Summit Strategies International (2004), 'Evaluation of the New gTLDs: Policy and Legal Issues' – Report prepared for ICANN <http://www.icann.org/tlds/new-gtld-eval-31aug 04.pdf> [accessed 6 August 2005]

Svensson, Jörgen S. and Frank Bannister (2004), 'Pirates, sharks and moral crusaders: Social control in peer-to-peer networks', First Monday 4th June 2004 <http://www.first monday.org/issues/issue9_6/svenssion/index.html> [accessed 14 April 2005]

Swire, Peter P. (2005), 'Elephants and Mice Revisited: Law and choice of law on the Internet', *University of Pennsylvania Law Review*, Vol. 153, pp. 1975-2001

Swire, Peter P. (1998), 'Of Elephants, Mice and Privacy: International Choice of Law and the Internet', *The International Lawyer*, Vol. 32, Issue 4, pp. 991-1026

Teubner, Gunther (ed.) (1997), *Global Law Without a State*, Dartmouth: United States

The Economist Special Report (2005), 'Crowned at last. A survey of consumer power' (2 April 2005) <http://www.economist.com/surveys> [accessed 27 April 2005]

Thirlway, H. (2001), 'Reflections on *Lex Ferenda*', in *Netherlands Yearbook of International Law*, TMC Asser Press: The Hague

Tilman, Vincent (2000), presentation on ECODIR at the Building Trust in the Online Environment: Business to Consumer Dispute Resolution Joint Conference of the OECD, HCOPIL, ICC held 11-12 December 2000 <http://www.oecd.org/> [accessed 13 July 2004]

Tilman, Vincent (1999), 'Arbitrage et nouvelles technologies: Alternative Cyberdispute resolution', *Revue Ubiquité*, Issue 2 <http://www.droit.fundp.ac.uk/crid/eclip/default.htm> [accessed 17 September 2003]

Trudel, Pierre (1988-89), 'Les effets juridique de l'autoréglementation', *Revue de droit de l'Université de Sherbrooke*, Vol. 19, pp. 247-286

Trudel, Pierre (2000), 'Quel Droit et quelle regulation dans le cyberespace?', *Sociologie et Sociétés*, Vol. 32, Issue 2, pp. 190-210

Trudel, Pierre (2001), 'La *Lex Electronica*', in Morand, Charles-Albert (ed.), *Le Droit saisi par la mondialisation*, Bruylant: Bruxelles

Van Tuijl, Peter (1999), 'NGOs and Human Rights: sources of Justice and Democracy', *Journal of International Affairs*, Vol. 52, Issue 2, pp. 493-513

Twining, William (2000), *Globalisation & Legal Theory*, Butterworths: London

D'Udekem-Gevers, Marie and Yves Poullet (2001-2), 'Internet Content Regulation'. Concerns from a European User Empowerment perspective about Internet Content Regulation: An Analysis of some recent statements – Part I, *Computer Law & Security Report*, Vol. 17, Issue 6, pp. 371-378 and Part II, *Computer Law & Security Report*, Vol. 18, Issue 1, pp. 11-23

UK Law Commission Report (2002), 'Defamation and the Internet – A preliminary investigation' <http://www.lawcom.gov.uk/files/defamation2.pdf> [accessed 20 November 2001]

UK National Consumer Council (2000), 'Models of Self-Regulation: an overview of models in business and the professions' <http://www.ncc.org.uk/pubs/pdf/models_self_regulation.pdf> [accessed 20 November 2001]

UK Office of Telecommunications (Oftel) (2003), 'Codes of practice: criteria for assessment and guidelines for content'. Doc. dated 17 February 2003

US Department of Commerce National Telecommunications and Information Administration (2005), 'US Statement of Principles on the Internet's Domain Name and Addressing System' (Doc. Dated 30 June 2005) <http://www.ntia.doc.gov/ntiahome/domainname/USDNSprinciples> [accessed 5 August 2005]

US Department of State Bureau of Economic and Business Affairs (2005), 'Comments of the United States of America on Internet Governance' (August 15, 2005) <http://www.state.gov/e/eb/rls/oths/2005/51063.htm> [accessed 5 September 2005]

US National Research Council of the National Academies (2005), 'Signposts in Cyberspace: the Domain Name System and Internet Navigation' – prepublication copy <http://www7.nationalacademies.org/cstb/dns_prepub.pdf> [accessed 6 August 2005]

Verweij, Marco (2000), 'Why is the River Rhine cleaner than the Great Lakes' (Despite Looser Regulation)?, *Law & Society Review*, Vol. 34, Issue 4, pp. 1007-1054

De Vey Mestdagh, C.N.J. and R.W. Rijgersberg (2006), 'Rethinking Accountability in the Cyber Age'. Paper presented at BILETA 2006, Malta 6th – 7th April 2006 later published in *International Review of Law, Computers and Technology* (Special Edition), March 2007, Vol. 21, Issue 1, pp. 27-38

Wagemans, Ton (2003), 'An introduction to the Labelling of Websites' (background paper prepared for DG Information Society conference 'Quality labels for websites-alternative approaches to content rating' 27 February 2003, Luxembourg.) <http://europa.eu.int/information_society/activities/sip/docs/pdf/reports/qual_lab_bkgd.pdf> [accessed 5 March 2004]

Wallace, John, Denise Ironfield and Jennifer Orr (2000), 'Analysis of Market Circumstances where industry self-regulation is likely to be most and least effective', report prepared for the Australian Commonwealth Treasury Doc. Date May 2000

Waltermann, Jens and Marcel Machill (eds) (2000), *Protection our Children on the Internet. Towards a New Culture of Responsibility*, Bertelsmann Foundation Publishers: Gütersloh, Germany.

Wapner, Paul (2002), 'the Democratic Accountability of Non-Governmental Organisations: Defending Accountability in NGOs', *Chicago Journal of International Law*, Vol. 3, pp. 197-205

Weiser, Philip J (2001), 'Internet Governance, standard setting, and self-regulation', *Northern Kentucky Law Review*, Vol. 28, Issue 4, pp. 882-846

Weyers, H.A.M. and J.N. Stamhuis (eds) (2003), *Zelfregulering*, Elsevier: Den Haag

The White House (1997), 'A framework for global electronic commerce' <http://www.technology.gov/digeconomy/framewrk.htm>

Williams, Nigel (1999), 'The Contribution of Hotlines to Combating Child Pornography on the Internet' <http://www.childnet-int.org/downloads/combating-child-pornography.pdf> [accessed 15 April 2005]

WIPO Press Release (2002), 'WIPO continues efforts to curb cybersquatting' Doc. Ref. PR/2002/303 (26th February 2002) <http://www.wipo.org/pressroom/en/release/2002/p303.htm> [accessed 6 December 2004]

WIPO report (1999), 'The Management of Internet Names and Addresses: Intellectual Property Issues'. Final Report of the WIPO Internet Domain Name Process (Doc. Dated 30 April 1999) <http://wipo2.wipo.int/process1/report/pdf/report.pdf> [accessed 4 August 2004]

Wolf, Martin (2004), *Why Globalization Works*, Yale University Press: New Haven, Connecticut

The Working Group on Internet Governance (2005a), 'Background Report' <http://www.wgig.org> [accessed 5 August 2005]

The Working Group on Internet Governance (2005b), 'Report of the Working Group on Internet Governance' (Doc. Dated June 2005) <http://www.wgig.org/docs/WGIGREPORT.pdf> [accessed 5 August 2005]

Yu, Peter K., (2003), 'The Neverending ccTLD Story', in Schlesinger Wass, Erica (ed.), *Addressing the world: national identity and Internet country code domains*, Rowman & Littlefield <http://ssrn.com/abstract=388980> [accessed 29 November 2004]

Zyglidopoulos, Stelios C. (2002), 'The Social and Environmental Responsibilities of Multinationals: Evidence from the Brent Spar Case', *Journal of Business Ethics*, Vol. 36, Issue 1, pp. 141-152

LIST OF LEGISLATION

Australian Broadcasting Services Act

Australian Spam Act 2003

Australian Telecommunications Act 1997

Council of Europe Convention on Cybercrime (ETS No. 185) opened for signature in Budapest, Hungary on 23 November 2001 and came into force on 1 July 2004 [accessible <http://conventions.coe.int/Treaty/en/treaties/html/185.htm>]

Council of Europe Recommendation (2001) 8 of the Committee of Ministers to Member States on Self-Regulation concerning cyber content (self-regulation and user protection against illegal or harmful content on new communications and information services. Adopted by the Committee of Ministers on 5 September 2001

EU Copyright Directive – Directive 2001/29/EC of the European Parliament and of the Council of 22 May 2001 on the harmonization of certain aspects of copyright and related rights in the information society (*OJ* L167 22 June 2001 p. 10)

EU Data Protection Directive – Directive 95/46/EC of the European Parliament and of the Council of 24 October 1995 on the protection of individuals with regard to the processing of personal data and on the free movement of such data (*OJ* L 281 23 November 1995 p. 31)

EU Data Retention Directive – Directive 2006/24/EC of the European Parliament and of the Council of 15 March 2006 on the retention of data generated or processed in connection with the provision of publicly available electronic communications services or of public communications networks and amending Directive 2002/58/EC (*OJ* L105 13 April 2006 p. 54)

EU E-Commerce Directive – Directive 2000/31/EC of the European Parliament and the Council of 8 June 2000 on certain aspects of information society services, in particular electronic commerce in the Internal Market (*OJ* L178 17 July 2000 p. 1)

EU Electronic Signatures Directive – Directive 1999/93/EC of the European Parliament and the Council of 13 December 1999 on a Community framework for electronic signatures (*OJ* L13 19 January 2000 p. 12)

EU Privacy and Electronic Communications Directive – Directive 2002/58/EC of the European Parliament and of the Council of 12 July 2002 concerning the processing of personal data and the protection of privacy in the electronic communications sector (*OJ* L201 31 July 2002 p. 37)

EU Commission Recommendation 2001/310/EC on the principles out-of-court bodies involved in the consensual resolution of consumer disputes (*OJ* L109 19 April 2001 p. 56)

EU Commission Recommendation 98/257/EC on the principles applicable to the bodies responsible for out-of-court settlement of consumer disputes (*OJ* L115 17 April 1998 p. 31)

EU Council Framework Decision 2004/68/JHA on combating the sexual exploitation of children and child pornography of 22 December 2003 (*OJ* L13 20 January 2004 p. 44)

EU Council Recommendation 98/560/EC promoting the development of national frameworks for self-regulation of content in the audiovisual and information services especially aimed at protecting human dignity and minors (*OJ* L270 7 October 1998 p. 48)

EU Parliament and Council Decision 283/1999EC of 25 January 1999 establishing a general framework for Community activities in favour of consumers (*OJ* L34 9 February 1999)

EU Parliament and Council Decision 276/1999EC of 25 January 1999 adopting a multiannual Community action plan on promoting safer use of the Internet by combating illegal and harmful content on global networks. (*OJ* L33 6 February 1999 p. 1)

German Jugendmedienschutz-Staatsvertrag

UK Consumer Protection (Distance Selling) regulations 2000

UK Data Protection Act

UK Regulation of Investigatory Powers Act 2000

US Digital Millennium Copyright Act 1998 [accessible <http://www.copyright.gov/legislation/dmca.pdf>]

U.S. Anticybersquatting Consumer Protection Act 1999

US Children's Internet Protection Act (CIPA) 2000

US Controlling the Assault of Non-Solicited Pornography and Marketing Act of 2003 [also know as the US CAN-SPAM Act 2003]

United Nations Framework Convention on Climate Change (adopted in 1992)

WIPO Copyright Treaty (adopted in Geneva, 20th December 1996) [accessible <http://www.wipo.int/treaties/en/ip/wct/trtdocs_wo033.html>]

INDEX

6

INFORMATION TECHNOLOGY & LAW SERIES

1. E-Government and its Implications for Administrative Law – Regulatory Initiatives in France, Germany, Norway and the United States (The Hague: T·M·C·ASSER PRESS, 2002)
   Editor: J.E.J. Prins / ISBN 978-90-6704-141-6
2. Digital Anonymity and the Law – Tensions and Dimensions (The Hague: T·M·C·ASSER PRESS, 2003)
   Editors: C. Nicoll, J.E.J. Prins and M.J.M. van Dellen / ISBN 978-90-6704-156-0
3. Protecting the Virtual Commons – Self-Organizing Open Source and Free Software Communities and Innovative Intellectual Property Regimes (The Hague: T·M·C· ASSER PRESS, 2003)
   Authors: R. van Wendel de Joode, J.A. de Bruijn and M.J.G. van Eeten / ISBN 978-90-6704-159-1
4. IT Support and the Judiciary – Australia, Singapore, Venezuela, Norway, The Netherlands and Italy (The Hague: T·M·C·ASSER PRESS, 2004)
   Editors: A. Oskamp, A.R. Lodder and M. Apistola / ISBN 978-90-6704-168-3
5. Electronic Signatures – Authentication Technology from a Legal Perspective (The Hague: T·M·C·ASSER PRESS, 2004)
   Author: M.H.M. Schellekens / ISBN 978-90-6704-174-4
6. Virtual Arguments – On the Design of Argument Assistants for Lawyers and Other Arguers (The Hague: T·M·C·ASSER PRESS, 2004)
   Author: B. Verheij / ISBN 978-90-6704-190-4
7. Reasonable Expectations of Privacy? – Eleven Country Reports on Camera Surveillance and Workplace Privacy (The Hague: T·M·C·ASSER PRESS, 2005)
   Editors: S. Nouwt, B.R. de Vries and J.E.J. Prins / ISBN 978-90-6704-198-0
8. Unravelling the Myth Around Open Source Licences – An Analysis from a Dutch and European Law Perspective (The Hague: T·M·C·ASSER PRESS, 2006)
   Authors: L. Guibault and O. van Daalen / ISBN 978-90-6704-214-7
9. Starting Points for ICT Regulation – Deconstructing Prevalent Policy One-Liners (The Hague: T·M·C·ASSER PRESS, 2006)
   Editors: B-J. Koops, M. Lips, J.E.J. Prins and M. Schellekens / ISBN 978-90-6704-216-1
10. Regulating Spam – A European Perspective after the Adoption of the E-Privacy Directive (The Hague: T·M·C·ASSER PRESS, 2006)
    Author: L.F. Asscher / ISBN 978-90-6704-220-8
11. Cybercrime and Jurisdiction – A Global Survey (The Hague: T·M·C·ASSER PRESS, 2006)
    Editors: B-J. Koops and Susan W. Brenner / ISBN 978-90-6704-221-5
12. Coding Regulation – Essays on the Normative Role of Information Technology (The Hague: T·M·C·ASSER PRESS, 2006)
    Editors: E.J. Dommering and L.F. Asscher / ISBN 978-90-6704-229-1
13. Customary Law of the Internet – In the Search for a Supranational Cyberspace Law (The Hague: T·M·C·ASSER PRESS, 2007)
    Author: P.P. Polánski / ISBN 978-90-6704-230-7
14. Fighting the War of File Sharing (The Hague: T·M·C·ASSER PRESS, 2007)
    Authors: A.H.J. Schmidt, W. Dolfsma and W. Keuvelaar / ISBN 978-90-6704-238-3
15. Constitutional Rights and New Technologies – A Comparative Study (The Hague: T·M·C·ASSER PRESS, 2008)
    Editors: R.E. Leenes, B.J. Koops and P. De Hert / ISBN 978-90-6704-246-8
16. Self-Regulation in Cyberspace (The Hague: T·M·C·ASSER PRESS, 2008)
    Author: J.P. Mifsud Bonnici / ISBN 978-90-6704-267-3